The Environment and Social Behavior

Privacy • Personal Space • Territory • Crowding

Lawrence S. Wrightsman,
Consulting Editor

The Environment and Social Behavior:
Privacy ● Personal Space ● Territory ● Crowding
Irwin Altman, The University of Utah

The Behavior of Women and Men
Kay Deaux, Purdue University

Research Projects in Social Psychology:
An Introduction to Methods
Michael King, California State University, Chico
Michael Ziegler, York University

Three Views of Man: Perspectives from
Sigmund Freud, B. F. Skinner, and Carl Rogers
Robert D. Nye, State University of New York, College at New Paltz

Theories of Personality
Duane Schultz, American University

Interpersonal Behavior
Harry C. Triandis, University of Illinois at Urbana-Champaign

The Environment and Social Behavior

Privacy • Personal Space • Territory • Crowding

Irwin Altman
The University of Utah

BROOKS/COLE PUBLISHING COMPANY
Monterey, California
A Division of Wadsworth Publishing Company, Inc.

ISBN: 0-8185-0168-5
L.C. Catalog Card No.: 75-14724
Printed in the United States of America

10 9 8 7 6 5 4 3 2

Production Editor: *Joan Marsh*
Interior & Cover Design: *John Edeen*
Illustrations: *Reed Sanger*
Typesetting: *Dharma Press, Emeryville, California*
Printing & Binding: *R. R. Donnelley & Sons Co., Crawfordsville, Indiana*

TO GLORIA

For her help through the inevitable ups and
downs, frustrations and elations,
certainties and uncertainties. For this, and for
all that she has given over the years, she
is as much the author as I.

Preface

This book presents an analysis of the concepts of privacy, crowding, territory, and personal space in humans. By tying together these concepts, I hope to make it easier for students to dig into the very broad environment and behavior field, for researchers to obtain some preliminary guides for their research and theorizing, and for practitioners to think about these issues in an integrated fashion.

General textbooks on environment and behavior are beginning to appear, but many cut an extremely wide swath, often treating some topics in only a superficial fashion. I have brought together research on four central issues in as comprehensive and as detailed a fashion as possible in order to provide needed conceptual handles and lend some coherence to at least part of the environment and behavior field.

This book can, therefore, serve as a textbook for undergraduates and graduate students taking introductory courses in environment and behavior, or it can be used as an adjunct to other textbooks for advanced undergraduate and graduate courses. This material is also applicable to courses in a variety of fields, including the practitioner disciplines of architecture and design and the various social and behavioral sciences. I have adopted a social-psychological perspective, but I have made an attempt to sample research and theory from many fields, to show how these concepts fit with the thinking of others. The book can also be used by researchers and practitioners as a resource, to help them integrate what is known about privacy, personal space, territory, and crowding into their professional activities.

Chapter 1 introduces the reader to my basic approach and briefly describes the four central concepts. Chapters 2 and 3 discuss privacy in terms of meaning, conceptions, mechanisms, and dynamics. Chapters 4 through 6 focus on personal space as it relates to meaning, theory, research, and special topics. Chapters 7 and 8 discuss territory, again from the perspective of theory and research knowledge. Chapters 9 and 10 follow a similar format in regard to crowding.

The final chapter examines some general implications of my analysis for the actual design of environments.

The following people read and commented on all or parts of the manuscript, and I am deeply indebted to them: Hugh Burgess of Arizona State University, Donald Conway of the American Institute of Architects, James Dabbs of Georgia State University, Julian Edney of Arizona State University, Aristide Esser of the North Bergen County Community Mental Health Center, New Jersey, Gary Evans of the University of California, Irvine, Ira Firestone of Wayne State University, Sam Franklin of California State University, Fresno, Robert Helmreich of the University of Texas, Austin, Stephan Hormuth, William Jackson of Bowling Green State University, Joseph B. Juhasz of the University of California, Santa Cruz, George Keiser of the University of Utah, Chalsa Loo of the University of California, Santa Cruz, Stephen Margulis of the U.S. Bureau of Standards, William Michelson of the University of Toronto, Arthur H. Patterson of Pennsylvania State University, Daniel Perlman of the University of Manitoba, Paul Rosenblatt of the University of Minnesota, Edward K. Sadalla of the University of California, Los Angeles, Lawrence J. Severy of the University of Florida, Daniel Stokols of the University of California, Irvine, Eric Sundstrom of the University of Tennessee, and Carol Werner of the University of Utah. I also owe a special word of thanks to Lawrence S. Wrightsman, my good friend, colleague, and Consulting Editor for Brooks/Cole. His patience, detailed comments, and good will are much appreciated.

To the staff at Brooks/Cole—William Hicks, Claire Verduin, Meredith Mullins, and Joan Marsh—I can only say "thanks." To have an honest, careful, and good-hearted publishing team is a boon—and I have it. Alice Rose provided much help in typing and retyping the manuscript; her dedication and competence are much appreciated. My family—Bill, Dave, and Gloria—provided constant support and encouragement during the writing of this book.

Irwin Altman

Contents

9 Crowding: Meaning, Theory, and Methods   146

10 The Effects of Crowding and Density   168

11 Implications for Environmental Design   194

Introduction

This is a book about human social behavior in relation to the physical environment. We will examine how people use the environment in the course of social interaction, especially in terms of the key concepts of privacy, personal space, territoriality, and crowding.

The study of environments and behavior has captured the attention of many writers and scholars, and work in this area has mushroomed in the last ten years. There are several features of this field that you should be aware of in order to understand the field better and to gain a perspective on the relationship between human behavior and the physical environment.

An Interdisciplinary Orientation

The field of environment and behavior is intrinsically interdisciplinary. Workers come from a variety of social- and natural-science disciplines, such as psychology, sociology, geography, biology, and anthropology, and from applied or practitioner disciplines, such as architecture, urban and community planning, interior design, and office and landscape architecture. A number of interdisciplinary organizations have been formed, in which people from these different backgrounds come together to exchange ideas, to work together, and to debate with one another. Professional journals, newsletters, and informal communication networks also serve as communication media. Furthermore, there are several universities that have established interdisciplinary courses of study in the environment and behavior field. Some of these courses of study involve whole new departments and colleges,

1

with faculty and students from a variety of fields brought together under one administrative unit. Others maintain traditional disciplinary identifications but have expanded their faculty to include fields other than the parent discipline. For example, some architecture departments have psychologist and sociologist faculty members.

Where do I stand on this issue? I agree with the need to view environment and behavior relationships from an interdisciplinary perspective, and so the material in this book draws on writings, research, and theory from several fields. For example, the concept of *privacy*, the central one from my point of view, has been treated by political scientists, philosophers, sociologists, and psychologists. *Personal space*, the area immediately surrounding the body, has been dealt with almost exclusively by psychologists. The concept of *territory* has been studied extensively by ethologists interested in animal social behavior and, recently, has been investigated by sociologists and psychologists. Finally, *crowding* and overpopulation have been of continuing concern to sociologists and other social and behavioral scientists. Environmental practitioners and designers have always been involved with these issues, but, because their work is problem-oriented and geared to the solution of immediate "real-world" problems, they have not often had the opportunity to conduct empirical research.

My goal is to draw on knowledge from as many disciplines as possible in regard to these four concepts and to summarize existing knowledge about each. Because these concepts have been treated separately in the past, often by different disciplines, their possible inter-relationships have not been closely explored. A major goal of this text will be to tie the four topics together, using an interdisciplinary perspective.

A Microinterpersonal Orientation

My integration of these four concepts will be from a particular perspective, which can be termed a "microinterpersonal orientation." To explain, the field of environment and behavior can be approached from many different levels of analysis. Some professionals are interested in understanding and designing environments at the level of cities or other large molar social units. They are concerned with how whole cities function, in terms of transportational, economic, political, and other subsystems. Others are interested in smaller social-environment units, such as the neighborhood, community, or urban housing development. In this book our interest will be in still smaller social units, which can include the family, a pair of people, or other small social groups. Using a social-psychological orientation, we will examine how people are affected by the physical environment in face-to-face interaction and how they actively use the environment to shape social inter-action with others. Thus we will approach the relationship between environment and behavior at a microlevel of analysis.

Emphasis on Four Key Concepts

Another feature of my approach is its focus on the inter-relationships of privacy, personal space, territoriality, and crowding. This book proposes a general theoretical approach that ties these concepts together and that reviews knowledge and theory about each. A major idea to be set forth is that the concept of *privacy* is central—that it provides the glue that binds the four concepts together. It will be proposed that privacy is a central regulatory process by which a person (or group) makes himself more or less accessible and open to others and that the concepts of personal space and territorial behavior are *mechanisms* that are set in motion to achieve desired levels of privacy. Crowding will be described as a social condition in which privacy mechanisms have not functioned effectively, resulting in an excess of undesired social contact.

The need for integrative thinking in the environment and behavior field has been eloquently discussed by Proshansky (1973). He noted that the time is not ripe for development of an elaborate and sophisticated theoretical system, perhaps because our knowledge base is not yet extensive or perhaps because of the interdisciplinary nature of the field and the collage of different approaches and ideas. Nevertheless, Proshansky called for three steps necessary to set the stage for more sophisticated theory in the field.

1. *Provide concept definition and elaboration*; that is, develop more precise meanings of terms in the field and uncover their properties and dimensions in an analytic fashion. Without some understanding of similarities and differences among terms and an identification of their crucial properties, we will not be able to proceed toward more sophisticated analyses. One major goal of this book is to provide such analytic definitions of the concepts of privacy, personal space, territoriality, and crowding.

2. *Establish linkages of environment and behavior concepts to ideas in various fields*. I will attempt to compare and relate the four focal concepts to other ideas in various disciplines—to emphasize the theme that the environment-behavior field can profit enormously by building bridges to already existing ideas, research, and theory.

3. *Where necessary, develop ideas unique to environment and behavior concepts*. A central notion to be proposed as a vehicle for linking the four key constructs is "interpersonal control" or "interpersonal boundary regulation." This notion refers to a person or group maintaining an appropriate and

desired level of interaction between itself and the external physical and social environment. I will offer the idea of self/other boundary regulation as an important theoretical process necessary to understanding certain features of environment-behavior relationships. Thus, although I will not state a full-blown theory in the usual sense of the term, I hope to take several necessary steps preliminary to the development of a sophisticated theory of environment and behavior relationships.

An Ecological or Social-Systems Orientation

Another feature of my approach is that the four concepts will be examined from an ecological, or social-systems, perspective, which has several properties.

1. Environment and behavior relationships are approached from a philosophical base that emphasizes *multiple levels of behavior*. For example, it will be argued that various degrees of privacy can be achieved through the use of a number of different behavioral mechanisms, including verbal behavior (content of speech), paraverbal behavior (voice intensity, tone and pitch, inflections), and environmentally related behaviors, such as personal spacing (distance from others) and territorial responses (personalizing and controlling geographical areas and objects). Thus, as I will propose, a full understanding of the dynamics of privacy regulation requires an appreciation of the functioning of the different levels of behavior that act in the service of privacy desires.

2. These several levels of privacy-related behaviors operate as a *coherent system*, sometimes substituting for one another (as when a nod of approval substitutes for a verbal statement), sometimes amplifying one another (as when an angry statement of "No!" is accompanied by a vigorous negative head nod and the slamming of a door), and sometimes modulating one another (as when the removal of someone from one's office is accompanied by a verbal apology). Thus these several levels of behavior act much like the separate sections of a symphony orchestra, which blend together as parts of a complex system to generate a coherent effect.

3. The privacy-regulation system is dynamic. The particular blend of verbal, nonverbal, and environmental behaviors that occur at any point in time are not static. As circumstances change, the pattern of behaviors may change. It is desirable, therefore, that we build a long-term, dynamic view of environment and behavior relationships in order to track their growth and change over time.

4. Finally, the social-systems perspective proposed here calls for a two-way view of environment and behavior relationships. A traditional approach is that the environment is treated as a complex of factors that affect

behavior in a causal sense; that is, the environment acts on and produces behavioral variations. This is undoubtedly the case when a particular environmental configuration, such as a housing arrangement, affects social interaction. However, it is also true that the environment can be viewed as the behavioral extension of an individual or a group—for example, when people establish territories through the use and arrangement of areas and objects or when people move closer to or away from one another. Thus my approach is to view the environment from a twofold perspective—as a determinant of behavior and as a form or extension of behavior.

Application of Environment-Behavior Knowledge

One final feature of my approach deals with the application of knowledge to the "real world" and to the solution of practical environmental-design problems. This book is written from the perspective of a social-psychologist researcher, and its primary goal is to develop a conceptual framework within which existing research knowledge about the four major concepts can be integrated. However, the last chapter takes a preliminary step in the direction of application and proposes some general design principles and ideas about working relationships between researchers and practitioners.

Synopsis of Theoretical Approach

The concepts of *privacy, personal space, territoriality,* and *crowding* are central to the study of environment and behavior relationships. Each has received increasing attention in the last few years for somewhat different reasons. The study of *crowding* has been spurred on by a burgeoning world population, and some writers are predicting ecological doom as more and more people consume decreasing resources and as pollution of air, water, and natural resources increases. Some social- and behavioral-science prophets of doom point to the interpersonal stresses that accrue from too much contact with too many people. For these reasons, it is likely that research on crowding will probably increase in the coming decade.

The topic of *territoriality*—the personalizing, ownership, and defense of geographic areas—has also received considerable attention in the past few years. Quite important to this area is the contribution of ecologists and ethologists, who point to the central role of territory in the social structure of animal groups, especially in regard to mating and bonding, controlling aggressive behavior, and dominance hierarchies. Controversy has surrounded the work of ethologists such as Lorenz (1966) and popular writers such as Ardrey (1966, 1970) because of their view that territorial behavior has an instinctive basis in animals and humans. Aside from the validity of this position, the concept of territoriality is exciting in its implication that human interpersonal events involve not only verbal exchange but an active use of the physical environment and that possession, ownership, and defense of geographic locales may be important vehicles of social exchange.

The third concept, *personal space*, has had much less of a "real-world" place in environmental research, although there are many more empirical studies of personal space than of the other concepts. Personal space refers to the "invisible bubble"—the area immediately around the body; intrusion into this space by others leads to discomfort or anxiety (Sommer, 1969; Hall, 1966). The importance of personal space was highlighted by the anthropologist Edward Hall (1959, 1966), who noted differences in interpersonal communication cues at close distances and at far distances. Research on personal space has grown steadily in the last few years.

Almost no empirical research has been done on the last concept, *privacy*. Conceptual analyses have been proposed by a few sociologists, political scientists, psychologists, philosophers, and lawyers. Beyond these, however, social and behavioral scientists have generally not seen the issue of privacy as central or as especially worthy of their empirically directed energies.

This book proposes that *the concept of privacy is central to understanding environment and behavior relationships; it provides a key link among the concepts of crowding, territorial behavior, and personal space.* Personal space and territorial behavior function in the service of privacy needs and, as such, are *mechanisms* used to achieve desired levels of personal or group privacy. Crowding and the related topic of social isolation will be described as resulting from breakdowns in achievement of desired levels of privacy.

Figure 1-1 outlines some hypothesized relationships among privacy, territoriality, crowding, and personal space. Briefly, privacy is conceived of as an *interpersonal boundary process* by which a person or group regulates interaction with others. By altering the degree of openness of the self to others, a hypothetical personal boundary is more or less receptive to social interaction with others. Privacy is, therefore, a dynamic process involving selective control over a self-boundary, either by an individual or by a group. Furthermore, as Figure 1-1 illustrates, a distinction is made between *desired* and *achieved* states of privacy. In the figure, I have hypothesized that a person subjectively desires an ideal level of privacy or contact with others at a given point in time. This ideal level is an internal, personal state in which a person or group develops momentary desires for certain levels of input and output to and from others. These desired levels of interaction can be low or high and can shift over time, as situations and interpersonal relationships change.

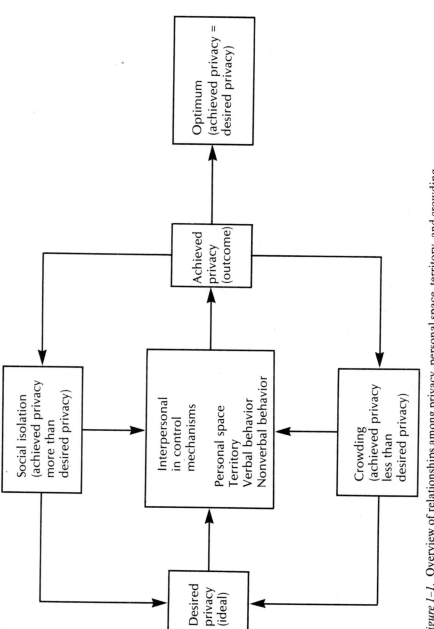

Figure 1-1. Overview of relationships among privacy, personal space, territory, and crowding.

7

Based on past experience, immediate possibilities, and general personal style, a person or group sets a series of *mechanisms* in motion to adjust self-boundaries so as to realize the momentary desired level of privacy.

Personal space—the area immediately surrounding the body—is one privacy-regulation mechanism whereby a person alters his or her distance and angle of orientation from others. By these alterations, one can effectively change communication with others. For example, moving close and maintaining face-to-face orientation markedly increases opportunities for touch, detailed visual contact, ability to smell the other person, and ability to feel bodily heat. At greater distances, richness of communication drops dramatically, so that personal space serves as an effective interpersonal boundary-control mechanism. Similarly, the person may employ territorial behaviors —possession, marking, and defense of objects and areas. By allowing others access to personal areas and objects, one permits greater opportunities for exposure of the self, provides information of a personal nature, and sets the stage for intimate contact. Preventing others from entering territories effectively lays down a boundary that limits the intimacy of social contact.

Another privacy-regulation mechanism is verbal behavior. This behavior includes content, or *what* people say to others to make themselves accessible or inaccessible, and form, or *how* they say things by means of pitch, intensity, inflection, and other stylistic features.

Employing this variety of boundary-control mechanisms results in the next step in Figure 1-1—an *achieved* privacy level, or an actual level of contact with others. If the achieved level of privacy or social interaction equals the desired level, then the boundary-regulation system is on target. But if the achieved level of privacy is greater than what was desired, then the person has been cut off from others to a greater extent than was hoped for. That is, the person is more socially isolated, bored, or alone than was intended. Or, conversely, if the achieved level of privacy falls short of what was desired, then the control of social interaction is inadequate and the person can be described as "crowded." Thus crowding is viewed as a particular kind of breakdown in privacy regulation—when an achieved level of interaction is more than is desired or when boundary-control mechanisms fail to prevent inputs and outputs from others.

A person may react to these imbalanced situations in any of several ways. An attempt may be made to use stronger or additional boundary-control mechanisms in a situation of crowding. The person may increase personal space or distance from others, may use more vigorous nonverbal-communication behaviors to communicate undesired intrusion, or may lay down firmer territorial markers and boundaries (such as slamming a door in the face of an intruder). Or attempts may be made to achieve more contact with others in situations in which too much privacy was achieved. After repeated failures to achieve a balance between achieved and desired levels of privacy, a person may accept the fact of inevitable and uncontrolled intrusion and/or separation. Another possibility is to shift the desired level of privacy in the direction of the achieved level. That is, a person or group may discover that an achieved level of privacy is really positive and thus worth having after all.

Regardless of which mode of adjustment or which mechanisms are used to regulate privacy, the person or group must pay some "price"; energy must be expended in boundary-regulation processes, much as any organism expends physical and biological energy in maintaining life processes. The more various the mechanisms that are employed in boundary regulation, the greater the price, in physical and psychological energies.

Organization of the Book

Chapters 2 and 3 consider the central concept of *privacy*. Chapter 2 analyzes privacy from a definitional and conceptual point of view, and Chapter 3 examines mechanisms, dynamics, and goals of privacy.

Chapters 4, 5, and 6 treat the topic of personal space. Chapter 4 describes personal space from a definitional and theoretical perspective. Chapter 5 summarizes research, and Chapter 6 presents some special issues surrounding personal space.

Chapters 7 and 8 discuss territorial behavior, again from definitional, theoretical, and research points of view. Chapters 9 and 10 examine the concept of crowding.

The final chapter in the book treats the application of my ideas to the design of environments. One part of the chapter examines the differing points of view and approaches taken by researchers and practitioners (architects, planners, and designers) as a backdrop to facilitating better communication. The other part of the chapter describes some general principles of environmental design that derive from the conceptual framework of the book.

Privacy:
Definitions
and
Properties

Introduction

In comparison with crowding, personal space, and territory, the concept of privacy has been neglected by social and behavioral scientists. Empirical research on privacy is essentially nonexistent, whereas there are about 200 studies of personal space and several dozen studies on human crowding and human territorial behavior. However, a number of theoretical and discursive analyses of privacy exist, done largely by political scientists, lawyers, philosophers, and, recently, sociologists. This chapter attempts to elevate the concept of privacy to a central place in the environment and behavior field. To telegraph our discussion, the following features of privacy will be considered.

1. Privacy is an interpersonal boundary-control process, which paces and regulates interaction with others. Privacy regulation by persons and groups is somewhat like the shifting permeability of a cell membrane. Sometimes the person or group is receptive to outside inputs, and sometimes the person or group closes off contact with the outside environment.

2. Two important aspects of privacy are *desired privacy* and *achieved privacy*. Desired privacy is a subjective statement of an ideal level of interaction with others—how much or how little contact is desired at some moment in time. Achieved privacy is the actual degree of contact that results from interaction with others. If the desired privacy is equal to the achieved privacy, an optimum state of privacy exists. If achieved privacy is lower or

higher than desired privacy—too much or too little contact—a state of imbalance exists.

3. Privacy is a *dialectic* process, which involves both a restriction of interaction and a seeking of interaction. A traditional view of privacy is that it is a shutting off of the self from others. My view is that privacy is profitably conceived of as an interplay of opposing forces—that is, different balances of opening and closing the self to others. Sometimes a person (or a group) wants to be alone and out of contact with others. At other times social interaction is desired. I believe that the whole range of openness-closedness of the person or group should be included in the idea of privacy. In fact, I shall argue that privacy is a dynamic process that has forces pushing toward a certain level of openness-closedness or accessibility-inaccessibility, with the relative strength of opposing forces shifting over time and with different circumstances.

4. Privacy is an *optimizing* process. In other words, there is an optimal degree of desired access of the self to others at any moment in time. And deviation from this optimum in the direction of either too much or too little interaction is unsatisfactory. For example, if a person wanted to have a hypothetical "fifty units" of interaction with another person, actual interaction outcomes of "zero units" or "one hundred units" of interaction would both be unsatisfactory. Thus the idea of privacy as an optimization process means that departures from an ideal in either of two directions—higher or lower—is unsatisfactory.

5. Privacy is an *input* and *output* process; people and groups attempt to regulate contacts coming *from* others and outputs they make *to* others. It is important to understand how people and groups regulate privacy with regard to what comes in from others and what goes out from the person or the group to others.

6. Privacy can involve different types of *social units*: individuals, families, mixed or homogeneous sex groups, and so on. Sometimes we speak of privacy in terms of one person's blocking off or seeking contact with another person. At other times we can speak of groups' seeking or avoiding contact with other groups or individuals. Thus privacy can involve a great diversity of social relationships—individuals and individuals, individuals and a group, groups and individuals, and so on.

7. Another aspect of my analysis concerns behavioral mechanisms used to achieve privacy goals. These mechanisms include (a) *verbal* and *paraverbal* behavior, or the content and style of verbal responses, (b) *personal space*, or the area immediately surrounding persons and groups, defined in terms of distance and angle of orientation from others, (c) *territory*, or the use, possession, and ownership of areas and objects in a geographical locale, and (d) *cultural mechanisms*, or the customs, norms, and styles of behavior by which members of different cultural groups regulate their contact with

others. And, most important, these different behaviors operate as a unified system, amplifying, substituting, and complementing one another.

8. A final feature of the discussion deals with *privacy functions*. Three basic components of privacy regulation are identified: (a) control and management of interpersonal interaction, (b) plans, roles, and strategies for dealing with others, and (c) features of self-identity.

The first section of the chapter portrays privacy processes in different cultures in order to provide some concrete anchors for the subsequent discussion. Next, definitions of privacy are discussed, with an eye toward identifying some general dimensions of the term. The chapter then summarizes some representative theoretical perspectives on privacy and follows with a statement of the theoretical approach of the book.

Privacy Around the World

A good way to begin an analysis of privacy is to see how people from different cultures regulate social contact among themselves. Naturally, cultures differ widely in behavior reflecting privacy, and, on first glance, some life-styles may seem to disregard privacy. But, on closer examination, I believe that all human cultures have behavioral mechanisms for managing the social accessibility of people to one another. What is different among cultures is how they accomplish control over interaction. The following are a few examples of some of these differences.

The Mehinacu Culture of Brazil

According to Roberts and Gregor (1971), the Mehinacu are a small tribal group who reside in an isolated tropical forest region in central Brazil. They live in small villages and apparently have little privacy. Everyone seems to know a great deal about everyone else, and people can easily see and hear one another. Dwellings are shared by several families and are built around an open plaza approximately 200 feet in diameter. Anyone in the plaza is quite visible, especially since people often sit working in their doorways. Paths from the central community lead to public bathing facilities and to agricultural fields. The paths are straight, and a person can be seen coming or going for long distances. The paths are also sandy, and people know one another's footprints, so that a person's whereabouts are known even if he or she isn't readily visible. The fields surrounding the community are side by side, also making for easy observation of others. Husbands and wives' quarrels and conversations are readily observed, since they live with relatives. The thatched walls of the homes do not shut out noises or sounds; poor performance or inappropriate social behavior is evident to all. Thus it is very difficult to conceal behavior.

Can it be said that the Mehinacu have no privacy—that individuals or groups cannot seclude themselves from others? Roberts and Gregor state that cultural vehicles do exist to permit people to have some control over contact with others. For example, although several families often live in one house, one family does not go into another family's area. Also, the men have a small building in the center of the village that serves as a combination social club and religious temple, from which women are barred. The natural geography is also used to permit people the opportunity to pace their contact with others. Roberts and Gregor describe a maze of hidden paths in the forest around the village that lead to secret clearings where people can go to hide, to make love, or to be alone.

A very elaborate child-rearing process, especially for boys, also bears on the control of social contact. A boy between 9 and 12 years of age leads a life of considerable social isolation. He stays inside the home during daylight hours, is taught social taboos and religious and food rituals, learns to speak quietly and to avoid emotionally intense behaviors and expressions, and generally has limited social contact. In addition, seclusion is a common practice on the death of a spouse and, for a man, at the birth of his first child. Roberts and Gregor estimated that a person during his lifetime can spend somewhere in the neighborhood of eight years in seclusion, in spite of the proximity and visibility of life to others. In addition, there are social norms to control contact; for example, people do not question one another about their possessions, sexual experiences, and lives; people are under pressure not to expose the inadequacies, bad conduct, or poor performance of others; falsehoods are commonly used to prevent others' knowing about one's activities.

Several features of Mehinacu life are important to this discussion of privacy. Although at first glance the Mehinacu seem to have no means for controlling social contact, a variety of cultural regulatory mechanisms exist. Moreover, the Mehinacu demonstrate the dialectic nature of privacy regulation. That is, privacy in their culture is a simultaneous blend of intrusion and nonintrusion, knowing and not knowing about others, being able to protect the self and not being able to protect the self from others. In addition, the Mehinacu demonstrate the multilevel nature of privacy regulation, which can involve the *physical environment* (knowing others' paths but also having hidden places; living together but still separating families and men from women), *verbal behavior* (limiting the probing of others, showing verbal reticence, speaking softly), and *nonverbal body behaviors* (suppressing emotional expression). Thus their privacy regulation is accomplished not by a single behavioral response but by a complex repertoire of finely tuned behaviors. Finally, the Mehinacu culture demonstrates how various social units must be included in a broad analysis of privacy. That is, individuals, families, and sex groups are all involved in various types of privacy regulation, each having its own mechanisms to achieve control over social interaction.

The Tuareg Culture of Northern Africa

Murphy (1964) discusses the Tuareg—a Moslem nomadic pastoral group, numbering about 250,000, who live in southern Algeria and the northern parts of Mali and Niger in Africa. They tend camels, sheep, goats, and, in some instances, cattle. They are loosely organized in tribal and subtribal groups, with the fundamental social unit consisting of approximately fifty to several hundred people. The social system has dominant noble tribes, vassal tribes, and slaves.

The Tuareg wear a sleeveless under-robe, a flowing outer garment that reaches from the shoulders to the ankles, and a turban and veil. The veil cloth is wrapped first around the head and then across the face; it covers the top of the nose and hangs below the chin, with only a narrow slit revealing the eyes. Only males wear a veil, and its position on the face is an important communication cue. The Tuareg wear the veil almost continuously—when eating or smoking, at home or away, in the evening and in the morning, and sometimes even during sleep. A man first wears the veil when he approaches manhood, at a time when it is believed shameful to show the mouth to others. Concealing the mouth presumably decreases a man's vulnerability by removing an important part of himself from interaction. Murphy (1964) feels that the veil serves as an explicit boundary separating the man from others but that it can be used to change the permeability of the self/other boundary by being raised and lowered, adjusted and readjusted, and tightened or loosened at its ends. For example, the Tuareg wear the veil highest and conceal most of their face when they interact with a high-status person, and they lower the veil when dealing with a lower-status person. Furthermore, the veil is only part of a complex communication system. The Tuareg rely heavily on cues from the eyes, body, and voice to judge the meaning of communications. When interacting, they stare steadily at each other; the wrinkles around the eyes and nose are quite visible, and these and body cues are central to communication.

The Tuareg communication system is important to our analysis of privacy in several ways. First, the veil as a literal boundary is related to the theme of privacy as a process for regulating interpersonal interaction. Second, the idea of opening and closing the self is compatible with the idea of privacy as more than a shutting off of the self from others; it is a process of achieving a balance between too much and too little interaction. Third, use of the veil and sensitivity to facial cues, verbal behaviors, and body positions illustrate the system-like quality of privacy-regulation mechanisms. That is, different types of behavior blend together to yield a profile aimed at some desired level of social contact.

Two Indonesian Societies: Bali and Java

Geertz (at a seminar presentation cited in Westin, 1970) described household privacy in Bali and Javanese societies:

> In Java people live in small, bamboo walled houses, each of which almost always contains a single nuclear family—i.e., mother, father, and unmarried children. . . . The houses face the street with a cleared front yard in front of them. There are no walls or fences around them, the house walls are thinly and loosely woven, and there are commonly not even doors. Within the house people wander freely just about any place any time, and even outsiders wander in fairly freely almost any time during the day and early evening. In brief, privacy in our terms is about as close to nonexistent as it can get. You may walk freely into a room where a man or woman is stretched out (clothed, of course) sleeping. You may enter from the rear of the house as well as from the front, with hardly more warning than a greeting announcing your presence. . . .
>
> The result is that their defenses are mostly psychological. Relationships even within the household are very restrained; people speak softly, hide their feelings and even in the bosom of a Javanese family you have the feeling that you are in the public square and must behave with appropriate decorum. Javanese shut people out with a wall of etiquette (patterns of politeness are very highly developed), with emotional restraint, and with a general lack of candor in both speech and behavior. It is not, in short, that the Javanese do not wish or value privacy; but merely that because they put up no physical or social barriers against the physical ingress of outsiders into their household life they must put up psychological ones and surround themselves with social barriers of a different sort. . . .
>
> Now, in Bali people live in house yards surrounded by high stone walls into which you enter by a narrow, half-blocked-off doorway. Inside such a yard lives some form of what anthropologists call a patrilineal extended family. Such a family may consist of from one to a dozen or so nuclear families of the Javanese sort whose heads are related patrilinearly: i.e., father, his two married sons, his two married brothers, *his* father. . . .
>
> In contrast to Java, nonkinsmen almost never enter one's houseyard. . . . Within the yard one is in one's castle and other people know better than to push their way in. . . . Other patrilineal relatives of yours may come around in the early evening to gossip and in some cases a close friend or two may do so, but except for these when you are in your houseyard you are free of the public. Only your immediate family is around [p. 16–17].[1]

Geertz goes on to say that the Balinese home is characterized by:

> ...a tremendous warmth, humor, [and] openness.... As soon as the Balinese steps through the doorway to the street and the public square, market and temples beyond, however, he becomes more or less like the Javanese [p. 17].

These descriptions are important in several respects. First, they illustrate that, although Javanese society seems to have an absence of privacy, closer examination reveals a number of mechanisms by which people regulate their contact with others. Across societies there appears to be a mix of different modes of behavior—environmental, verbal, nonverbal, and psychological—that assist in the regulation of interaction. While the mix and repertoires may differ across cultures, the results are similar. People, groups, and societies use a variety of behaviors to achieve changing balances of openness/closedness and accessibility/impermeability to others.

The Strip Teaser

A final and perhaps bizarre "anthropological" analysis of the strip teaser (Silber, 1971) illustrates how a seemingly nonprivate situation may actually reflect effective interpersonal-boundary control:

> The strip teaser would seem to forfeit, by virtue of her professional calling, the privacy of her body. She has, it might seem, no private parts, since she has contracted for their public display. But in the blank, dead expression on the face of the dancer one sees the closed door, the wall, behind which she hides an intense, if limited, privacy. She wears her fig leaf on her face. With eyes that disclose nothing—least of all an interest in what she is doing or in those who are watching her—she preserves some part of her individuality from public gaze. Some dancers exhibit such powers of withdrawal that they succeed in totally estranging themselves from the audience. Because she does not value the intimate disclosure of her body, because she makes her body available with such utter indifference, that rare dancer may even convey to a stupid and drunken audience the stark realization that in seeing all they have seen nothing. What is offered publicly to an audience becomes private once again [p. 228].[2]

Similar anthropological descriptions could be obtained for other societies, but it is not necessary to be anthropologically comprehensive. The point is to give some concrete examples of principles and themes that will be emphasized in this chapter. Beyond the themes already cited, there is an important capstone thought in regard to privacy regulation. Most societies

[2]From "Masks and Fig Leaves," by J. R. Silber, in J. R. Pennock and J. W. Chapman (Eds.), *Privacy*. Reprinted by permission of the publishers, Lieber-Atherton, Inc. Copyright © 1971. All rights reserved.

have evolved means for allowing persons and groups to regulate social interaction. While the mechanisms may differ across societies, there appears to be a "cultural universal" that people in groups can shut off and open themselves to contact with others at different times. A viable society probably cannot exist if many members are totally and permanently out of contact with others. But it is also probable that few societies exist where people have no barriers against others. What appears to be different among societies is not the absence of interpersonal-boundary processes but the specific behavioral mechanisms by which some degree of control is achieved. With these concrete examples in mind, we now proceed with an analysis of the concept of privacy.

Definitions of Privacy

The concept of privacy appears in the writings of several disciplines —psychology, sociology, anthropology, political science, law, and architecture. But its meaning varies widely. Some writers use definitions of privacy that emphasize seclusion, withdrawal, and avoidance of interaction. For example:

> ". . . a person's feeling that others should be excluded from something which is of concern to him, and also recognition that others have a right to do this" [Bates, 1964].
> A value to be by oneself—relief from the pressures of the presence of others [Chapin, 1951].
> ". . . an outcome of a person's wish to withhold from others certain knowledge as to his past and present experience and action and his intention for the future . . . a desire to be an enigma to others or, more generally, a desire to control others' perceptions and beliefs *vis à vis* the self-concealing person" [Jourard, 1966b].
> Avoiding interaction and intrusion by means of visual, auditory, etc. channels, and combinations thereof [Kira, 1966; Kuper, 1953].

Another group of definitions has less of a "keep-out" character and emphasizes the idea of control—opening and closing of the self to others and freedom of choice regarding personal accessibility. Such broader definitions of privacy are compatible with my theoretical framework. For example:

> ". . . The right of the individual to decide what information about himself should be communicated to others and under what conditions" [Westin, 1970].
> The ability to control interaction, to have options, devices, and mechanisms to prevent unwanted interaction, and to achieve desired interaction [Rapoport, 1972].
> Obtaining freedom of choice or options to achieve goals in order to control what (and to whom) information is communicated about oneself [Ittelson, Proshansky, & Rivlin, 1970].

". . . Control of stimulus input from others, degree of mutual knowledge and separateness of people from one another" [Simmel, 1950b].

". . . Control of movement of information across a boundary from person to person, person to group, group to group, or group to individual" [Shils, 1966].

For my purposes, privacy will be defined as *selective control of access to the self or to one's group*. This definition contains several properties that are central to the approach taken in this book. First, the proposed definition allows for a variety of social units—for example, individuals dealing with other individuals, individuals relating to groups, and so on. Second, it permits analysis of privacy as a bidirectional process—that is, inputs from others to the self and outputs from the self to others. Third, the definition implies selective control, or an active and dynamic process, in which privacy can change over time and with different circumstances.

Before launching into a theoretical analysis, I will briefly describe several existing approaches.

Some Theoretical Approaches to Privacy

Westin (1970) provided a systematic analysis of privacy by categorizing four types and four functions of privacy. The first type of privacy is *solitude*, whereby a person is alone and free from observation by others and, as such, is in the most extreme condition of privacy. *Intimacy*, the second privacy state, occurs when a small group—for example, a husband and wife—separate themselves from outsiders in order to be alone. *Anonymity* occurs when a person is "lost in a crowd"; he is in a public place with others present but does not expect to be recognized. The person may be in the physical presence of many other people but is still private in the sense that others do not engage in more than casual interaction. Examples include going to a movie alone or walking alone in a crowded downtown area. The fourth state of privacy described by Westin is *reserve*, which includes ". . . the creation of a psychological barrier against unwanted intrusion" (1970, p. 32). Here, one literally "tunes other people out." Whether in the presence of one other person or one hundred other people, we have all learned how not to listen to others and how to ignore them psychologically, often without anyone even knowing. Many of us have been in a situation with another person who chattered unceasingly but with whom we learned to cope by tuning them out and thinking about other things. (We are sometimes caught at this game when they ask us a question and we have no idea what they're talking about.)

Westin's analysis is important to our framework, because it indicates how different size social units (individuals and groups) are involved in privacy and how settings make a difference and because he suggests the operation of various mechanisms to achieve different degrees of privacy.

Westin also describes four functions of privacy. The first, *personal autonomy*, deals with the central core of the self and the important issues of self-worth, self-independence, and self-identity. As we will discuss later, both successful and unsuccessful privacy regulation help people define what they are, how they relate to the world, and where and when they can control interaction with others. *Emotional release* is a second function of privacy; it permits people to relax from social roles, to be "off stage," and to deviate from rules and customs in a protected fashion. Being alone and not worrying how one looks or dresses, relaxing in speech, picking one's nose, or doing personal things that are typically avoided in public are a part of Westin's notion of emotional release. *Self-evaluation* involves the integration of experiences and the opportunity to plan future actions. By being out of the public limelight, a person or group can assess their experiences, plan strategies for how to act in the future, and generally meditate about themselves in relation to the world. Physical separation from others facilitates the process of self-evaluation. The fourth function of privacy is *limited and protected communication*. Privacy provides the opportunity to be alone with another person or a small group of persons and to share confidences with them. The private meetings of decision-makers or confidants or the time alone spent by lovers or spouses to discuss a problem or their relationship is, according to Westin, an important function of privacy. These functions of privacy will be discussed further in Chapter 3.

Westin also stated that individuals and groups seek a balance between openness and closedness. Furthermore, too much or too little separation is undesirable. Thus, he alluded to the optimizational, dialectic approach to privacy that is central to the framework of my analysis. In this regard, he and I draw on the writings of Simmel (1950b, 1950c), a sociologist who wrote near the turn of the century. Simmel emphasized the dialectic quality of social exchange and proposed that any social bond involved dialectic interplays between various forces—helping and harming, harmony and conflict, openness and closedness, and exchange of intimacies and trivia. Simmel felt that without such an interplay a social relationship could not be viable. For example, to be always intimate with another person would be unwieldy for most people. No matter how close they are to each other, most people end up exchanging trivial information and intimacies in some balanced arrangement. Similarly, close relationships probably cannot be viable without some balanced interplay of the members' being together and apart, thereby sometimes being individuals and sometimes being members of a group but never in either role *all* the time. The dialectic and optimizational approach to privacy implied by Westin, which derives from Simmel, forms a central feature of my theoretical approach.

Pastalan (1970a, 1970b) extended Westin's analysis and described events that precipitate individuals to seek various forms of privacy. These include (1) antecedent social events, such as social relations and role responsibilities, (2) organismic or personal factors, such as motivation to escape identification and desire to be free from observation, (3) mechanisms to achieve privacy, such as physical withdrawal, use of nonverbal behavior, and psychological barriers, and (4) environmental factors, such as crowdedness, confinement, and environmental arrangements. This analysis points to surrounding circumstances, such as one's status relations with others, the crowdedness of the environment, individual needs, and so on, that trip off various privacy desires. Thus, it is useful because it casts the concept of privacy in a broader context and attempts a first approximation at factors that may lead to various forms of privacy and toward selection of behavioral mechanisms to achieve privacy.

Another analysis that fits well with my way of thinking is that of Proshansky, Ittelson, and Rivlin (1970). They proposed that privacy maximizes freedom of choice and behavioral options and thereby allows a person or group to have control over their activities. They also noted that important factors in maintaining options are to control space—that is, territory—and to determine what will and will not take place in territories. Proshansky and his associates (1970) stated the case perfectly when they said that "territoriality thus becomes one mechanism whereby [a person] can increase the range of options open to him and maximize his freedom of choice in the given situation" (p. 181). In agreement with their analysis, we shall approach territoriality as one of several behavioral mechanisms used to satisfy privacy needs.

Laufer, Proshansky, and Wolfe (1973) and Wolfe and Laufer (1974) extended this line of thinking by pointing to several dimensions of privacy: (1) *self-ego dimension*, which refers to the idea that social development involves the growth of autonomy and an individual's learning when and how to be with or to be separate from others, (2) *interaction dimension*, which deals with the role of privacy in coming together with others and being apart from others in a balanced sense and which deals with privacy as a boundary-control process, (3) *life-cycle dimension*, which implies that privacy is not a static process but shifts over the life history of people and as social roles and social responsibility change, (4) *biography-history dimensions*, or differences in personality and personal histories that may make people differentially sensitive to various privacy needs and regulation mechanisms, and (5) *control dimension*, or freedom of choice—freedom of access and interaction with others—which is also a central idea in my approach. As Laufer and his associates point out, control does not rule out stimulation. Rather, it is concerned with regulation and freedom to either increase or decrease contact with others. (6) *Ecology-culture dimension* refers to the way in which the physical environment can be used or not used to achieve control over interaction, (7) *task orientation* and (8) *ritual privacy dimensions* refer to tasks and behaviors that are typically accomplished in nonpublic places, and (9) *phenomenological dimension* includes the idea that privacy is not only a behavioral phenomenon but also a "unique psychological experience." I shall draw heavily on this analysis, especially in regard to self-identity functions of privacy, the idea of privacy as concerned with control and regulation of social interaction, and privacy as a dialectic—that is, an optimizational process involving the balance between increasing and decreasing stimulation from others.

The idea of control—freedom of choice to pursue or not to pursue interaction, or the ability to regulate self/other boundaries—is an emerging theme. For example, Kelvin (1973) views privacy in terms of individual independence, vulnerability, and power that others have or do not have over a person. For Kelvin, privacy involves protecting oneself from the influence and power of others. Thus social isolation is a negative state, because a person's presumed freedom and desire to have contact with others is blocked. The positive condition of "privacy" may involve the same shutoff of interaction, but the shutoff occurs in circumstances in which the person wants such a low-contact state. Our ability to regulate interaction and to achieve desired states gives others less power over us, in Kelvin's terms, and thereby makes us less vulnerable.

Much the same line of thinking has been offered by Johnson (1974), using the construct of *personal control*. Johnson deals with four aspects of personal control in privacy regulation: (1) *outcome-choice control* includes choice of a goal to be achieved or, in my terms, a desired level of privacy; (2) *behavior-selection control* deals with one's ability to select behaviors to reach a desired outcome. (My concept of behavioral mechanisms of territoriality, personal space, nonverbal behavior, and verbal behavior is identical with this aspect of Johnson's thinking.) (3) *Outcome-effectiveness control* and (4) *outcome-realization control* deal with the effectiveness of behaviors in achieving desired levels of interaction and one's perceptions and evaluations of outcomes in relation to desires. In my terms, these processes involve desired and achieved privacy levels, and determining whether one has succeeded in effectively implementing what one wanted.

Several other writers have written about privacy, and if you want to delve further you should examine the writings of Westin (1970), Pennock and Chapman (1971), Schwartz (1968), and Margulis (1974).

A Conceptual Analysis of Privacy

The following analysis is anchored around several aspects of privacy: social units (which vary from individuals to groups), the dialectic quality of privacy, the optimization nature of privacy, and privacy as a boundary-regulation process.

Units of Privacy

Privacy is usually an interpersonal event, involving relationships among people. Person-to-person, person-to-group, group-to-person, or group-to-group social units can be involved. For example, college room-mates (a group) studying for an exam may wish to avoid contact with other persons or groups for a period of time. Or a lonely senior citizen may join social organizations and clubs in order to be identified with a group and to meet other people. Or a family group may want to be alone to discuss a problem, or individual family members may wish to reflect on some matter alone and out of the presence of others. Thus there can be a variety of person-group social units involved in privacy. And privacy processes may or may not be similar for all these combinations of social units.

One dimension of Westin's (1970) four states of privacy deals with social units. For example, solitude (being away from others), anonymity (being lost in a crowd), and reserve (psychological separation) all relate to a single person's desires to be separate from others. However, Westin's fourth state, intimacy, concerns a group of people who wish to deal with one another out of the range of contact with others. Thus a potentially important feature of privacy concerns differences in dynamics for various social units.

The Dialectic Nature of Privacy

> We become what we are not only by establishing boundaries around our-selves but also by a periodic opening of these boundaries to nourishment, to learning, and to intimacy [A. Simmel, 1971, p. 81].

> It is essential that a person be able to set boundaries for himself, but freely, so that he can raise the boundaries again and remove himself from them [G. Simmel, cited in Schwartz, 1968].

These quotations say that social interaction is a continuing interplay or dialectic between forces, driving people to come together and to move apart. There are times when people want to be alone and out of contact with others and there are times when others are sought out, to be heard and to hear, to talk and to listen (upper part of Figure 2–3).[3] For example, many husbands and wives work out an arrangement, explicitly or implicitly, for times in their lives to be away from each other. Sometimes this is done on a daily basis; they go to different places in the home to read, to work on hobbies, or just to sit quietly. Sometimes this is done on a longer-range basis, in the form of separate vacations or separate interests that they turn to periodically.

Permanent separation from others, especially liked or loved ones, is not

---

[3]I am indebted to Ira Firestone for suggesting these figures.

Figure 2-1. Sometimes people want to be alone and out of contact with others . . .,

a wholly desirable state of affairs. In fact, forced separation, such as solitary confinement in prison, is a very serious punishment and something likely to be harmful to people in the long run. Thus, privacy is not solely a "keep-out" or "let-in" process; it involves a synthesis of being in contact with others and being out of contact with others. The desire for social interaction or noninteraction changes over time and with different circumstances. The idea of privacy as a dialectic process, therefore, means that there is a balancing of opposing forces—to be open and accessible to others and to be shut off or closed to others—and that the net strength of these competing forces changes over time.

My dialectic approach to privacy is somewhat broader than the approaches that view privacy solely as a withdrawal process—those in which people seek to avoid stimulus overload (Milgram, 1970), prevent intrusions (Schwartz, 1968), or search for freedom from interference (Jourard, 1966b, 1971b). This dialectic way of thinking about privacy is implicit in other conceptual approaches. For example, Proshansky and his associates (1970) spoke of privacy as involving freedom of choice or options to use the environment to regulate interaction. Furthermore, the concept of opposing dialectic forces is implicit in a long history of scientific, religious, and philo-

Figure 2-2. . . . and sometimes they want to be with others. (Figure 2-1 photograph by Jim Pinckney; Figure 2-2 photograph by Howard E. Harrison.)

sophical thought. The idea of good and evil as aspects of the same phenomenon is an old philosophical issue; the layman's idea of love and hate as being close together reflects a dialectic theme. In physics, the principle of there being an opposite reaction to every physical action (a Newtonian principle) reflects the idea of opposing forces. The ancient practice of acupuncture as a medical therapy has a philosophical underpinning concerned with regulating opposing bodily forces. And Freud's basic concepts of the id as a source of primitive, negative psychic energy, balanced by the superego, or social norms and conscience, by means of an executive or regulatory ego, convey a dialectic way of thinking. In a word, the idea of dialectic theorizing is as old as human beings' conception of their own being, of the world, and of the universe and pervades scientific and philosophical theorizing. It also seems to me to be a useful way for examining the concept of privacy.

The Optimization Nature of Privacy

A related feature of privacy is that too much or too little privacy is unsatisfactory and that persons or groups seek varying optimal levels of social interaction. The lower diagram in Figure 2–3 illustrates how the optimization and dialectic properties of privacy fit together. At Time 2 in the lower diagram, for example, a person desires a relatively high level of interaction with others, which results from some net balance of forces to want and to avoid contact. If that level of desired interaction is actually achieved, then the social system is in a state of balance or equilibrium. But if *either* more or less contact occurs, then the situation is not in balance. A similar state of affairs can occur for Time 4, when a generally low level of interaction was desired. Here, also, any deviation from the optimum is undesirable. If a person desires a lot of interaction with another person and gets only a little, then he feels lonely, isolated, or cut off. And if he actually receives more interaction than he originally desired, then he feels intruded upon, crowded, or overloaded. However, what is too much, too little, or ideal shifts with time and circumstances, so what is optimum depends on where one is on the continuum of desired privacy. If I want to be alone, a colleague who comes into my office and talks for fifteen minutes is intruding and staying too long. If I want to interact with others, the same fifteen-minute conversation may be far too brief. In summary, the dialectic idea points to the net level of desired contact with others, which can be high or low. The optimization quality of privacy deals with deviations from this ideal.

Several writers proposed similar ideas. Smith, Downer, Lynch, and Winter (1969), Schwartz (1968), McGinley (1959), Bates (1964), Jacobs (1961), Jourard (1966b, 1971b), Rapoport (1972), Westin (1970), Wohlwill (1974), and others point to the need to maintain some optimum balance between seclusion and interaction, under- and over-stimulation, or social isolation and stimulus overload. In fact, adaptation level (Helson, 1964) and comparison level (Thibaut & Kelley, 1959) are central ideas in psychology and involve neutral or optimum points of stimulation, above and below which stimuli are undesirable or are differentially discriminated.

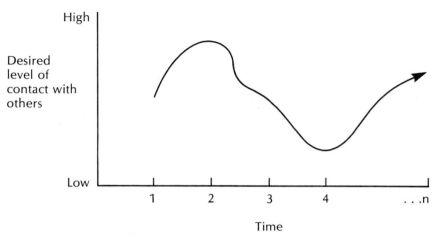

1a. Privacy as a Dialectic Process

High

Desired
level of
contact with
others

Low

1   2   3   4   . . .n

Time

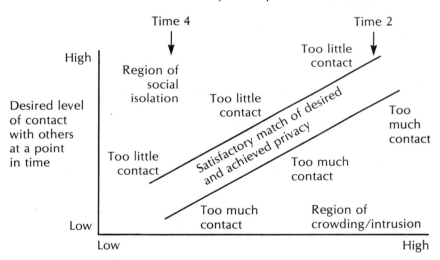

1b. Privacy as an Optimization Process

Time 4   Time 2

High

Desired level
of contact
with others
at a point
in time

Region of
social
isolation

Too little
contact

Too little
contact

Too little
contact

Satisfactory match of desired
and achieved privacy

Too
much
contact

Too much
contact

Too much
contact

Low

Too much
contact

Region of
crowding/intrusion

Low   High

Achieved or actual contact with
others at a point in time

Figure 2-3. Dialectic and Optimization Properties of Privacy.

Privacy as a Boundary-Regulation Process

Many definitions of privacy use such terms as "reveal," "know about," "intrude," or "separation from others." The connotation is that privacy involves a distinction between the self or group and others. To use Hutton's

(1972) terminology, there are *boundaries* or *barriers* that are used by a person or group to control access by others. An analogy is the cell membrane, the boundary properties of which vary with the state of the outside environment and with internal cell dynamics. The cell membrane is differentially permeable to the outside; its boundary properties shift to achieve a viable level of functioning. One feature of privacy proposed here is that it is an interpersonal-boundary process, whereby accessibility and openness-closedness of a person or group are regulated as circumstances change.

The notion of boundaries is not new to the environment and behavior field. For example, territory implies a bounded area that an organism defends and preserves as its own. Similarly, personal space involves an invisible boundary around the self, intrusion into which creates tension or discomfort. Furthermore, all manner of social units—families, communities, cities, and nations—define their existence, in part, by boundaries in the form of walls, fences, rivers, and natural geographical and man-made barriers. In a broad sense, the concept of boundary is a distinction between the self and nonself—literally, the interface of the self and nonself.

Some Boundary-Regulation Processes

Desired and Achieved Privacy.   As a regulatory process, privacy can be viewed from two perspectives: (1) a personally defined ideal level of interaction that a person or group desires and (2) a resulting outcome or achieved amount of actual interaction, which may or may not match what was desired.

The regulation of social interaction involves various relationships between desired and achieved privacy. When achieved privacy equals desired privacy (that is, when the person obtains the ideal level of social interaction, low or high), an optimum degree of privacy exists. When achieved privacy is less than desired privacy (that is, too little privacy obtained), more contact occurred than was desired. Such situations are typically labeled as intrusion, invasion of privacy, or crowding. When achieved privacy is greater than desired privacy, one commonly speaks of boredom, loneliness, or isolation.

Input and Output Processes.   My framework also hypothesizes a two-way privacy process, involving control over both *inputs* and *outputs.* Boundary regulation includes control over inputs from persons and stimuli outside the self, ranging from zero input on some occasions to maximum input on other occasions. Social inputs deal with stimulation coming from others to the self—from the outside in. Being called to the telephone, listening to a radio, and having others talk to you represent inputs from others. Privacy also includes *outputs* from the self to others. A person may seek out others, may wish to have them listen to his or her views, or may enlist their help in solving a personal problem. In one sense, social outputs involve an active seeking of others to become part of the psychological environment of the self. To use the cell-membrane analogy again, I speak here of a two-way exchange with the environment—sometimes from the inside of the cell out to the environment and sometimes from the environment into the cell.

Profiles of Regulatory Processes.   Figure 2-4 presents eight privacy situations based on boundary regulation, desired and achieved privacy, and input-output processes. P refers to a person or a group; E refers to another person or group or to general environmental stimulation. The boundary around P can be either closed (solid line) or open and permeable (dashed line). Cases 1 to 4 portray relationships between desired and achieved privacy in regard to inputs from others; Cases 5 to 8 deal with outputs from the self to others. In order to simplify, assume a single person (P) is relating to another person (E).

In Cases 1 and 2, P desired certain levels of contact with E and was able to achieve those levels. Thus desired privacy is equal to achieved privacy and the person should be satisfied. In Case 1, P wanted inputs from E; P opened the self-boundaries, and E entered the self-zone of P. The boundary could have been opened by P's actions (for example, opening a door and welcoming E), but it was also necessary that other events allow the boundary to be crossed (for example, the door wasn't stuck closed, E was not geographically isolated from P).

Case 2 is a prototype of the traditional successful privacy situation, in which P, viewing E's inputs as undesirable, laid down a boundary designed to be impermeable to E and succeeded in keeping E away. Again, desired privacy equals achieved privacy. Cases 1 and 2 both reflect adequate privacy situations—one in which P wanted contact and received it and the other in which P wanted to avoid contact and was successful.

In the next two cases, P was unsuccessful in achieving a desired degree of privacy. In Case 3, P was intruded upon by E; in Case 4, P was unable to achieve a desired level of contact with E. In Case 3, P closed the self-boundary, but E crossed the boundary against P's wishes. For example, P may have closed the door, but E came through the door, or P may have turned away from E to avoid interaction, but E ignored the cue and interacted with P in a way that could not be avoided.

Case 4 is a different type of boundary-countrol failure. Here E is viewed as a positive source of stimulation, but E did not move into the proximity of P, in spite of P's having taken steps to be accessible. E may have been prevented from interacting with P, or E may not have wanted to deal with P. From P's perspective, the achieved level of privacy is *greater* than the desired level of privacy. In summary, the optimal situations of Cases 1 and 2 reflect

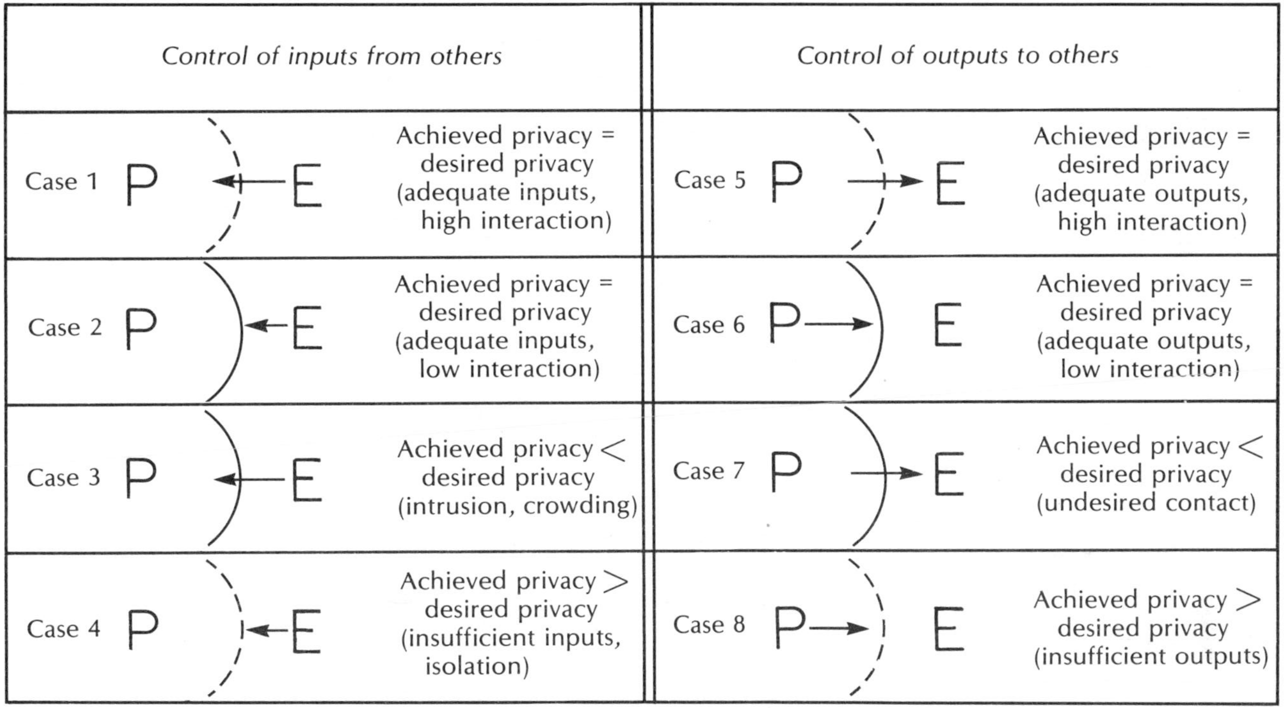

Control of inputs from others

Case 1   P — E

Achieved privacy =
desired privacy
(adequate inputs,
high interaction)

Case 2   P — E

Achieved privacy =
desired privacy
(adequate inputs,
low interaction)

Case 3   P — E

Achieved privacy <
desired privacy
(intrusion, crowding)

Case 4   P — E

Achieved privacy >
desired privacy
(insufficient inputs,
isolation)

Control of outputs to others

Case 5   P — E

Achieved privacy =
desired privacy
(adequate outputs,
high interaction)

Case 6   P — E

Achieved privacy =
desired privacy
(adequate outputs,
low interaction)

Case 7   P — E

Achieved privacy <
desired privacy
(undesired contact)

Case 8   P — E

Achieved privacy >
desired privacy
(insufficient outputs)

Figure 2–4. Relationships between achieved and desired privacy as a function of interpersonal boundary-control processes.

satisfactory self/other boundary-regulation processes, and the nonoptimal situations of Cases 3 and 4 reflect instances in which P was unable to regulate boundaries around the self. These examples show that satisfactory privacy is not only the successful exclusion of unwanted others (Case 2) but is also the successful inclusion of someone with whom interaction is desired (Case 1). Furthermore, privacy failures can also be viewed as either the inability to keep someone away from the self (Case 3) or the inability to interact with a person when one wants to (Case 4).

Cases 5 to 8 parallel the first four profiles but deal with P's desire to direct *outputs* to E. In Hutton's terms (1972), Case 5 involves instances in which P successfully gained access to a positive goal. An example of a successful Case-5 privacy situation is when a person telephones another person, finds that person in, and talks about a serious problem or even just chats about superficial matters. That is, P wanted to move into the area of E's self and direct outputs to E and was successful in so doing. In Case 6, P arranged a boundary system to prevent self-movement toward E. By not calling E, by avoiding places where E might be, and by being hesitant, aloof, and distant in the presence of E, P was successful in maintaining a desired low level of contact with E. Thus, Cases 5 and 6 are successful privacy-regulation situations in regard to outputs from the self to others and are directly parallel to Cases 1 and 2. Case 5 portrays achievement of high levels of output, and Case 6 reflects successful control over low levels of interaction.

Cases 7 and 8 parallel Cases 3 and 4, respectively, and all represent failures of privacy systems. Case 7 is an instance in which P hoped to avoid contact with E, but the boundary system failed, and P ended up in the presence of E. Case 7's counterpart, Case 3, involved E's actively breaking through P's boundaries, not P's moving toward E. But both cases have the same result—intrusion by E beyond P's self-boundary. Finally, Case 8 parallels Case 4, in which desired contact with a positive E was not achieved. In Case 8, P actively solicited contact with E but failed. For example, E was not at home when P called, E was not receptive to P's advances, or E was prevented from receiving outputs from P because of the presence of other people. In Case 4, P was ready to accept E's inputs, but they never materialized. Thus, both cases involve less interaction than desired.

These eight cases oversimplify the complexity of privacy regulation. At a slightly more complicated level, one can generate various privacy-management situations from Cases 1 to 8. For example, an optimum-exclusion situation exists when P arranges matters so that E's inputs are excluded (Case 2), and P is able to control outputs to E (Case 6). But a form of intrusion occurs if P is able to control outputs to an undesired E (Case 6) by, say, conveying a general distaste for interaction with E, but E manages to force P to listen (Case 3). That is, I might be able to avoid telling you about me (Case

6) but still be forced to listen to you tell about yourself (Case 3). Or consider a mix of Cases 1 and 8. In Case 1, P is receptive to E; P opens the self-boundaries, listens to E's problems, permits E access to physical areas, and so on. But in Case 8, P hopes to reciprocate; P wants E to listen in return but is rebuffed. Thus I listen to you (Case 1) but you refuse to listen to me in return (Case 8). Both of these combinations turn out to be undesirable, because P does not give or get exactly what was desired.

The conception of privacy discussed in this chapter emphasizes certain themes: (1) privacy as an interpersonal process with several classes of potential actors, (2) privacy as a bidirectional process involving incoming and outgoing contacts, (3) privacy as a regulatory process involving adjustments of self-boundaries to permit various levels of contact with others, (4) privacy as a multifaceted process involving achieved and desired levels, which fit together to yield optimal or nonoptimal privacy states, (5) privacy as an optimization process, with too little privacy represented by more contacts than desired and too much privacy reflected in fewer contacts than desired, and (6) privacy as a dialectic process, with open/closed and accessible/inaccessible forces operating in a simultaneous and dynamic fashion. The next chapter examines privacy goals and functions and privacy mechanisms used to assist in boundary regulation.

Privacy
Mechanisms
and
Functions

This chapter first deals with behavioral mechanisms used by people and groups to achieve ideal levels of privacy and then discusses functions that privacy serves, such as interpersonal-boundary control, the interface of the self and others, and, most important, self-identity.

Privacy Mechanisms

People attempt to implement desired levels of privacy by using behavioral mechanisms such as verbal behavior, nonverbal use of the body, environmental behaviors (for example, personal space and territory), and culturally defined norms and practices. These mechanisms operate as an integrated system in much the same way as the instruments and sections of a symphony orchestra yield an integrated result. For example, verbal and nonverbal behavior sometimes substitute for each other (a head nod can substitute for words of praise), sometimes complement each other (a smile, a head nod, and verbal praise can combine to reflect strong agreement), and sometimes conflict and thereby convey ambivalence or nongenuineness (verbal agreement or praise can occur with a hostile glance or nonrelaxed body posture).

In addition, privacy mechanisms can change over time and are responsive to the situation at hand. Thus if a person cannot achieve a desired level of boundary regulation, additional mechanisms may be mobilized. For example, if a closed door is ignored, the intruder might be told to leave, might be given nonverbal cues of disapproval, or might even be tossed out bodily.

Thus privacy regulation involves a complex feedback system in which resources are mobilized over time to move the system toward a match between desires and outcomes.

Verbal Privacy Mechanisms

A main vehicle of social interaction is verbal communication; words convey all kinds of personal states and desires. Verbal behavior can be considered from two perspectives: content and structure.

Verbal content refers to the substance of verbal communications or "what" is said (for example, "keep out," "come in," "I'd like to be alone," "I'd like to have you listen to what I say"). People use verbal content to convey discrepancies between desired and achieved privacy: "You're too noisy," "Don't you know what a closed door means?" "I called you, and you didn't come when I needed you." Such statements include expressions of desired levels of interaction and assessments of outcomes. People also negotiate about privacy at a verbal level—for example, when a parent says to a child "Leave me alone now; I'll talk with you later when I finish the newspaper" or when a friend interrupts and says "Can I just have a few minutes of your time, and then I will leave." Relatively little work on verbal-content features of privacy regulation is available, although voluminous analyses of verbal interaction exist from problem-solving groups, in psychotherapy situations, and so on.

Structural aspects of verbal behavior include what have been termed paraverbal, paralinguistic or linguistic features of speech (Argyle & Kendon, 1967; Duncan, 1969; Mahl & Schultze, 1964; Birdwhistell, 1970). For example, Mahl and Schultze (1964) proposed a classification based on (1) *language style,* which includes verb/adjective ratios, parts of speech, verb tense, (2) *vocabulary selection and diversity,* which concerns the type of speech relative to the amount of output, (3) *pronunciation and dialect,* (4) *voice dynamics,* such as quality, rhythm, continuity, or pauses and intrusions, (5) *speech rates,* (6) *temporal phenomena,* such as speech duration and latency, (7) *verbal output,* (8) *voice quality,* which includes pitch, rate, and loudness, and (9) *vocalizations,* such as yawning and crying.

Only a few, general studies of verbal structure relate to privacy. For instance, Davis and Olesen (1971) observed that residents of an Israeli kibbutz often lapsed into their native languages, other than Hebrew, when they wanted to have private conversations. Other examples include parental use of a native tongue in the presence of children and children's use of pig-Latin and other spontaneous "languages," special linguistic styles, and words.

There are also analyses of structural features of verbal behavior that have implications for privacy. For example, Altman and Taylor (1973) examined the development of friendships by considering how people allow themselves to become mutually accessible. The research showed increased *amounts* and *intimacy* of verbal output as relationships grew. Thus volume and quality of verbal output may reflect privacy mechanisms. Other work in the general area of verbal openness and self-disclosure has been done by Jourard (1971b, 1971c).

Another approach distinguishes between *immediacy* and *nonimmediacy* in verbal communication (Mehrabian, 1967a, 1967b, 1968a, 1968b, 1969, 1971; Mehrabian & Weiner, 1966; Weiner & Mehrabian, 1968). Verbal immediacy or closeness to another person is reflected in intense and direct personal references ("I," "we," or "ours" as opposed to "some people" or "others"), assumption of personal responsibility for feelings ("my opinion is . . ." or "I feel . . ." versus "some people think . . ." or "I have heard that . . ."), and use of active rather than passive speech forms ("I like you" versus "My feelings for you are positive"). Mehrabian also found that people who used more immediate forms of expression were better liked.

Nonverbal Privacy Mechanisms

Nonverbal behavior, popularly termed "body language," involves the use of various parts of the body to communicate. Some research emphasizes body language such as arm and leg positions, body postures, broad gestures, and head movements. Other studies do detailed analyses of specific behaviors or body areas. For example, Ekman, Ellsworth, and Friesen (1972) and Ekman, Friesen, and Tomkins (1971) examined minute facial behaviors associated with emotions of anger, happiness, and sadness. They categorized specific patterns of musculature in the forehead, nasal, and mouth areas of the face according to the role of each area in specific emotions. Ekman and Friesen (1972) did a similar analysis of hand movements.

There is relatively little direct research on nonverbal aspects of privacy, except for a few studies of reactions to spatial intrusion. For example, Patterson, Mullens, and Romano (1971) observed that the closer an invader sat to subjects in a library the greater the subjects' reactions of glaring, leaning away, blocking themselves off (placement of hands or elbows between their bodies and the invader's) and reorienting their bodies away from the intruder. In a similar study, Felipe and Sommer (1966) found that the closer an intrusion the greater the probability of flight and the greater the use of various nonverbal behaviors, such as turning away or pulling in elbows. Thus, nonverbal behaviors in reaction to unwanted "immediacy" of others reflect attempts to restore acceptable boundaries around the self. And when we inadvertently come too close to others, we use all manner of nonverbal cues to display our discomfort and often our apology. For example, in a crowded elevator where we are forced to be close to strangers, we typically keep our hands at our sides, hold our bodies rigid and immobile, breathe quietly, and look up at the floor-designation numbers, look down at the floor, or stare blankly ahead. It is as if we are conveying the message "We are all intruding on one another, so all we can do is show our discomfort and demonstrate that we are doing our best not to inappropriately intrude on one another." Beyond these studies and examples there is relatively little research on nonverbal behavior as a privacy-regulation mechanism. However, general nonverbal research and theory are worth examining for their potential application to privacy.

Ekman and Friesen (1969, 1972) proposed a classification of nonverbal behaviors based on *origin* (how the behaviors became part of behavioral repertoires), *usage,* and *interpersonal significance.* They described five types of nonverbal behavior: (1) emblems, (2) illustrators, (3) affect displays, (4) regulators, and (5) adaptive behaviors. *Emblems* are often substitutes for words—for example, fist-shaking as a hostile communication or the silent language of the deaf. *Illustrators* complement verbal statements—for example, sketching a path or direction of thought, or pointing to objects. *Affect displays* convey emotions, and *regulators* manage and pace interaction—for example, head nods, patterns of eye contact, and postural shifts. *Adaptors,* such as covering the eyes, face, or mouth, are remnants of earlier behaviors and are unique to a person.

This schema might be adapted to understand privacy mechanisms. For example, people use many "keep-away" and "come-forward" emblems and illustrators, such as keeping their hands open and in front of their bodies in a "stop" motion as opposed to keeping their palms open and extended upward with outstretched arms. Certain regulators are associated with exclusion and inclusion, such as gaze aversion and direct eye contact, formal postures involving arm-and-leg symmetry and body rigidity as opposed to more relaxed, asymmetrical, slouching positions that reflect attraction and liking, or general body fidgeting to signal boredom or desire to terminate an interaction. And people use idiosyncratic adaptors, such as facial expressions reflecting discomfort or nervous habits and movements peculiar to them (biting pencils and the like), that others learn to interpret as signals of interest or boredom.

Argyle and Kendon (1967) described nonverbal behaviors in terms of *standing features* and *dynamic features.* Standing features change infrequently during the interaction; for example, physical distance, body orientation, and postures are relatively stable. These features set the structure within which dynamic events occur, including movements of the body, changes of facial expression, and eye contact. Eye contact, for example, has been a heavily researched area in relation to regulation of interaction. Argyle and Dean (1965) proposed several interpersonal functions of eye contact, such as seeking information from others, signaling open channels, and providing feedback. They posited an equilibrium level of eye contact involving social approach and avoidance forces and demonstrated that eye contact and interpersonal distance form an integrated behavioral set; the closer the distance between people, the less their eye contact. That is, closeness of bodies and resulting changes in eye contact are mechanisms to maintain an appropriate level of intimacy (see also Goldberg, Kiesler, & Collins, 1969). In work related to privacy, Exline, Gray, and Schuette (1965) found reduced eye contact when persons disclosed intimate information—as if they were opening a verbal channel to the self but holding a nonverbal one closed. In another study, Exline and Eldridge (1967) found that people had greater trust in a speaker who looked at his audience and that there was more eye contact in cooperative (rather than competitive) situations. Perhaps a cooperative situation permits a lowering of personal boundaries, whereas competition leads to strong barriers between people.

In another series of studies, Mehrabian examined nonverbal behavior and interpersonal attraction (Mehrabian, 1968a, 1968b, 1969; Mehrabian & Diamond, 1970, 1971; Mehrabian & Ferris, 1967; Mehrabian & Williams, 1969). The more favorable a social relationship, the closer the distance between people. There also was greater eye contact, more smiling, and greater forward body lean. Thus being involved in a positive relationship creates more permeable boundaries around the self, as reflected in a variety of nonverbal behaviors.

In summary, there is a vast array of nonverbal behaviors that are potentially relevant to privacy regulation. The task remains to document such nonverbal mechanisms and to determine their relationship with other levels of behavior.

Environmental Privacy Mechanisms

The role of the physical environment as a privacy mechanism is quite complex. To break the problem down, I will first focus on aspects of the environment closest to the person (such as clothing), then move to personal space, and then to distant features of the environment (such as territories, areas, and objects).

Clothing and Adornment.   Anthropologists and home economists have studied clothing far more than have other social scientists. It is quite evident that different age, occupational, and status groups adopt styles of clothing or "uniforms" to tell the world who they are, to help define situations, and to reflect their status roles. For example, one usually dresses formally at weddings and casually at picnics; one wears suits and ties to business offices and informal clothing at home. Those who dress according to common standards of appropriateness convey their acceptance of a situation and their communality with others who do likewise. Those who do not dress in "good taste" indicate either their momentary misreading of the situation or their deliberate rejection of norms and customs. Status is also reflected in dress. Middle-management office workers wear shirts, ties, and jackets more often than factory workers; generals in the army have different status symbols on their uniforms from privates; teachers usually dress more formally than students; and the President of the United States and other high officials typically dress conservatively.

People also use clothing to signal their approachability. For example, as described earlier, male members of the Tuareg culture (Murphy, 1964) wear a veil to cover their face, and the veil is constantly adjusted according to the social situation—to reflect status and approachability. Goffman's (1961) analysis of life in a mental institution illustrates the lack of control allowed patients over their personal selves, clothing, and possessions. Many private possessions are taken away from patients and are made available only with staff permission; periodic inspections of personal effects can occur at any time; a patient's body can be examined by the staff at any time. This lack of personal control is also present in military training camps, where recruits' heads are shaved, wearing of personal clothing is restricted, and new clothing is provided. Such restrictions on a person's use of clothing, adornments, and possessions are infringements on privacy-regulation mechanisms. As such they prevent the self from being under the control of the individual.

Personal Space.   The next layer of the self that serves as a privacy mechanism is personal space—that is, the invisible boundary surrounding the self; intrusion into this space creates tension or discomfort (Hall, 1966; Sommer, 1969; see Chapters 4, 5, and 6 for a full treatment of this topic).

In some early theorizing Hall linked four distance zones to interpersonal intimacy. (1) Intimate distance, ranging from body contact to a distance of about 18 inches, is usually appropriate to intimate relationships in private situations, permitting extensive communication involving touch, heat, sound, and smell. (2) Personal distance spans the area from 1½ to 4 feet and also permits considerable exchange of cues. (3) Social distance, 4 to 12 feet, occurs in impersonal, work, or casual relationships. (4) A public zone, beyond 12 feet, is appropriate to formal meetings and interactions with higher-status persons. According to Hall these zones are used to regulate interaction and to avoid inappropriate intrusions. For example, Hall described how people from Middle Eastern and Mediterranean cultures are accustomed to interacting at very close distances, including exchange of visual, touch, smell, and sound cues, often to the dismay of American and British people. In terms of the model described earlier, this situation represents a case in which one party wishes to approach closely (inside the other's boundaries), and the other person attempts to prevent inputs from reaching the self. Thus personal space may serve as a privacy-regulation vehicle, sometimes opening the self to others and sometimes closing the self off from interaction.

The privacy mechanisms of clothing and personal space are literally close to peoples' bodies. Territorial behavior and the use of the more distant environment will be treated in detail in Chapters 7 and 8, and I will describe them only briefly here.

Anthropological studies of poor families in Mexico by Lewis (1959, 1961) illustrate how environments are used (and sometimes fail) to regulate privacy. In one poor family, in which parents and seven children were living in a single room, the adults located their bed, to achieve privacy, in a far corner of the kitchen area behind a wall built out of empty crates. In a second family (tenement dwellers), privacy was achieved by a norm of not visiting neighbors and a custom of always keeping outside doors closed. But inside, life was plagued by lack of privacy, especially in regard to the toilet, which was located near the kitchen and eating area. The toilet had only a half-shutter swinging door, which did not produce any real separation. A rule was developed (but never really enforced) that the bathroom was not to be used while the family was eating because of the noise, teasing, and general indelicacy that inevitably arose. In wealthier families (those who had more space), there was a greater variety of environmental-control options. In another poor Mexican family (Lewis, 1961), privacy was a serious problem. The family members could rarely act separately from one another—dressing or undressing, listening to a radio program, waking up and going to bed—because of the limited space and facilities and the lack of control by anyone. Using the bathroom was a major trauma because there was no visual and auditory privacy, and teasing was prevalent. In these case studies, there seems to be almost a total absence of ability to use the physical environment to shut the self off from others.

Other analyses of family life also illustrate the role of the physical environment in privacy. For example, Jourard (1966b) noted the importance of family members' having rooms of their own, where they could be alone and away from others. Hill (1969) demonstrated how bedroom windows and curtains are used to adjust noises and visual inputs; Schwartz (1968) described how such things as doors, fences, and signs are used to protect people from unwanted intrusion. Kuper (1953) analyzed an English housing development and noted that flimsy common walls between adjoining family bedrooms, and the design and location of toilets, doors, and paths made privacy difficult to manage. In a more historical vein, McGinley (1959) noted that privacy was a treasured possession and a mark of status in many earlier civilizations (as it is in contemporary society). To protect themselves from unwanted intrusion, affluent Egyptians had vine-hung gardens, Greeks used porticoes, Romans had various enclosures, and the wealthy British had country homes guarded by stone walls and parks. We probably use other settings to achieve comparable separation—for instance, the automobile, the bathroom, or the bedroom. Along these lines, Chermayeff and Alexander (1963) suggested that homes should allow a firm boundary from the outside world and that the interior design should allow a family to have balanced contact with nature on the outside and family interaction on the inside. They also stress the importance of privately owned homes for families, areas that separate adults and children, access routes that are direct and private to various parts of the home, and acoustic and visual isolation of certain areas. Their approach is not only to establish physical boundaries between the family and the outside and among family members but to have access options whereby the members of the family can come together or go apart, depending on the circumstances.

A similar direction of thinking has been applied in other settings, such as communes, collectives, and mental hospitals. For example, Davis and Olesen (1971) observed that residents of an Israeli kibbutz developed a number of techniques to separate themselves from others. These included applying for overtime work in isolated settings, volunteering for undesirable tasks, taking meals alone, and showering or washing at times when others were not apt to be present. All these behaviors were designed to allow the person to seek environmental settings in which boundaries between the self and others could be established.

As another example, Osmond (1957) called for patient privacy as an essential feature of mental-health therapy. Ideally, he stated, patients must have sanctuaries or private places, analogous to animal nests, where they can withdraw from social pressures and stimulation. But there must also be environments that are gradated in opportunity for interaction, so that patients can achieve a level of interaction appropriate to their condition and momentary needs. That is, the therapeutic environment must have a series of boundaries that vary in their permeability and into which patients can gradually move to achieve desired interaction. This idea is analogous to Goffman's (1959) theory of front and back regions. In front regions—that is, "on stage"—people act out roles to fit their expectations about how to behave properly. In back regions—that is, "off stage" (bathrooms, bedrooms, dressing rooms)—masks are dropped and the actors relax, permitting themselves to rest and behave in ways appropriate to being "in private," where they know they are free from observation. Goffman also noted that back regions are often physically separated from front regions and are connected by passageways and doors.

In a different analysis, Goffman (1961) described how patients in mental hospitals are often unable to use ordinary environmental privacy mechanisms. For example, in the situation he observed, patients were often forced to undress, were required to have their hair cut on schedule, and were stripped of possessions. Toilet articles were either taken away or given to the patient in circumscribed settings. In addition, patients were often unable to achieve privacy in a physical sense. Doors on toilets were often absent, urination and defecation were often scheduled by the staff, there were often no private places to store possessions, physical contact with others was often forced, and physical examinations and property inspections were conducted whenever the staff wanted. Thus, much of a patient's life and physical and personal boundaries, which most people take for granted, were no longer under the control of the patient. Another type of boundary violation, termed "looping" by Goffman, was equally pervasive. Most people are more or less able to separate the different roles in their lives; their functioning in one situation (for example, as a husband or father) is separate from their role in other settings (for example, as a business executive). Goffman found that role separation was not possible for mental patients. They were always under observation; their behavior in one situation was never separated from that in another setting. Thus they were constantly confronted with inconsistencies in their behavior and were fully accountable to the same people for all aspects of behavior. Such widespread practices may well be a deterrent to rehabilitation, because they expose the self, eliminate a number of normal self-boundary control processes, and make the person extremely vulnerable to others.

The verbal, nonverbal, and environmental mechanisms used to regulate privacy that have been described thus far have the common goal of adjusting boundaries between self and nonself in accord with a desired level of interaction. There is also another set of mechanisms that partly overlaps those discussed to this point—namely, cultural specifications of behaviors, or norms and modes of regulating privacy.

Culturally Based Privacy Mechanisms

It is easy to point to several obvious ways in which Western culture has certain norms and customs to facilitate privacy management. For example, Schwartz (1968), Kira (1966), and Bossard and Boll (1950) pointed to the sacred role of the bathroom in our culture—a place where people can be quite certain of not being intruded on when the door is closed. In a recent survey, Altman, Nelson, and Lett (1972) also found bathrooms with closed doors to have an aura of sanctity. People typically knocked on closed bathroom doors rather than barging in, and the more intimate the activity (for example, using the toilet), the less likely it was that others were permitted to use the bathroom. In fact, these writers all noted the general sanctity of closed doors to bedrooms, dens, and offices in Western culture, with the message of "leave me alone" or "knock before entering" almost universally communicated. Thus our culture places considerable importance on physical barriers as privacy mechanisms. These include fences, hedges, and separators of various types. Furthermore, our culture emphasizes formal status as a modifier of privacy ranks. For example, children or low-status persons are entitled to fewer privacy mechanisms than higher-status persons. Thus the higher the person's rank in an organization, the more private his or her office and the more barriers (passageways, secretaries) between the person and others. In Altman and his associates' study (1972), parents' closed bedroom doors were rarely passed through without knocking. However, as Bates (1964) noted, parents typically had rights to enter young children's rooms almost at will. And (as already indicated) the staff in mental hospitals often have the right to intrude on patients' possessions and areas, although the reverse is obviously not so.

Several analyses of city life reflect how privacy norms and customs operate. The stereotype of the city-dweller as aloof, cold, uninvolved with others, and impervious to the needs of others goes back to early sociological analyses of urban life by Simmel (1951), Wirth (1938), and others. Milgram (1970) recently postulated the operation of a series of mechanisms that may give rise to such stereotypes. For example, he hypothesized that the city dweller's exposure to such intense and voluminous masses of stimulation from others leads to a general lowering of time given to others and an appearance of brusqueness because of the need to process so much information. Furthermore, the appearance of aloofness and nonconcern with others may derive from a filtering process in which only really important things are attended to and in which other less important inputs are ignored or treated superficially. Other strategies described by Milgram involve blocking inputs and preventing even minimal communication, as, for example, in the use of unlisted telephone numbers. Another mechanism is the more delimited definition of one's personal responsibility to others, which can result in a person's ignoring needs for aid by strangers. This behavior is typified by the anecdote about the big-city pedestrians who literally trample to death someone who momentarily stumbles while walking along the street. Obviously, such mechanisms need to be confirmed and analyzed empirically, but these theoretical speculations illustrate how cultures evolve ways for regulating their interaction with others.

Beyond Western culture there are also customs that have evolved to facilitate privacy regulation. Westin's (1970) analysis of privacy in other cultures is probably the most comprehensive. Most dramatic is the contrast between Western society and either those cultures that have no apparent privacy mechanisms or those that seem to have very elaborate ones. Lee (cited in Westin) reported that members of the Tikopia culture of Polynesia had little physical privacy, with people sleeping side by side in crowded conditions and only infrequently working or being alone. Mead's (cited in

Westin) analysis of Samoan culture also illustrated an apparent lack of privacy. Nudity was common, people were not alone at even birth or death, and houses had few inside or outside walls. Geertz (cited in Westin) illustrated how Javanese culture apparently had little privacy. Homes did not have walls or fences, people wandered in and out, and interiors were not strictly subdivided. Still other cultures have highly structured customs to regulate interpersonal boundaries—for example, the use of the veil around the Tuareg man's face (Murphy, 1964). Geertz reported extreme privacy mechanisms in Bali, with homes surrounded by high walls and people only infrequently entering other homes, much like Lewis's (1959) Mexican tenement families. And as Canter and Canter (1971) noted, the Japanese home is carefully designed to maximize privacy. There are high walls around homes, careful lot and site location ensure against visual access by outsiders, and shifting room and wall arrangements are designed to achieve differential privacy for various situations.

But privacy-regulation mechanisms do not always involve environmental manipulations; they often depend on general styles of behavior. For example, in Javanese society there are few physical symbols of privacy, but a variety of psychological techniques are used to maintain boundaries. Relationships are restrained, people do not express feelings easily, etiquette and politeness are important, and people speak softly. In England, people do not often have private offices or exclusive ownership of places (Hall, 1966), but they obtain privacy by a type of interpersonal reserve; they speak less loudly than Americans, they direct their voices and remarks carefully, and they use nonverbal and verbal means for achieving boundary control. And the Navajo do not use elaborate physical mechanisms to achieve privacy, but there is a pervasive norm concerning individual autonomy and freedom of decision-making (Lee, 1959). People do not coerce one another (including children); the individual is inviolate and is allowed considerable freedom from intrusion.

From such analyses, is it proper to say that some societies are highly private and others are nonprivate? According to Westin's (1970) research and to my approach, the answer is probably "no." Rather, if one examines carefully a culture with seemingly little privacy, privacy mechanisms will eventually be uncovered. Such mechanisms may be nonverbal or verbal, or they may be a blend of these with environmental techniques. Thus I believe that they exist in some form in *all* cultures. To put the point more dramatically, it might be said that mechanisms for separating the self and nonself—that is, for regulating interpersonal boundaries to achieve a desired level of privacy—are universal and present in all societies. Some cultures may appear to have little privacy, but this is probably due to a traditional view of privacy as solely a physical-environment process and not a complex behavioral system that draws on many levels of functioning.

Dynamics of Privacy Regulation

The sequential chain of events of privacy regulation includes, first, a subjective or desired level of privacy in a specific situation. Based on this subjective ideal, a mix of behavioral mechanisms is put into play to achieve the desired privacy state. These mechanisms include various blends of verbal, paraverbal, nonverbal, and environmental behaviors, as well as cultural norms and styles. As discussed earlier, actually achieved levels of privacy might match desired levels, yielding a state of balance. Or the privacy-regulation mechanisms may not have worked too well, resulting in a discrepancy between desired and achieved privacy. More achieved privacy than desired creates a situation of being isolated from others; less achieved privacy than desired creates a state of being crowded or intruded upon.

But boundary-regulation systems are not static; they change over time and have feedback loops that permit readjustments. As situations develop or as a certain level of stimulation is achieved, needs and desires for social contact may change. A person may want to be alone for a while to think through a problem, to organize thoughts, or to ponder an important incident. But after having been alone for a while, the desire to seek stimulation may grow. Thus in the normal course of events the dialectic quality of needs for high interaction and needs for low interaction will vary, and interpersonal boundaries will cycle between being open and closed. Furthermore, as permeability shifts, different blends of behavioral mechanisms may be used. For example, at one point a person may rely heavily on verbal and nonverbal behaviors; at another time personal space and verbal behaviors may predominate.

Privacy situations are not always easy to control successfully. For example, a person may seek solitude by closing a door to a room. However, intrusion may still occur if someone barges in and demands attention. In the face of such an interruption several actions are possible. The person can convey nonverbal cues of dissatisfaction (dirty looks, unpleasant expressions), ignore the intruder, or verbally express a desire to be alone. If none of these work, the person might raise his or her voice to a yell or a shriek or even leave the situation. Thus it is sometimes necessary to escalate responses and make adjustments in self/other boundaries because of misestimates of the effectiveness of the boundary or because of misreadings of the social situation. The situation can also be viewed from the perspective of the hypothetical intruder, who may have a serious problem and desire advice. By all manner of behavior—a forceful entry, pleading expressions, nonverbal behaviors reflecting deference and apology, looks of pain and worry—the intruder may try to show the openness of his boundary system and thus seek to include the other person. From both parties' perspectives, the boundary-

"That's right. Don't bother to knock. Just barge the hell in."

Figure 3-1. Responses to violations of desired levels of privacy can take many forms. Drawing by Stevenson. © 1959 The New Yorker Magazine, Inc. Reprinted by permission.

control systems were not working very well, and adjustments were made to meet individually desired levels of interaction.

One possibility to resolve discrepancies between desired and achieved privacy is to attempt to maintain the original goal—that is, to reach the originally desired degree of privacy—by expending new energies and mechanisms. Another possibility is to shift the original goal. You may discover that the achieved outcome is, in fact, rewarding. For example, giving in to the desires of the intruder in the example may prove to be quite pleasant; you might help the other person, learn more about him or her, and advance a social relationship further. Or being forced to be alone when you initially sought advice may stimulate you to solve the problem in a different and beneficial way. In summary, forces are always present to move the self/other boundary system toward greater openness or closedness, and there is continual adjustment, with shifts in the situation or in personal and group motivations.

These adjustments also require energy expenditure—"costs" and "prices." Such costs may involve physical and psychological energy. Thus the sheer exertion of shrieking or of bodily removing an intruder requires physical energy. And there may be physiological costs such as heightened adrenal-gland functioning or excessive cardiovascular activity. Furthermore, there may be psychological costs as the boundary system fails, including stress, tension, and anxiety. If such costs are incurred over long periods of time the person may well end up in a deteriorated condition. Moreover, even if boundaries are maintained, costs might accumulate if enormous personal and behavioral resources are required. For example, when a person or group must maintain a constant vigil to keep others at a desired interaction distance or must work unceasingly to gain contact and maintain desired levels of interaction, costs may be excessive. Furthermore, these processes need to be understood in terms of an intensity-time effect. It may require little energy to maintain boundaries in an elevator or restaurant, since time in the situation is usually brief. But continual, long-term attempts to manage interpersonal boundaries—as in a home with many family members and few rooms, or in a poorly insulated, noisy, dense work situation with an intrusive, nosy co-worker—in which one spends unending energy in regulating interaction, may yield very high costs to the individual.

In summary, an understanding of privacy as a boundary-regulation system requires study of mechanisms that are used to achieve privacy, changing mixes and patterns of mechanisms, and associated consequences. And very important, the privacy-regulation system is a dynamic one; properties and operation shift over time and with changing circumstances.

Functions of Privacy

Thus far we have examined privacy from three perspectives: (1) a conceptual perspective, with primary emphasis on its interpersonal-boundary properties, (2) a behavioral perspective, with emphasis on mechanisms used to implement privacy, (3) and a perspective that emphasizes dynamics of privacy regulation. Next we will consider privacy in terms of functions or goals. What needs does privacy regulation serve? What is its purpose? What does it do for individuals or groups? It will be proposed that privacy is concerned with three important goals (see Figure 3-2). These goals are: (1) relationships between a person or group and the social world, (2) the interface of the self and social world, and (3) self-definition and self-identity.

Privacy goals are hypothesized to vary on a continuum of "closeness to the self" at one end and "closeness to the social environment" at the other

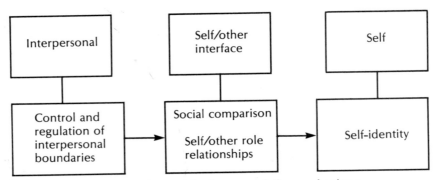

Figure 3-2. Functions of privacy and privacy-regulation mechanisms.

end. This dimension is similar to Altman and Taylor's (1973) idea of inter-personal relationships as involving inside-the-skin processes (perceptions and motivations), boundary-of-the-skin processes (clothing and adornment), and interpersonal events (such as verbal and nonverbal interactions).

We will assume that these functions are cumulative from the outside in. That is, the outermost function of privacy is to regulate interaction with others (along the lines of what has been emphasized in this chapter). This process contributes to the second function—namely, the interface between the self and nonself, or how a person relates to others. This aspect of privacy deals with plans and strategies for relating to others. It also lays the ground-work for the most central function of privacy, the definition of the self.

Interpersonal Functions of Privacy

A major function of privacy is regulation of interaction with the social environment. While the interpersonal function of privacy is important in and of itself, it also acts in the eventual service of the very central goals of self-definition and self-identity. Self-identity is partly dependent on the abil-ity of a person to define his or her own limits and boundaries. A child is born not knowing where it begins and where it ends. It does not discriminate between itself and the environment. It behaves as if the world revolves around it; only gradually does the child learn to separate itself from other persons. It may even be said that the beginnings of becoming a "person" occur when a child learns to distinguish between itself and other persons. This happens as a result of interaction with others, when mutual contact is controlled and regulated, when one's own behavior is separable from others' behavior, and when contacts with others are paced and regulated.

Thus the ability or failure to regulate self/other boundaries is an im-portant contributor to self-definition because it is a source of self-knowledge based directly on overt ongoing interaction. That is, if I see that I cannot control interaction with others in ways that I desire, then I am provided with important negative information about my competence to deal with the world. If I fail to implement my desired contact repeatedly and in many situations, then I gradually will develop a self-definition quite different (and probably more negative) than if I were reasonably successful in regulating interaction with others. Therefore, interpersonal-boundary regulation is an important privacy function, especially in its implications for more fundamental goals.

The Interface of the Self and Nonself

Several writers suggest that privacy serves important functions in interpersonal strategies, roles, plans, and assessment of the self in relation to others. For example, Westin (1970) pointed to *self-evaluation* as a privacy goal. This means that when a person is not in the presence of others, experiences can be integrated, information received from interactions can be processed, and alternative plans for future behavior can be formulated and assessed. As Westin put it, self-evaluation is analogous to a religious retreat or to the exile of political leaders. Separation from others permits assimilation of experiences and examination of possible future relationships with others. Other writers speak of privacy as allowing thinking, reflection, interpretation, and meditation (Kira, 1966; Chapin, 1951; Chermayeff & Alexander, 1963; Jourard, 1966b).

This self-evaluation function of privacy also fits with *social-comparison theory* (Festinger, 1954). The basic idea of this theory, substantiated by considerable research, is that people have a "need" to evaluate themselves, others, and situations. This need for social comparison is particularly evident in ambiguous situations, in which people are inexperienced or momentarily uncertain. Examples include attitudes toward others, emotional states, and reactions to new and strange situations, especially threatening ones. To test this idea, experiments were designed to generate fear, uncertainty, and unusual physical conditions in subjects. In such ambiguous circumstances, which are ever present in our lives, social-comparison theory hypothesizes that we seek other people out to help us define situations, interpret uncertainty, and check our views and opinions. We use other people to help label our feelings and define our perceptions. It might be said, therefore, that one function of privacy is to assist in the social-comparison process—at the interface of the self and others. As such, privacy regulation may enable the person to decide on courses of action, to apply meanings to various interpersonal events, and to build a set of norms or standards for interpreting self/other relations.

A specific area at the interface of the self and others concerns status relations between people. Schwartz (1968) noted that privacy assists in the maintenance of status relationships between superiors and subordinates. High-status people often have the right to intrude on others, but the opposite is usually not the case. Put in more general terms, if my status can be manifested by my ability to control boundaries, then I and others have an indication of who we are *vis à vis* one another. Conversely, a particular role relationship may have a set of agreed-upon boundaries. Hall (1966) gives an interesting example from Theodore White's *The Making of the President: 1960* of how new role relationships are translated into interpersonal boundaries. In 1960, at the time of the presidential convention, John F. Kennedy and his advisors were all gathered together awaiting the outcome of the balloting. As Kennedy came into the group after the victory news was announced, they all rushed to congratulate him but hesitated at the last moment. It was as if they suddenly realized that a new role relationship had been established, that he might become the next president, and that getting too close to him might no longer be appropriate. Only after he beckoned them toward him did they approach. Thus Kennedy had new boundary-control opportunities by virtue of his new status.

All manner of other role relationships can be reflected in boundary processes. Being a good friend implies a role relationship in which mutual boundaries are different from those of casual acquaintances. Being an aloof person implies fewer possibilities for access by others. Thus an important privacy function concerns the nature of relationships one has with other people. In summary, privacy mechanisms not only aid in the regulation of interpersonal interaction but also contribute to the development of interpersonal roles, and toward general strategies and plans for dealing with others.

Self-Identity

This function of privacy has its roots deep inside the self and has at least two aspects: *self-observation* and *self-identity*.

Self-observation involves the opportunity for persons or groups to see, describe, and evaluate themselves, usually when they are out of the presence of others. Self-observation includes the person's dropping social masks of various types, being able to try out new behaviors, and then watching the self exhibit those behaviors. This is what has been termed "being off stage" (Goffman, 1959)—the exhibiting and protecting of vulnerable aspects of behavior (Bates, 1964; Schwartz, 1968) and emotional release (Westin, 1970) and the general laying aside of social roles. An example of this process is the young child or teenager who spends time in front of the mirror trying out various expressions and stances to convey a range of moods, as if they were being practiced alone in readiness for a crucial moment of interaction with another real person. Or intimate group members may try out various roles *vis à vis* one another in a private setting or describe themselves to one another as a basis for greater "we" feeling.

Such self-observations are in the service of self-worth and self-identity. Self-identity is a person or group's cognitive, psychological, and emotional definitions and understanding of themselves as beings. It includes persons' knowing where they begin and where they end, which aspects of the physical world are parts of the self, and which aspects are parts of others. It encompasses self-understanding of one's capabilities and limitations, strengths and weaknesses, emotions and cognitions, beliefs and disbeliefs. Furthermore, self-identity has a strong evaluative (positive or negative) component; that is, am I a worthwhile person to myself and others, and, if so, why?

Privacy in the service of self-identity appears in the writings of many people. For example, Westin (1970) described *personal autonomy*, or an individual's sense of integrity and independence and the ability to avoid being manipulated by others, as a major function of privacy and as "basically an instrument for achieving individual goals of self-realization" (p. 39). Pennock (1971), Beardsley (1971), and Gross (1971) speak of invasions of privacy as especially harmful because they destroy individual autonomy, self-respect, and dignity by taking control of a person's life away from the person and in a sense demeaning the worth of the person. Thus it is a loss of control to others that is serious, not so much the mere exposure of information.

Simmel (1971) captured well the theme of privacy and self-identity:

> We need to be a part of others, of intimate circles, families, communities, nations, part of humanity, and we need to be so recognized by others, to be supported by their approval for our affiliation and our likeness to them. But we also need to confirm our distinctness from others, to assert our individuality, to proclaim our capacity to enjoy, or even suffer, the conflicts that result from such assertions of individuality [p. 73].

He goes on to say how social-comparison and self-identity processes link together:

> It is in part because the self needs periodic conceptual validation from others that its sense of separateness from them is painful and it must lower its boundaries occasionally. On the other hand, because there can be no self without some boundaries, no self without some differences from . . . others, . . . the self sometimes seeks out and sharpens tensions with others [p. 74].[1]

[1]From "Privacy Is Not an Isolated Freedom," by A. Simmel, in J. R. Pennock and J. W. Chapman (Eds.), *Privacy*. Reprinted by permission of the publishers, Lieber-Atherton, Inc. Copyright © 1971. All rights reserved.

Goffman (1961) and Jourard (1966b, 1971a) pointed to the critical effect of a mental patient's privacy on self-identity. As described earlier, Goffman postulated that the violation of the physical and biological self of patients may well retard rehabilitation, since it contributes to the degradation of the self and to a loss and confusion of self-identity and self-esteem.

Others have also treated this theme. Bates (1964) wrote of privacy as serving self-esteem in the setting of personal goals; Proshansky, Ittelson, and Rivlin (1970) emphasized the need for a place where a person could evaluate and find himself; Chapin (1951) noted the importance of privacy for self-respect and self-freedom.

In my view, self-identity is central to human existence. For a person to function effectively in interaction with others requires some understanding of what the self is, where it ends and begins, and when self-interest and self-expression can be exhibited. If one's self is perceived as worthless and if the self has no boundaries and no control over who has access, then the person is literally "nothing." It is difficult to conceive of a person with such feelings as being able to function very well. Or at the other extreme, if everything is viewed as part of the self and controlled by the self (for example, the young child who does not separate the world from the self), then there is also no sense of self-identity; the self is "everything" and knows no uniqueness or separation from others.

The essence of this discussion is that privacy mechanisms define the limits and boundaries of the self. When the permeability of those boundaries is under the control of a person, a sense of individuality develops. But it is not the inclusion or exclusion of others that is vital to self-definition; it is the ability to regulate contact when desired. If I can control what is me and not me, if I can define what is me and not me, and if I can observe the limits and scope of my control, then I have taken major steps toward understanding and defining what I am. Thus privacy mechanisms serve to help me define me. Furthermore, the peripheral functions toward which control is directed—regulation of interpersonal interaction and self/other interface processes—ultimately serve the goal of self-identity.

Chapter 3 described mechanisms or vehicles used to implement desired levels of privacy. These included (1) verbal and paraverbal behavior or the content and form of verbal behavior, (2) personal space or the use of distance/angle of orientation from others (to be reviewed in Chapters 4 through 6), (3) territorial behavior or the use of areas and objects in the environment (to be reviewed in Chapters 7 and 8), and a series of culturally based norms and customs. Thus personal space and territorial behavior function as mechanisms in the service of privacy goals. Privacy mechanisms were hypothesized to operate as a system, sometimes substituting for and sometimes amplifying one another. Thus persons and groups use different mixes of these behaviors at different times and in different circumstances.

It was also noted that privacy mechanisms sometimes fail and that intrusion and crowding occur when insufficient boundary control is achieved. (Crowding will be discussed in detail in Chapters 9 and 10.)

The privacy-regulation system is dynamic, with adjustments and readjustments occurring over time. These changes result from new desired levels of privacy and attempts to maintain desired levels when mechanisms overshoot or undershoot the mark. One effect of adjustment processes is costs of various types—physical, physiological, and psychological—which are often translated into illness, stress, and anxiety.

Chapter 3 also considered goals of privacy regulation. One goal is interpersonal and is concerned with the management of self/other boundaries. A second goal concerns the interface of the self and others—how people use social interaction to define self/other roles and to interpret the self in relation to others. Most central, with its locus in the self, is the goal of self-identity. It was proposed that histories of ability to regulate interaction and privacy contribute to an understanding of the self—where it begins and ends and its capabilities and limitations. They also contribute to the power to control and regulate one's life, and a general sense of self-esteem.

Subsequent chapters are extensions of the ideas presented thus far. Territoriality and personal space are considered vehicles in the service of achieving privacy goals, and crowding is viewed as a condition resulting from privacy goals' being underachieved or achieved at unusual costs.

Personal Space: Meaning, Methods, and Theory

The next three chapters discuss the concept of personal space. In Chapter 4, I will analyze the meaning of the term, examine research methodologies applied to its study, and consider some theoretical positions. Chapter 5 reviews research evidence on individual, cultural, interpersonal, and situational factors associated with personal space. And Chapter 6 deals with special topics such as spatial proximity, personal-space invasion, and the system-like quality of personal-space behaviors.

Historically, more attention has been devoted to personal space than to privacy, territoriality, or crowding. The concept of personal space has roots in the work of ethologists, who have studied the natural life and habits of animals for many years. Hediger (1950) noted that animals often maintain distances from other members of their species or group and that these distances are remarkably constant; for instance, birds sitting on a fence or on a telephone wire seem to have paced off exactly the space between themselves and their neighbors. But there are also other spacing distances used by animals. "Flight distance" refers to the acceptable degree of closeness of another animal, which, if bypassed, is threatening and often leads to escape. There is also a closer "fight or attack distance," which occurs when another animal comes very close; if escape is not possible, the intruder may be attacked.

At a more general level, Hall (1966) described an interplay of *personal distance*, or "the normal spacing that noncontact animals maintain between themselves and their fellows," and *social distance*, or a psychological distance beyond which the organism feels anxious because of a need to be in contact with others. Thus various distances involve simultaneous forces toward separation from others and toward being in contact with others, a dialectic compatible with the notions of privacy discussed in Chapter 2.

The idea of personal space, therefore, deals with the boundary around the self, described by Sommer (1969) as follows:

> Personal space refers to an area with an invisible boundary surrounding the person's body into which intruders may not come. Like the porcupines in Schopenhauer's fable, people like to be close enough to obtain warmth and comradeship but far enough away to avoid pricking one another. Personal space is not necessarily spherical in shape, nor does it extend equally in all directions. . . . It has been likened to a snail shell, a soap bubble, an aura, and "breathing room" [p. 26].

In another definition, Goffman (1971) described personal space as "the space surrounding an individual where within which an entering other causes the individual to feel encroached upon, leading him to show displeasure and sometimes to withdraw" (p. 30).

Several properties of personal space are implicit in these definitions. First, personal space is an "invisible" boundary or separation between the

Figure 4–1. Personal spacing is a common thing among humans and is readily seen in many public situations. (Photograph by Jim Pinckney.)

self and others. Second, it is literally "attached" to the self. As Sommer and DeWar (1963) stated, personal space is carried everywhere one goes, whereas the notion of *territory* usually implies a fixed, geographically immobile region. Third, personal-space regulation is a dynamic process that permits differential access to the self as situations change. Fourth, when someone crosses a personal-space boundary, anxiety or stress often results, or even flight and aggression. Thus personal space is directly related to interpersonal distance, although the angle of orientation from others (face to face, side to side, front to back) is also part of the concept.

Personal Space in the Context of Privacy, Territory, and Crowding

Chapters 2 and 3 portray privacy as a dynamic boundary-regulation process. The self opens to others when interaction is desired, and the self closes itself off if the interaction is more than what is desired or is undesired. As described earlier, privacy regulation is achieved through a series of behavioral mechanisms, including verbal and paraverbal behaviors, nonverbal behaviors involving use of the body, and environmentally oriented behaviors of personal space and territory. Thus personal space is a mechanism used to regulate interpersonal interaction and to achieve a desired level of privacy.

Personal space is often translated into physical distance from others. Hall (1966) emphasized that distance itself is not important; it is the communication cues possible at various distances that lend significance to the concept of personal space. For example, at a distance of 6 inches from another person I can smell, touch, and see fine facial skin textures, whereas at 12 feet my cues about that person and my possibilities for communication are quite different. Personal space and distance serve as a milieu within which different degrees and forms of social contact are possible.

Methods for Studying Personal Space

Three general methods are used to study personal space. The most frequently used and oldest techniques are "simulation" methods; figures or symbols *representing* persons are presented to subjects, who then arrange them or make judgments about the distances between them. A second procedure is the "laboratory" method. This usually involves a laboratory setting where subjects select or respond to actual distances from others. For example, they may be asked to approach another person or to allow another person to approach them to some point of discomfort. The third method is the "field/naturalistic" technique. Here personal-space measurements are obtained in natural environments, with little experimenter intrusion. The subjects often do not even know they are being observed. This technique has been used in schoolyards, in zoos, on street corners, and in other natural settings.

Figure 4–2 is a cumulative distribution of methods used in approximately 200 personal-space studies conducted since the early 1960s, when empirical research first began on a large scale. From the data presented, it is evident that research on personal space is growing at a steady rate. Simulation methods are clearly the most popular strategy, with laboratory methods close behind and field/naturalistic strategies only recently used. However, use of the latter two methods is increasing, and continued growth is likely.

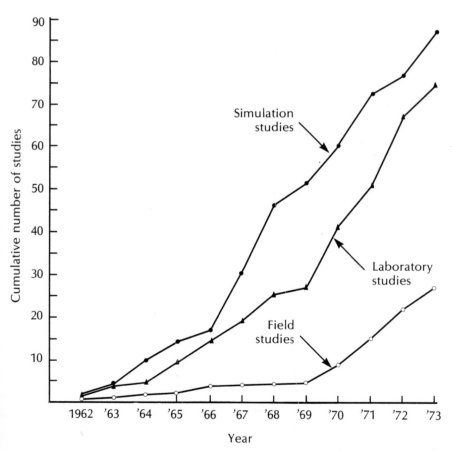

Figure 4–2. Cumulative rates of occurrence of simulation, laboratory, and field studies of personal space.

A methodological issue concerns personal space as a dependent variable or as an independent variable. Theoretically, personal space can serve either as a predictor (or independent variable) or as a behavioral outcome (or dependent variable). Thus we could ask an independent-variable question: "What are the effects of different personal spaces on outcomes such as liking, perceptions, and so on?" To answer such a question, distances between people are experimentally varied and effects measured by questionnaire responses, behavior alterations, or other procedures. Only about 20% of the studies I examined used personal space as an independent variable. Most research focuses on personal space as a dependent variable or behavioral outcome. Here distance between people is studied as an outcome rather than as a predictor variable, with the following types of questions in mind: "What is the effect of interpersonal attraction or liking on interpersonal distance?" or "Do people with emotional disturbances use different personal-space zones than so-called normals?"

Simulation Techniques

The earliest and most popular simulation strategy was developed by Kuethe (1962a, 1962b) and his colleagues at Johns Hopkins University in the late 1950s and early 1960s. The technique was based on the idea of "social schemata," or culturally shared perceptions about how things and people go together spatially. To study these schemata, Kuethe used 7-inch to 10-inch flannel, cut-out figures of men, women, children, animals, and rectangles. The subjects were to place groups of these objects on a flannel board in any formats desired. From these early studies it was discovered that certain figures were grouped together in certain ways: (1) figures were usually placed vertically, (2) woman-child combinations were placed closer together than man-child pairs, (3) figures were often ordered by height, (4) dogs were often placed nearer to men than to women, and (5) rectangles were rarely placed between a man and a woman.

The format of study just described is a *free-placement* technique, in which figures can be placed anywhere, the measure being either how figures are grouped or actual distances between them. Another approach used by Kuethe was a *reconstruction* or *replacement* task. Here decks of figures were presented to the subject for a short period in already-fixed arrangements. The figures were then removed from the board and the subject's task was to replace them as they were originally located.

Variations of this basic procedure include groups of human silhouettes, line drawings of figures in various postures (reclining, sitting, leaning forward), miniature statues or dolls, and overhead drawings of figures or heads to convey distance zones around the person. Another variant of the technique uses abstract symbols (such as circles or triangles) to represent people, with the subject asked to arrange them in lines, inside or outside various spatial zones.

Laboratory Techniques

Laboratory techniques are second in popularity to simulation methods. However, they are likely to be used more and more as researchers begin to tap actual spatial behavior rather than simulated representations of behavior. There are three key features of laboratory techniques. (1) Subjects are placed in a laboratory situation, which is not typically part of their natural environment, and they are often aware that their spatial behavior is being observed. (2) Some control is exerted by the experimenter over the situation or over the types of responses that subjects can exhibit. (3) As with simulation methods, distance is the primary measure of personal space, and not much attention has been paid to angles of orientation between people.

An early laboratory technique was developed by Horowitz, Duff, and Stratton (1964), who examined the spatial habits of schizophrenic patients, nonschizophrenic patients, and "normal" persons. Subjects physically approached either another person or a hat rack (an inanimate object), and measurements were made of the distance they stopped from the stimulus target. Subjects approached targets frontally, sideways, or diagonally.

In other variants of this technique, subjects approached a target person or object to the point beyond which they no longer felt "comfortable," or sometimes a target person (often a confederate) approached subjects to the point at which the subject told the person to stop.

Other laboratory techniques include chair selection or manipulation by the experimenter of chair and seating arrangements. For example, several studies observed which of several chairs or seating locations subjects chose when conversing with others. Other studies reversed the situation and varied the distance a confederate sat from a subject—for example, across the long side of a table, diagonally, or across the short side of a table—and then studied the impact on behaviors such as eye contact and feelings of comfort.

Field/Naturalistic Techniques

The study of personal space in naturalistic settings has only recently begun, but the coming years will probably show a sharp increase in this methodological strategy. Field techniques involve studying personal space in everyday situations, such as school playgrounds, classrooms, libraries, parks, or cafeterias. Furthermore, the persons observed usually are not aware that they are part of a research study, since measurement is often done unobtrusively; for example, observation of distances maintained by children in a playground may involve use of telephoto lenses, or the coding of distances between people watching animals in a zoo may be done from several yards away.

Field/naturalistic methods, like simulation and laboratory techniques, can be used to study personal space from either an independent- or dependent-variable perspective. Some investigations of personal-space invasion were made from an independent-variable perspective by approaching people at close or far distances and then observing reactions. In a dependent-variable strategy, studies have examined spacing behaviors of various groups (children versus adults, ethnic and sex groups) as a result of diverse conditions.

Theoretical Approaches to Personal Space

These research techniques reflect several theoretical approaches to personal space. However, much of the research on this topic was stimulated by the observations of Edward Hall, an anthropologist who wrote a book in 1966 entitled *The Hidden Dimension*. This book pointed to the fact (a fact then not so obvious to many social and behavioral scientists) that people make very active use of space in communicating with one another and that cultures have different customs regarding space usage. Hall proposed a science of "proxemics," or the study of man's use of space as a communication vehicle. It is probably fair to say that his writings and astute observations have been the single most important impetus for research on personal space, in spite of the fact that he typically relied on qualitative descriptions of personal space rather than on quantitative empirical research.

Hall's theory of personal space falls into two areas. First, he proposed a scheme of proxemics that could be applied to the analysis of spatial zones used by people in different social relationships and settings. Second, he offered some general observations about how different cultures make use of space and how conflict can result from interpretations of others' spatial practices.

Interpersonal Distance Zones

Hall spoke of four spatial zones used in social interaction. The first zone, *intimate distance,* covers the range of 0 to 18 inches. According to Hall:

> At intimate distance the presence of the other person is unmistakable and may at times be overwhelming because of the greatly stepped up sensory input.

Sight (often distorted), olfaction, heat from the other person's body, sound, smell, and feel of the breath all combine to signal unmistakable involvement with another body [p. 110].

In the close phase of the zone (0 to 6 inches), physical contact is considerable. Hall describes this distance as one at which "lovemaking and wrestling, comforting, and protecting" could easily occur. Think for a moment what it is like to be facing another person eye to eye at a distance of 6 inches or less (or even 18 inches or less). The possibilities for receiving and conveying communication cues are extraordinary. You can see a great deal—the texture of the skin, wrinkles and blemishes on the face, eye color, the degree of whiteness of the eyeball, and slight twitches of the eyebrows or mouth. And there is more than seeing at such distances. You can touch almost any part of the body of the other person, or you can easily embrace them. You can also smell the other person—breath, lotions, and perfumes. Body heat and breathing rates are also distinguishable and can be important cues about general arousal. Thus this intimate zone is a rich one in terms of its potential for communication; it exposes much about a person. It is perhaps for these reasons that Hall said this distance is usually reserved for intimates, lovers, and spouses and, even among them, is frowned on in public.

While this zone is pleasant in some situations, as when one is interacting with a loved one, it can be quite unpleasant in other situations. For example, when people are forced involuntarily into proximity, as in a crowded elevator, they often become immobile and rigid, looking up nervously at the floor numbers or down at the floor, perhaps as a signal that they realize they are violating one another's intimate distances but are trying to do their best to avoid inappropriate interaction.

Hall termed a second zone *personal distance*, which spans the range from 1½ to 4 feet. This distance is the characteristic spacing people use with one another; intrusion beyond this distance is uncomfortable. The close phase of the zone (1½ to 2½ feet) still permits rich exchange of touch, smell, sight, and other cues, although there is by no means as much exchange as occurs in the intimate zone. Fine musculature of the face, pores, and facial hair are still visible, and there is considerable potential for touch at less than arm's length. As with the intimate zone, Hall feels that the close phase of this personal distance zone is reserved for intimates. The far phase covers about 2½ to 4 feet and extends from a point that is just outside easy touching distance by one person to a point at which two people can touch hands if they extend their arms. "Beyond it, a person cannot easily 'get his hands on' someone else" (Hall, p. 113). At this range, fine grain communications can be observed, including hair color, skin texture, and general facial features. Voice cues are also rich, although smell and body heat typically cannot be detected unless perfume is used. The personal-distance zone is transitional between intimate contact and rather formal, public behavior.

The third zone, *social distance*, ranges from about 4 feet to 12 feet and is the normal distance at which business and general social contact occur. An examination of office reception areas and desk and public furniture arrangements will reveal that this zone is rather widely used. For example, the typical office desk is 2½ feet wide. When chair locations on either side are taken into account, the distance between people will be in the neighborhood of 4 feet or more. (We also know that the higher one's status, the larger the desk, so that important people are often located at the upper ranges of this zone).

In the near part of the social zone (4 to 7 feet) visual contact is not as finely tuned as in the other zones (the visual range encompasses the head, shoulders, and upper trunk). Vocal cues such as loudness or pitch can be easily detected, but heat, olfactory, and touch cues become relatively unimportant. Interaction among people who work closely together and among casual acquaintances often occurs at this distance, and it is an acceptable and appropriate distance in public settings. Hall and others observed that people in airports, in public conversation on street corners, or in offices often maintained distances from one another in this range. The far phase of the zone (7 to 12 feet) is considerably more formal; fine visual details are often lost, although the full figure is easily perceived. And heat, touch, and smell are usually no longer available at this distance.

The last zone, *public distance*, varies from 12 to 25 feet and is the distance at which communication cues become quite gross; the richness of most communication channels is much less than that of the preceding zones. Such distances are typically reserved for formal occasions or for public speakers or high-status persons. Lecterns in classrooms and arrangements for speakers usually place the person at least 12 feet away from even the front row of an audience. And speakers are often elevated above the audience or put behind tables and lecterns. I often find myself stepping down from a platform or pushing a lectern closer to the audience, trying to get closer to them in order to pick up cues from them and to make available a greater range of cues from me. Such formal arrangements often occur at official dinners; that is, the head tables and dignitaries are somewhat remote from others. Courtrooms also establish formality by the location and distance of the judge, jurors, defendants, and attorneys.

Several ideas are explicit in Hall's analysis of distance zones: (1) the zones are not necessarily universal, and there are wide cultural variations in what behaviors are permissible in each zone and in what distances are appropriate with certain persons in certain settings. (2) The zones are not important in terms of physical distance per se; they are important because of the interpersonal communication possibilities they offer. They are milieus within which a variety of behavioral possibilities and communication chan-

Figure 4–3. Social distance—a zone used widely in public settings. (Photograph by Jim Pinckney.)

nels are embedded. In line with this idea, Hall (1966) called for categorization of behaviors in each zone as follows:

1. Postural-sex identifiers: standing, sitting, squatting.
2. Sociofugal-sociopedal orientation: body angle or facing positions.
3. Kinesthetic factors or the potentiality for touch.
4. Touching.
5. Visual possibilities.
6. Thermal or heat cues.
7. Olfactory or smell cues.
8. Voice loudness.

My conceptual framework meshes nicely with Hall's thinking. The various space zones represent boundaries around the self that allow various degrees of openness to others. By moving closer to or away from other people, we change their accessibility to us. By moving away we signal a desire for more privacy and use personal space as a mechanism to shut off certain channels of communication. By moving closer to someone, we permit greater access to our self and open up an increasing richness of communication. Thus Hall's distance zones serve to regulate contact with others and make self/other boundaries more or less permeable.

In several parts of the next chapter I will refer to research that bears on Hall's distance zones. Briefly, the evidence is generally supportive of Hall's thinking, although not all zones have been studied rigorously. For example, studies of personal-space intrusion confirm the idea that close contact with strangers, within about 2 feet, is aversive and leads to discomfort. Studies of close contact between friends support the idea that very close distances are appropriate for people in an intimate relationship. Although very few studies have examined social and public zones, there are some suggestive results indicating that, in interaction among persons who are not friends, both overly intimate and overly formal distance zones are avoided. Thus Hall's ideas about intimate and personal distances are generally confirmed—not in specific inches or feet but within a reasonable range. However, relatively little is known about the other two zones or about which distances are used in which settings by people in various social relationships.

Cultural Differences in Personal Space

The second facet of Hall's interest was related to cross-cultural differences in use of space. He observed that the norms and customs of different ethnic and cultural groups were reflected in their use of space—furniture arrangements, home configurations, and distances and angles of orientation that people maintained from one another. He described, in a qualitative way, how members of various cultural groups differed in spatial habits. According to Hall, Germans are much more sensitive to intrusion, have larger personal-space bubbles, and are more concerned with physical separation than Americans, and they go to considerable lengths to maintain privacy by means of doors and physical layouts. The English, Hall states, are also private people but manage their psychological distance from others by verbal and nonverbal means (such as voice characteristics and eye contact) rather than by physical and environmental means. Even the well-to-do often grow up in less-than-spacious circumstances, and so they are not accustomed to having totally private places. Hall described the well-known English reserve and reticence as including psychological, nonverbal, and verbal mechanisms for achieving desired contact with others. The French, on the other hand, interact in a much more involved, sensory fashion, again partly as a function of life-style and experiences.

Hall also described Arabic cultures as highly sensory, with people interacting at very close quarters—nose to nose, breathing in one another's faces, touching, and the like. For Arabic, Mediterranean, and Latin cultures, sensory input from all channels is important. Hall observed that these cultures tend to be more "contact" oriented than Northern European and Western cultures—at least in public settings and with strangers. Close distances and cues of touch, olfaction, and body heat seem to be more prevalent in contact cultures; this closeness often creates communication difficulties for those not accustomed to having someone breathe in their face, touch them, or emit a variety of odors normally hidden in Western cultures by soaps, deodorants, sprays, and perfumes.

Finally, Hall observed that the Japanese use space in an elaborate way, perhaps in response to their dense population. Japanese families have a great deal of close interpersonal contact; they often sleep together in crowded arrangements or use the same space for many activities. Spatial arrangement of gardens, landscaping, and artwork is a highly developed activity, designed to illustrate man's unity with nature, the interplay of all the senses, and the importance of relationships between people and the environment.

Hall's observations promoted research on cross-cultural differences in personal space (reviewed in the next chapter). In general, the results lend some plausibility to Hall's qualitative observations, but the question of cross-national differences in personal space has not been researched to any great extent.

Beyond Hall, theoretical positions are mostly preliminary and recent. For example, Leibman (1970) proposed a model in which perceptions and attributions of individuals are central features of personal space. That is, she proposed a "psychological" rather than a strictly physicalistic approach. According to Leibman, personal space involves expectations about interpersonal goals, which are then related to distance and position in space. Such goals include formality, intimacy, privacy, and so on. Personal space, therefore, deals with how people *expect* space to be used. Leibman also called for an integrative analysis of personal space as part of a coherent behavioral system in which verbal, nonverbal, and body behaviors join together to facilitate goal attainment. The idea that personal space is integrated with other levels of behavior is, of course, central to our thinking.

Argyle and Dean (1965) also took a systems approach and postulated an equilibrium hypothesis regarding level of intimacy of social interaction. Increased intimacy was hypothesized to be associated with a combination of behaviors, including eye contact, physical distance, and personal disclosures. In their model, if one behavioral component shifts and if a particular level of intimacy is to be achieved, then another behavior will change to restore the equilibrium. For example, as distance between people decreases, eye contact decreases, and vice versa. Thus they proposed a compensatory model in which various aspects of behavior join together in different combinations to achieve a desired level of exchange. Argyle and Dean presented these ideas several years ago, and a number of studies generally support their compensatory model of personal space (Goldberg, Kiesler, & Collins, 1969; Argyle & Ingham, 1972; Aiello, 1972).

In another theoretical statement, Duke and Nowicki (1972) proposed a social-learning model of personal space. They believe that distancing is learned (an idea probably acceptable to most theoreticians) and that learning occurs because of reinforcements and expectancies about reinforcements. A person's history of reinforcement results in a general personality orientation regarding internal/external causation. That is, some people view reinforcements as being under the control of the self (internal orientation), while others see reinforcements as under the control of some external source (external orientation). They compared the distancing of persons with internal or external locus-of-control orientations and hypothesized that internally oriented people would distance *less* from strangers. That is, those who rely on others for reinforcement ("externals") should desire more distance from others when they know little about them (perhaps because they feel more vulnerable), whereas "internals" should not keep as much distance from strangers, since they are less dependent on others for social gratification (and may feel less threatened by them). The results of one study confirmed these predictions. While this approach is at its barest beginnings, it suggests that a personality-oriented, social-learning model may be useful.

It should be obvious that theorizing about personal space is at an early stage. Except for Hall's global framework, the points of view are only recently developed and not extensively researched. My framework is also general and views personal space as one of a series of self/other boundary mechanisms that function in the service of desired levels of interaction. This way of thinking does not rule out any other theoretical direction. Leibman's expectancy theory, if developed further, could possibly describe how boundary-control mechanisms are set in motion; the equilibrium hypothesis proposed by Argyle and Dean deals with the rules of combination of various behaviors and the circumstances under which different behaviors compensate, substitute, or enhance one another. And the social-learning/personality-theory approach of Duke and Nowicki can provide valuable information about how personal-space mechanisms are used and how they relate to personality differences. In a very real sense, these are not competing theoretical approaches. Rather, they each tap a different facet of the process, and each needs to be pursued further.

In summary, research on personal space has led to a large number of empirical studies, often without any theoretical underpinning. Methodological development has also received considerable attention, and properly so. However, the time is at hand not only to integrate findings from all these studies but to take aggressive steps toward general theory development. The framework of this volume presents one general way of thinking about personal space, but it now remains to identify useful theoretical constructs at a more detailed level. And as my sampling of emergent theories and methods indicates, it would be helpful to use ideas from other parts of the social and behavioral sciences, such as role theory, expectancy concepts, and social-learning theory, to understand better the concepts of personal space, crowding, territory, and privacy.

This chapter considered representative definitional, methodological, and theoretical issues concerning personal space, which is one of several privacy-regulation mechanisms. A number of methods for doing research on personal space were described, including simulation methods, laboratory methods, and field/naturalistic methods. Some theoretical approaches to personal space were also discussed, the most prominent of which is the spatial-zones approach. Others included an equilibrium model, a social-learning hypothesis, and a psychological-expectation approach. Chapter 4 is summarized in greater detail along with Chapters 5 and 6 at the end of Chapter 6.

Factors Related to Personal Space

This chapter examines three broad classes of factors that affect or are affected by personal space: (1) individual factors, (2) interpersonal factors, and (3) situational factors.[1]

Individual factors deal with properties of specific persons: biographical variables such as age and sex, cultural variables such as socioeconomic, ethnic, and racial characteristics, personal-skill factors such as creativity and intelligence, personality factors such as need achievement and need affiliation, personality disorders and abnormality, and personal handicaps such as speech and physical disorders. Research on these factors deals with differences among types of people in their personal-space boundaries and the permeability of those boundaries.

Interpersonal factors refer to social relationships among people in regard to attraction, cohesion and liking, interpersonal influence, group composition (with attention to sex and ethnic variables), and group structural factors such as size and status. This research asks about the permeability of personal-space boundaries for people who differ in their relationships with one another.

Situational factors deal with the general setting within which people or groups function, including physical factors such as seating arrangements, the formality of situations, and public versus private settings. Here, interest is on the impact of settings on regulation of personal-space boundaries.

[1]Recent reviews of personal-space research have also been done by Evans and Howard (1973) and Pedersen and Shears (1973).

Individual Factors in Personal Space

Research on individual differences occurred early in the history of personal-space studies, perhaps because some of the differences, such as age, sex, and other biographical, cultural, and personality differences, were easily measured. With few exceptions much of this research was "shotgun," atheoretical, and based on an "I wonder what will happen" approach rather than derived from ordered conceptualizations or theory. As we might expect in a new field, most early research on individual factors was a preliminary probe designed to assess the feasibility of research in this field and to identify potentially fruitful areas and methods of study. My review will emphasize reasonably well-researched individual factors including (1) age and developmental processes, (2) sex, (3) personality factors, including various traits and abnormal/normal comparisons, and (4) cultural differences.

Age and Developmental Processes

Edward Hall, who stimulated much of the work on personal space, once presented a talk with slides that illustrated beautifully how children learn spacing mechanisms. The candid photographs that he showed from different cultures demonstrated that parents actually positioned their young children at various distances from themselves as they talked with them—moving them closer or farther away—thereby indicating to the children where and how to stand. Those who have been around young children know that they often come too close or not close enough in different instances. Sometimes they breathe in your face as they talk; at other times they blurt out intimacies in loud voices at great distances. Children seem to learn only gradually the appropriate distances to maintain from others in different social situations. But the available research data indicate that they do learn how to manage personal space and that the learning is quite comprehensive and parallel to their learning of other social skills. Furthermore, the data suggest that boys and girls learn boundary-regulation rules at different times, an indication of the differences in sex-role training in our society.

One line of research has been spearheaded by Guardo and Meisels and their associates, using the Kuethe simulation technique described in Chapter 4. They found that young children had stable social schemata, with figures labeled as strangers placed farther away than figures representing friends or persons who liked one another (Meisels & Guardo, 1969; Estes & Rush, 1971; Guardo & Meisels, 1971b). Thus even young children reflected more open personal-space boundaries for intimate others versus nonintimate others.

There is also some evidence concerning when and how self/other boundaries develop. For example, Guardo and Meisels (1971b) compared boys and girls in the third through the tenth grades (ages 8 to 16) and found more well-established figure placements in older children (seventh through tenth grades) and more rapid development of stable placements in girls. Fewer differences among girls at different ages than among boys suggested a systematic and an earlier cultural training of girls in regard to rules of social interaction. (These data are also congruent with the fact that girls in our culture have greater social maturity at an earlier age.) They also reported that girls typically put larger distances between figures than boys (and had generally less-permeable self/other boundaries). By the ninth or tenth grades, there were few differences between the sexes in space usage. Their results also suggested that greater distances were kept from opposite-sex figures in earlier grades than in later grades (after the sixth grade). This developmental process is supported by general observations that children often avoid too much contact with the opposite sex until they discover new virtues in one another, around the period of adolescence.

While the data are not extensive, they suggest that the process of learning self/other boundary control begins early in the socialization process, as children have contact with one another in a variety of situations. By adolescence the personal-space boundary system is probably well established, although elements of it seem operative earlier.

A somewhat different approach to developmental processes was taken by Long, Henderson, and Ziller (1967). In one study of children 6 to 12 years old, individuation (measured by the subject's choosing a circle of a particular size to represent himself) increased with age, as did self-esteem (preference ranking of a self symbol in relationship to symbols representing others), identification (placement of a self symbol in close relations with others), and dependency (perception of a self symbol as part of a group). There was, in my terms, greater boundary articulation as children became older and a greater sensitivity to where and when self/other boundaries were to be open or closed.

Koslin, Koslin, Pargament, and Bird (1971) used line drawings of figures to track children's developmental patterns in personal space. In grades one through four, children placed figures differing in sex farther apart than those differing in race, whereas, in the higher grades, racial differences were more important than sex differences. These occurrences fit with other research that indicates children only gradually learn to develop social distance from other ethnic groups and that such separation is often established by adolescence.

In summary, the volume of research on developmental processes is small, although the results are orderly and fit with other information about childhood socialization. Personal spacing seems to stabilize reasonably early in life, but it isn't until adolescence that the system is finely tuned to handle a variety of situations and social relationships.

Personality Abnormality

One of the most popular areas in the early days of personal-space research involved personality—especially personality disorders. Most studies used simulation techniques and a few used laboratory methods to contrast the personal-space behaviors of people with social-emotional disorders—for example, schizophrenics, psychotics, neurotics, and drug addicts. These studies often examined the hypothesis that emotionally disturbed people would have different personal-space zones and that their deviant social behavior would be reflected in deviant spatial behavior. In my terms, it might be expected that the boundary-control mechanisms of unusual populations would be different from those of most people. In some instances, members of atypical groups may be more open; in other cases, they may be less open, suggesting a distorted or differently operating self/other control system. Such a control system is compatible with anecdotal observations that disturbed people are not only "weird" in their verbal and social behavior but are different in their willingness to touch or be touched or to approach or be approached by others. It is as if they have "different" self/other boundary systems from most people. Research results generally substantiate these expectations, although the issue is not as simple as it first appears to be.

In an early study, Horowitz, Duff, and Stratton (1964) compared hospitalized schizophrenics with other groups. Under the guise of conducting an equilibrium test, they asked subjects to approach a person and a hat rack. Schizophrenics and other psychiatric patients went closer to the hat rack than to the person. Furthermore, schizophrenics' approach distances were more variable; they approached the targets either more closely or more distantly than others. In another facet of this study, schizophrenics and "normals" approached the person and hat rack from several angles (frontally, backwards, sideways). Here, schizophrenics showed a greater variability and also stayed at greater distances from either object. In another setting, subjects were given an overhead drawing of a figure representing themselves; they then drew a line around the figure to indicate the distance they would like to keep between themselves and others. Schizophrenics drew lines keeping people at greater distances than nonschizophrenics. In still another study, Horowitz (1968) asked newly admitted mental patients to approach another person to a point of discomfort. This procedure was repeated every three weeks until the patient was discharged. Schizophrenics initially maintained the most distance compared with other psychotic groups, but they moved closer when their clinical state had been independently judged to be improved. Depressed patients maintained closer distances than schizophrenics but moved even closer as they approached their discharge date. Thus, with successful therapy, the self/other boundary processes of patients gradually became similar to those of nonpatients.

In a study of seating preferences, Sommer (1959) found that schizophrenics chose distant diagonal or immediately adjacent seats relative to a target person at a table, whereas normals preferred intermediate distances or corner-to-corner seating. Thus some data show disturbed persons' using greater distances from others than normals, other data report their using smaller distances, and there is an indication of greater variability in distance placements by abnormal persons.

Historically, studies of personality disorder and personal space relied heavily on simulation techniques. For example, Blumenthal and Meltzoff (1967) gave schizophrenics a task in which they were first shown figures at a certain distance apart and were then asked to replace them in the same relationship. The results indicated that schizophrenics were less accurate than normals in reproducing the original distances. And their errors were either overestimates or underestimates. Using a test involving placement of symbols representing people, Ziller, Megas, and DiCencio (1964) and Ziller and Grossman (1967) found that hospitalized psychotics placed themselves lower than normals on an ordering of symbols from left to right (low self-esteem) and placed symbols representing themselves farther from other symbols, the distance increasing with age. Similar results were obtained by Long, Ziller, and Bankes (1970) in an analysis of problem-behavior adolescents.

A series of studies investigated the personal-space behavior of children with social and emotional disturbances. Weinstein (1965) and Fisher (1967) found that disturbed children placed a greater distance between figures than normals did. These findings were supported by the studies of DuHamel and Jarmon (1971) and Newman and Pollack (1973), the latter study dealing with teenagers who had behavior problems. Tolor (1968) did not obtain such results but noted that disturbed children exhibited more response variability than normals.

Moving away from strict psychological disorders, a few studies looked at the behavior of convicted prisoners. Kuethe and Weingartner (1964) found that homosexual prisoners placed male figures closer together than did nonhomosexuals and also placed rectangles between men and women figures more often than normals. Kinzel (1970) worked with prisoners who were classified (according to their prior histories) as having high and low aggression. He found, by observing how closely the prisoners allowed others to approach them, that the more violent prisoners had larger body-buffer zones. Similar results were obtained by Hildreth, Derogatis, and McCusker (1971). Those prisoners classified as "violent" or "aggressive" may have a self/other boundary system that is less permeable than that of most people. They may, therefore, have been intruded upon often (by their personal definition) and reacted quite negatively to others who came too close, however inadvertently it may have happened. The old clichés about a person's "needing elbow room" and "keeping others at arm's length" may be part of the dynamics underlying data on aggressive tendencies in personal space.

Abnormality, in any of several forms, is associated with either (1) greater interpersonal distance from others or (2) greater variability in distance kept from others. I am more comfortable, at this stage of knowledge, with the idea that personality abnormality or social deviance may be associated with greater distortion in personal spacing than with the unidirectional "greater distance" notion. The idea that social deviancy is associated only with greater distances seems unwarranted by the present pool of knowledge. In the terms of my framework, those with social-emotional problems probably have personal-boundary processes that are different from those of nondeviant groups.

Reactions to Those with "Abnormalities"

A small but interesting cluster of studies has tackled the issue from the other side of the coin; that is, "How do others react to those with an abnormality or defect?" Kleck, Buck, Goller, London, Pfeiffer, and Vukcevic (1968) demonstrated that people maintain greater distance from those labeled as having some type of social stigma (for example, amputees, epileptics, or mental patients) than from nonstigmatized persons. In one test, subjects placed rectangles representing the self and various others, and in another test they selected chairs arranged at various distances from others who either were labeled as epileptics or were not so labeled. In both situations greater distances were maintained from stigmatized people. Furthermore, on a figure-placement task, greater distances were kept from those with nonvisible stigma (for example, epileptics and mental patients) versus those with readily observed stigma (such as amputees). Similar results were obtained by Wolfgang and Wolfgang (1971). They used a figure-placement task with the self placed in relation to others who were obese, drug users, homosexuals, and physically handicapped. Again, those with stigma were placed farther from the self than "normals." Wolfgang and Wolfgang (1968) also found a relationship between the type of physical handicap and distance, which they attributed to a handicap "threat" quality. Figures with broken arms were placed closest to a self figure, amputees and clubfoots were placed at intermediate distances, and obese figures were placed farthest away. Similar results were obtained with children in grades one through three; these children kept obese figures at greater distances than thin or well-built ones

(Lerner, 1973), which suggests that we learn to respond negatively to deviant people early in life. Also, Comer and Piliavin (1972) reported that, in a face-to-face interview, subjects stayed at a greater distance from a physically disabled person. And physically disabled subjects also exhibited strained behavior in an interview with a nondisabled person; they smiled less, avoided eye contact, ended the conversation sooner, and were more rigid in their body behavior. Thus these studies suggest that people try to seal themselves off from unusual people. Many people feel quite uncomfortable in the presence of a person who has some social stigma. This discomfort and attempt to put up a barrier against an unusual person not only occurs through words and nonverbal behavior but also seems evident in personal-space control mechanisms.

If the data on the behavior of disturbed persons are pieced together with reactions to such persons by others, it seems clear that we are dealing with an interpersonal "system," in which it is difficult to partial out simple cause and effect. Social deviants both react to others and are reacted to by others; this process yields a mutual boundary system, which does not function in the same way as the boundary system does for interaction among normals. But the etiology is probably not in either party alone; it likely resides in the relationship between them. Therefore, to understand personal-space mechanisms, we must move in directions that account for the joint regulation of boundaries by both partners of an exchange.

Personality Correlates of Personal Space

Moving away from personal deviance, several studies investigated personality correlates of personal space. For example, do people with outgoing, expansive personalities also have personal-space boundaries that are permeable to others? Are fear of others, anxiety, introversion, and a low self-image also reflected in resistance to making the self spatially accessible?

One thrust of research in this area concerns anxiety. Several studies generally confirm the idea that anxiety-prone people place greater distance between themselves and others, that close distances are perceived as more anxiety-provoking, and that stress-producing conditions yield greater distances from others. For example, Smith (1953, 1954) found that highly anxious subjects placed photographs of others at a greater distance from themselves than did less anxious persons. Similar results were obtained by Luft (1966), Weinstein (1968), Patterson (1973b), Karabenick and Meisels (1972), and Bailey, Hartnett, and Gibson (1972), all of whom used questionnaire measures of anxiety.

Other studies demonstrated an interaction of anxiety-provoking situations and personality. For example, using a laboratory technique, Meisels and Dosey (1971) found that interpersonally defensive people maintained greater distances from others, especially when they were provoked to anger. In another experiment (Dosey & Meisels, 1969), those in a stressful condition (they were told that their physical and sexual attractiveness was being studied), also kept greater distances from others. Similar results were obtained by Dinges and Oetting (1972); subjects rated the anxiety portrayed by people (in photographs) who were at various distances and in different counseling situations.

In another realm of study, there are some data to support the obvious idea that extroverts (outgoing, high-social-contact, people-seeking persons) maintain closer personal space than introverts (withdrawn, inward-type persons). Williams (1971) found that introverts preferred greater distances from others, as expected, but there were no differences in actual chair selection in a discussion with a confederate. Cook (1970), as well as Patterson and Holmes (1966), found that extroverts sat closer to others in a variety of discussion situations. However, Meisels and Canter (1970) did not obtain such results.

Beyond the work reported here, the literature on personality correlates of personal space loses its coherence, as if research proceeded in a "shotgun" strategy, seeking out person-linked correlates of personal space almost willy-nilly. For example, a variety of studies found the following:

1. Self-directed people were more willing to approach strangers and authority figures than were those more dependent on external reinforcements from others (from a simulation-task study by Duke and Nowicki, 1972).
2. Persons with high self-esteem and low authoritarianism approached others more closely than did authoritarians and those with low self-esteem (from a laboratory-task study by Frankel and Barrett, 1971).
3. Those with high self-concepts approached others closely on a simulation task but not on a laboratory task (Stratton, Tekippe, and Flick, 1973).
4. Racially prejudiced persons did not group different ethnic figures together as often as did unprejudiced people (from a simulation-task study by Kuethe, 1964).
5. People with a clear sense of their body boundary, as measured by an ink-blot test, were willing to have closer contact with others than were those with a less definite body barrier (from a simulation-task study by Frede, Gautney, and Baxter, 1968).
6. Firstborn children placed themselves closer to their fathers and more distant from their mothers and siblings than laterborns (from a simulation-task study by Hamid, 1970).
7. Those with predispositions for high affiliation sat closer to others than did low affiliators (from a laboratory-task study by Mehrabian and Diamond, 1971).

Research on personality correlates of personal space is suggestive but by no means unequivocal. There are certain reasonably confirmed relationships; for example, emotional disorders are associated with greater and/or distorted boundary processes, and threatened or anxious people maintain greater distances from others. However, because results are not always unequivocal from study to study, future research might profitably examine the interaction of other variables on personal space: (1) personality characteristics and self/other boundary styles of *all* parties to an interaction (for example, reactions to stigmatized persons by others are likely to affect how stigmatized persons will regulate their contact with others) and (2) the nature of the setting within which interaction takes place, as illustrated in studies that vary the stress quality of situations.

In summary, there is sufficient empirical evidence to suggest that personality characteristics are reflected in how people regulate their personal-space boundaries. If personality, however crudely defined, contains the idea of desired or ideal levels of contact with others, then personal space can be viewed as a mechanism that acts in the service of the central governing process. Variations in personal space of the type discussed here may then provide a window to understanding such personality processes, in terms of regulation of self/other interactions.

Sex Differences

As indicated previously, early studies examined relationships between personal space and several biographical factors, including sex. And data on the sex variable continue to be collected. In spite of the volume of research, however, sex differences have occupied a secondary place in personal-space research. Most studies have not been primarily interested in sex differences per se but bow to the likelihood that they are important and embed them within other experimental conditions. Furthermore, these studies are so diverse in methodological approach and other variables that it is difficult to draw out any pervasive themes. Some authors compare the responses of males and females to various situations, some work with homogeneous sex pairs, some study mixed-sex pairs, some blend in setting and age differences, and some work with sex and ethnic differences. The result is a fair degree of confusion.

Concerning overall sex differences, the thrust of the data is that males have larger personal-space zones than females and that people generally maintain greater distance from males than from females.[2] However, this is an oversimplification. Sex differences really need to be understood in terms of whether males or females are interacting with males or with females.

[2]Several studies reported greater separation of males using a variety of methods and settings—for example, approach of female versus male friends on a college campus (Edwards, 1972); subjects approaching or being approached by a confederate (Hartnett, Bailey, & Gibson, 1970); a questionnaire analysis of the accessibility to the touching of one's body (Jourard, 1966a); seating selection (Leibman, 1970); an analysis of different cultural groups (Little, 1968); a paper-and-pencil distance measure (Duke & Nowicki, 1972); and a face-to-face interaction study (Mehrabian & Diamond, 1972).

For different sex combinations, the results seem generally consistent. Members of mixed-sex dyads have typically been found to be in closer proximity to one another than members of same-sex pairs (Kuethe and Stricker, 1963; Kuethe, 1962a, 1962b). Jourard (1966a), Hartnett, Bailey, and Gibson (1970), and Duke and Nowicki (1972) also reported closer distances in heterosexual pairs, primarily between same-race figures. However, Kuethe (1964) found that male homosexuals were an exception in that they more frequently placed pairs of male figures closer together. A number of so-called "intrusion" studies are also affected by sex characteristics. These studies, reviewed in detail in the next chapter, generally involve a subject's being approached inappropriately closely by a stranger. Garfinkel (1964) found that males were more upset than females when they were invaded; Patterson, Mullens, and Romano (1971) reported that both sexes responded negatively to intrusion, but males showed more discomfort. Furthermore, Argyle and Dean (1965) observed that females were more willing than males to engage in eye contact, even at close distances. And in a group-intrusion situation, Knowles (1972) noted that mixed-sex dyads were most impervious to intrusion; for instance, when walking down a street, mixed-couple members moved jointly out of the path of a potential intruder, female pairs were the next most resistant to penetration, and male pairs were the most willing to allow their group to be split. Similar results were obtained by Cheyne and Efran (1972), who demonstrated that mixed-sex pairs were least often intruded upon, followed by female and then male dyads, respectively.

But the whole sex picture clouds somewhat when other factors are considered, such as age, ethnic composition, and situational factors. For example, Jones (1971) reported that females from black, Puerto Rican, Chinese, and white groups exhibited more direct facing orientation to one another than males. Similar results were obtained by Jones and Aiello (1973) in a study of grade-school children, although they found that black females stood closest to one another and white females stood farthest apart, with males of both ethnic groups intermediate. Aiello and Jones (1971) reported no differences in male/female distances for Puerto Rican and black children, whereas white males maintained greater distances than white females. Baxter (1970) found, for blacks and whites in a zoo setting, greatest spacing among males, with female pairs intermediate and mixed-sex pairs closest. For Mexican-American pairs, however, there was a reversal, with the closest spacing among females. So there are combinations of sex-composition and ethnic factors. And if one looks at cross-ethnic compositions, the complexity of the issue increases. For example, a study by Koslin, Koslin, Pargament, and Bird (1971) indicated that children placed mixed-sex, different-racial figures at maximum distance from one another.

I have not cited all the studies that deal with sex facets of personal space. For every study cited that reports sex differences, I could probably cite another study with no sex differences. To really understand the effects of sex characteristics, it is necessary to develop a program of research with sex as a central focus rather than a secondary factor.

Cultural Factors

Edward Hall's ideas set the foundation for much research on personal space. He hypothesized four personal-space zones, and he pointed to cross-cultural differences in personal space. He observed qualitatively that people from so-called "contact cultures"—Middle Eastern, Mediterranean, and Latin American—were accustomed to using closer distances when interacting with others than were people from Northern and Western European cultures. And naturally, the closeness is associated with different types of communication cues, with touch, heat, and smell more evident the closer the contact between people.

The question for us is whether Hall's ideas have been confirmed by subsequent research. As of this writing, the data base is not very extensive, although the few studies that are available lend plausibility to some of his ideas.

An early empirical test of Hall's notions compared the use of space by Arabs with that of Americans (Watson & Graves, 1966). Observations were made of discussion groups composed of either Arabs or Americans. Distance among group members, angle of orientation, touching, physical contact, thermal and olfactory cues, and voice behaviors were all taken into account. The results supported the idea that Arabs would show more direct face-to-face orientation, less distance between each other, more touching, more direct visual contact, and greater voice loudness. On the other hand, Forston and Larson (1968) compared Latins and North Americans and did not find any differences in spatial behavior, although Latin Americans showed more variability in their responses.

Other cross-national studies used the questionnaire approach or simulation techniques. For example, Little (1968) had subjects from five countries (the United States, Sweden, southern Italy, Scotland, and Greece) place doll figures in relationship to one another, with the figures differing in sex and status. The general hypothesis was confirmed; those from Mediterranean cultures showed closer interaction distances, and so-called "noncontact" cultures (Sweden and Scotland) exhibited larger distances. Americans were intermediate. Using a questionnaire approach, Sommer (1968) had American, English, Swedish, Dutch, and Pakistani college students rate various seating arrangements (corner to corner, side by side, opposite) on intimacy. All samples rated side-by-side seating as most intimate, followed by corner-to-corner and opposite seating. The more distant arrangements were rated as least intimate. Ratings by American, English, and Swedish groups were quite similar; the Dutch differed in that they viewed corner seating as less intimate than Americans. Pakistani students perceived opposite seating as quite distant. In one other study, Ziller, Long, Ramana, and Reddy (1968) found that Asian Indian students had higher self-esteem, social interest, identification with parents, and self-centrality than Americans, based on their placement of symbols representing the self and others in various spatial locations. Finally, Engebretson and Fullmer (1970) reported few differences in the use of distance by native Japanese, Hawaiian Japanese, and Caucasian Americans.

From this small cluster of studies there is only some support for Hall's general thesis. It might be said that the data show both similarities and differences among cultures in personal-space styles and that future research should seek out not only differences among cultures but also similarities.

The idea of seeking out both cultural similarities and differences is also applicable to a series of recent studies that compared the spatial behavior of various ethnic groups in the United States. The goal of these studies was to search for different styles of space usage among such groups as white Americans, Mexican-Americans, black Americans, and others. The results of these studies show that although some differences may exist, there are also similarities among the groups in use of space. And more important, there is evidence indicating that the underlying factor associated with *apparent* differences may not be ethnic-related but socioeconomic-related. I telegraph this conclusion to emphasize the idea that research in this area should be as attentive to similarities among groups as it is to the discovery of differences. In the search for knowledge there is a tendency for scientists to emphasize differences among people and groups. In some ways this can lead to an ignoring of the ways in which we are all alike. Admittedly, this is a personal value question, but it is one that I feel is worthy of consideration.[3]

One line of research comparing ethnic groups in the United States began with a field study (Willis, 1966) that reported marginal evidence that blacks maintain greater conversation distances than whites. Baxter (1970) did a study in the Houston zoo and found that Mexican-Americans stood closest together at exhibits, whites were intermediate, and blacks were most distant, confirming Willis's preliminary findings and substantiating Hall's thesis that Latin American and Mediterranean cultures used close physical contact. But Baxter also found interactions varying with sex; for instance, members of white and black mixed-sex groups were closest to one another, whereas, among Mexican-American groups, female-pair members were closest and male-pair members were most distant. Behavior in different settings also varied, with Mexican-Americans interacting most closely in outdoor settings and blacks closest in indoor settings. In another field study, Thompson and

---

[3]I am indebted to Lawrence Wrightsman for making this issue salient in his review of an earlier draft of this material.

Baxter (1973) observed the spatial behavior of whites, Mexican-Americans, and blacks on the school grounds of high schools and in a hospital canteen. They charted forward and backward movement of subjects as they conversed. The data suggested that, in mixed-ethnic interactions, blacks tended to move backward and away from the other person, Mexican-Americans tended to move forward, and whites were intermediate.

A series of studies by Aiello and Jones and a very recent study by Scherer (1974) are somewhat in disagreement with these findings, suggesting that cultural differences are not as simple as we might be led to expect. In the first study (Jones, 1971), observations were made of blacks, Puerto Ricans, Italians, and Chinese in New York, with photographs taken of interacting pairs in various neighborhoods. In two separate studies, no differences were found in the distance and/or angle of orientation among different groups. In subsequent studies, however, differences among groups were found. Aiello and Jones (1971) tracked the spatial behavior of first- and second-grade black, Puerto Rican, and white children in a schoolyard and demonstrated that middle-class white children stood farther apart than lower-class blacks and Puerto Ricans, with no differences among the latter groups. Black children showed less-direct body orientations, but again there were no differences in this respect among blacks and Puerto Ricans. These results are confusing for two reasons. First, the age groups of subjects were not always comparable. Second, there was no clear specification or consistency among or within studies on socioeconomic levels of the different groups. Thus, it is not easy to draw conclusions.

In an attempt to unravel some of these factors, recent studies by Aiello and Jones and Scherer are instructive. Aiello and Jones (1973) conducted an experiment that compared the spatial behavior of upper-lower-class blacks and middle-middle-class whites, expecting to find that blacks from this socioeconomic level would stand closer than whites but would be less direct in orientation. Based on observations of first-, third-, and fifth-grade children in a free-discussion setting, there was an interaction of ethnic background, grade, and sex. In the first grade, black children stood closer together, but this difference disappeared by the third grade and even seemed to reverse itself by the fifth grade. Also, there were complicated sex differences, with black females staying closest to one another and white females most distant. The angle of facing confirmed expectations, with black children at all grades facing one another less directly than whites. The results of these and other studies begin to fit together; at least there is a useful direction to pursue—that is, age and developmental differences coupled with sex and cultural differences. These results suggest potentially early developmental differences in cultural groups that may shift with maturation and acculturation, yielding either no differences and/or even reversals from early developmental stages.

One very unclear issue in all these studies involves noncomparable socioeconomic levels of cultural groups. To deal with this issue, Scherer (1974) conducted two field studies in schoolyards. In one study he compared black and white schoolchildren in grades one through four, who were all at a low socioeconomic level. No differences between ethnic groups appeared. In a second study, black and white, middle- and low-socioeconomic children were compared. The results indicated that middle-class children stood farther apart from one another than did lower-class children for both white and black groups, although the differences were reliable only for white groups. There were no distance differences between white and black middle-class children or between white and black lower-class children. Sherer's study is a very significant one; it is the first to systematically separate cultural and socioeconomic factors and the first to suggest that the previously obtained differences among blacks and whites may be partly a function of socioeconomic factors. Thus the apparent differences in space usage among ethnic groups may be as much (or more) a result of socioeconomic factors, age, sex, and other variables as of ethnic differences. This is not to say that culture makes *no* difference, but we need to be careful in jumping to conclusions about such differences and, in the process, ignoring the similarities among cultures.

Other studies have also addressed differences in black and white personal-space behaviors. For example, Frankel and Barrett (1971) found that white subjects allowed a white confederate to approach more closely than a black confederate and that the distance maintained from blacks was greater for low-self-esteem, high-authoritarian whites. No data were collected regarding black subjects' responses to whites or to homogeneous racial groups.

One is left with some uncertainty about the role of cultural factors on personal space. There is empirical evidence to suggest the plausibility of cultural differences, but we now know, after a number of studies, that the nature of such differences may be difficult to unravel. Social settings, age and sex of participants, and socioeconomic factors are not inconsequential issues. Until these and other variables are disentangled, I can say only that the hypothesis of cultural differences in personal space is plausible, but so is the hypothesis of considerable similarity among cultures and ethnic groups.

Interpersonal Relations and Personal Space

Up to this point we have examined the relationship between individual characteristics and personal space. Here we turn to the impact of different types of social bonds. As a mechanism designed to help regulate self/other boundaries, personal space will probably be different across social relationships. The person or group members should make themselves more accessible when interaction with others is sought out, and they should seek to close themselves off from others with whom interaction is not desired. Generally speaking, research supports this simple idea. Many studies on interpersonal relationships indicate that (1) positive relationships between people are associated with closer interpersonal distances or smaller personal-space zones, and (2) people located at close (but not overly close) distances are viewed as having good interpersonal relationships. These two general propositions are perhaps the most well-established and longest-standing findings in the field and have been reported consistently using a variety of methods and settings.

There are several ways in which these basic propositions have been researched, as well as a number of qualifications that we will consider in the following discussion. Before examining the studies, however, some general features of this research are worth noting. First, there are several different types of studies. One series examined the effect of various interpersonal factors on spacing, with distance treated as a dependent or behavioral variable. This type of study was done by manipulating social relationships (for example, praise versus blame) or by comparing existing relationships (for instance, friends versus strangers) in terms of personal space. These are the most popular types of studies by a ratio of about two to one. In a second group of studies, personal space was treated as an independent, predictor variable. Here the question "What are the effects of variations in personal space on liking or social interaction?" was posed. The typical procedure in these studies was to have people or symbols located at different distances and to then examine how they interacted or how well they liked one another.

A second feature of this research is that personal space has typically been defined in terms of distance, as is the case for most studies in the field. Angle of orientation and other personal-space dimensions have not been treated extensively. Third, while several facets of interpersonal relationships have been explored, most research has dealt with interpersonal affect— positive and negative feelings toward someone, liking and disliking, compatibility and hostility.

Now let's consider specific research studies. One general strategy is to compare the spacing of strangers, casual acquaintances, and close friends —either actual persons or symbolic representations of people. For example, in an early study (Little, 1965), line drawings of figures were described as good friends, casual acquaintances, or strangers, the task being to place them in relation to one another. The closer the social bond, the closer the figures were placed to one another. The same findings were obtained when a subject physically placed live actresses at different distances from one another when they were portrayed as having different degrees of friendship. Several studies used simulation techniques with many different types of subjects and corroborated these results. Korner and Misra (1967) used teenage boys in a

Figure 5-1. Personal space between friends, acquaintances, or people who just met? (Photograph by Jim Pinckney.)

figure-placement task, Long and Henderson (1968) studied rural Southern schoolchildren, and Meisels and Guardo (1969) and Guardo and Meisels (1971b) used a figure-silhouette approach with third- through tenth-grade children, as did Bass and Weinstein (1971) with 5- to 9-year-olds. Jourard (1966a) used a diagram technique to determine who could touch what part of one's body. All these studies obtained essentially similar results.

Several laboratory and field studies also demonstrated that friends kept a closer distance among one another than did acquaintances or strangers. Willis (1966) measured approach distances in naturalistic settings on a college campus and found that friends consistently approached closer than ac-quaintances. Edwards (1972) obtained similar results (primarily for females) on a South African campus. Aiello and Cooper (1972) observed eighth graders in an unobtrusive classroom setting and obtained similar results, as did Duke and Nowicki (1972), using a questionnaire technique. Kleck (1967) also confirmed these findings, using photographs of a subject and others.

A second type of study comes a bit closer to the substance of interper-sonal relationships and personal space. Rather than infer content of ex-change among friends and strangers, several studies systematically varied the actual content of ongoing interaction—for example, positive versus negative responses, praise versus reproof, or friendly behavior versus threat. Or they varied certain features of positive and negative interaction—for example, presenting pleasant stimuli or describing someone as popular or unpopular, warm or cold, and the like. The goal of these studies was to approach more closely the outcomes of social interaction along a positive/negative dimension. For instance, Smith (1953, 1954) presented subjects with photographs of figures that had pleasant and unpleasant expressions and found greater distance placement for less pleasant figures. Tolor and Salafia (1971) reported that figures about whom a variety of unfavorable personal attributes were made (low intelligence, low prestige, low personal adjustment) were placed at more distant locations than were figures to whom positive traits were assigned. Little, Ulehla, and Henderson (1968) found that figures having similar political opinions were sometimes (but not always) placed closer to one another than were those holding divergent views. However, in a face-to-face laboratory test, Tesch, Huston, and Indenbaum (1973) found no differences in seating proximity for subjects who believed that a confederate held similar rather than different views from them. Another nonsupportive study was conducted by Tolor (1971), using a figure-placement task, in which unpopular children placed figures closer together than did popular children.

The studies described so far emphasized attitudes, feelings of liking, and other subjective states as factors related to distance. Another cluster of studies worked with ongoing social interaction and found that favorable social exchange is associated with closer distances than is unfavorable exchange. For example, Rosenfeld (1965) asked subjects to role play or act in a way to gain approval or avoid approval of a confederate. In the approval condition, subjects showed more eye contact, used more positive gestures, smiled more, and placed their chairs closer to the confederate. Thus they made themselves more receptive to the other person and signaled their own boundary permeability. Similar results were obtained by Mehrabian (1968a, 1968b). King (1966) studied children in a free-play situation and demonstrated that those who behaved in an unfriendly way were not approached as closely as those with a history of friendly contact. Guardo and Meisels (1971a) reported a simulation study in which parent-child figures were placed closer together when the parent was described as praising rather than criticizing the child.

In two studies, Dosey and Meisels (1969) and Meisels and Dosey (1971) looked at the effect of stress and anger on personal space. In one situation, subjects used silhouette drawings, approached one another, and chose seats under conditions of stress (produced by highlighting the interpersonal threat value of their behavior) or nonstress. Two of the three distance measures indicated greater distance from others under stress conditions. In a similar study, Karabenick and Meisels (1972) reported that subjects maintained greater distances from a confederate when they were told that their performance on a task was not very good. But Meisels and Dosey (1971) induced anger in some subjects by insulting them and found that angered subjects approached more closely than nonangered subjects, a result that was inter-

•reted as having retaliatory significance and was somewhat contrary to the nain thrust of studies in this area. All these studies suggest that, in one form •r another, close proximity between people is associated with positive social •onds. Those who like one another or are positive toward one another make hemselves more accessible and more open by the simple mechanism of •ersonal spacing.

A second line of research treats personal space as an independent or predictor variable. Here personal space is varied and its effects on other aspects of behavior are studied. Once again, the conclusion is relatively straightforward. People located at close distances are perceived to be more friendly, more positive toward one another, and more accessible and open to one another compared with those at greater distances. Several simulation studies demonstrate this relationship. Goldring (1967) presented subjects with silhouette figures in various postures and distances and found that closer pairs were guessed to be warmer and as liking one another more. Haase and Pepper (1972) and Kelly (1972) obtained similar results using photographs of client-counselor interviews. Counselors who used more eye contact, leaned forward toward the client, and had a more direct body orientation and closer distance were rated as more empathic and understanding. And Mehrabian (1968a, 1968b) found certain nonverbal behaviors and distances to be associated with positive affect. Looking at someone, facing someone, opening the arms and legs (rather than tightly folding the limbs against the body), relaxing the body in an asymmetrical fashion leaning, arms and legs not parallel), and getting close to someone will probably produce a picture of positive relationships. Thus a whole cluster of bodily behaviors and distance combine to yield an impression of liking or positive contact among people.

Several other studies confirm these findings. For example, Haase (1970) reported that distances of 30 to 50 inches were most preferred by subjects in counseling situations and that distances of 66 to 88 inches were least preferred. Being too far away implies noncontact and may lead to a feeling of unpleasantness and probably nonreceptivity. And Kleck (1970) found that subjects did more positive head nodding when a confederate agreed with them at close rather than far distances. But subjects were also more nervous at close distances, as illustrated by more self-manipulation (rubbing the body and face). Thus close distances can yield a mixture of positive and negative reactions, suggesting that closeness may signal approval in some situations and intrusion in others. Other studies related to the impact of very close distances will be considered in the next chapter, when we discuss personal-space intrusion.

Before leaving the topic of interpersonal relations and personal space, t might be noted that a number of studies have operated at a more molar level—friendship formation and residential proximity in apartments, neighborhoods, and communities (see Chapter 6 for details of this work). Again, the general finding is that friendship formation is often associated with residential proximity. Those who live near one another seem to be friendlier, based on studies in dormitories, housing developments, suburban areas, classrooms, and the like.

Situational Determinants of Personal Space

There is relatively little research on situational aspects of personal space, although a few studies touched on the effects of formality or informality of settings, familiarity or strangeness of situations, and different places such as streets, offices, and living rooms.

Little (1965) examined doll placement and positioning of live actresses in different settings. The more formal the setting (for example, office versus street corner versus living room), the greater the distance of placement. Similar results were obtained by Bass and Weinstein (1971), who used a figure-placement task with 5- to 9-year-old children. Every child (except the youngest ones) placed figures farther apart when they were portrayed as being in a school principal's office than when in a living room. Thus people who find themselves in formal settings probably act in a restrained and "proper" way, which might mean having formal relationships, adopting stylized roles and modes of behavior, using barriers such as distance, and thereby not making the self very accessible to others.

Degree of familiarity of a place often affects personal space. For example, Castell (1970) tested 1½- to 3-year-old children in their own homes as opposed to in a strange environment. As might be expected, children stayed closer to their mothers in the strange environment. In a laboratory study, Edney (1972a) gave some subjects experience with a laboratory room (they were in it for about a half hour, while others were not). Also, some subjects expected to be in the room again, and others did not. Those who had prior exposure to the room rated its size as smaller, and those who anticipated being in the room again stood closer to a confederate. Finally, Felipe and Sommer (1966) conducted an intrusion study in a mental hospital and observed flight reaction. Those who were invaded in a park-like area fled more rapidly and showed more discomfort than when the intrusion took place in a more familiar location on the patients' ward. In summary, when people are in places where they have had previous experience, they are more willing to be in closer contact with others, perhaps because they feel that they can control their contacts in such settings.

A few other studies examined additional setting factors. Moving figures (walking, horseback riding) were placed farther apart than were stationary figures (Lewit & Joy, 1967); white ethnic-group members interacted at similar distances both outside and inside at the zoo, while Mexican-Americans interacted more closely in outdoor settings, and blacks interacted more closely indoors (Baxter, 1970). And subjects allowed a confederate to approach more closely in a wide room and in a long narrow room than in a very large or a very small room (Daves & Swaffer, 1971).

Beyond these few studies, the impact of setting differences on personal space is an untapped area and one waiting to be researched.

This chapter examined empirical research on factors related to personal space including (1) individual characteristics such as biographical variables, personality characteristics, and abnormality, (2) interpersonal factors such as liking and friendship, and (3) situational variables such as setting formality. The next chapter completes our analysis of personal space and deals with the issues of intrusion and compensatory or system-like qualities of personal space.

Intrusion, Proximity, and Compensatory Aspects of Personal Space

This chapter continues my analysis of personal space as a boundary-regulation process. One issue to be discussed concerns personal-space intrusion, or the unwanted violation of self/other boundaries. As part of this analysis I will propose a general framework that ties together research on intrusion, attraction, and personal space. I will also examine a body of knowledge dealing with spatial proximity. This research does not, strictly speaking, deal with personal space in the sense of small distances between people, but it is quite relevant to much of what has been discussed so far. Finally, I will discuss the system-like quality of privacy-regulation mechanisms, or how personal space fits together with other behaviors as part of a total response system.

Personal-Space Intrusion

Personal space was described as a boundary around a person, intrusion into which is often uncomfortable and not generally permitted. One way to study personal space is to examine the impact of someone's getting overly close to someone else and inappropriately bypassing self/other boundaries. Goffman (1971), Lyman and Scott (1967), and others describe various forms of personal-space intrusion or invasion. My emphasis will be on intrusion of personal-space barriers rather than on territorial or "place" invasion. Goffman (1971) described one form of intrusion as "ecological placement of the body" near another person and inappropriate use of the various parts of another person by touching or sexually molesting him or her. Also, intrusions can occur by means of eye gazes, intrusive looks, interference with what someone else is doing, certain kinds of questioning, and various kinds of defilement such as body or breath. Thus not only can I intrude on you by getting very close but I can touch you in an inappropriate way, stare at your eyes or other parts of your body, breathe on you, or force you to smell me because of my closeness. Goffman (1961) observed (as described in Chapters 2 and 3) that intrusions in mental hospitals often take the form of lack of bathroom privacy for patients and forced medication and physical examinations. Leibman (1970) defined three types of personal-space violation, which overlap the preceding: (1) overly close physical distances, (2) inappropriate body positions, and (3) behaviors that result in excessive symbolic intimacy.

In an early demonstration, Garfinkel (1964) looked at the effect of violations of everyday norms and customs. In one illustrative episode he had students suddenly place their faces inches away from the faces of others, almost to the point of nose touching nose. The result was embarrassment, anger, and bewilderment on the part of the persons invaded (and often by the student invaders as well), with particularly strong reactions by males. In a more systematic field experiment, Felipe and Sommer (1966) examined the reactions of mental patients to personal-space intrusion in key settings—a public-park area and a day-ward room. Confederates sat beside patients with a shoulder-to-shoulder distance of about six inches. The results were striking. First, invaded subjects in the park area fled rather quickly. About one-third of the patients left the bench within two minutes, about 50% left within nine minutes, and two-thirds fled within 20 minutes. Furthermore, many showed signs of discomfort, such as facing away from the intruder, mumbling, shifting postures and fidgeting, and nervously rubbing parts of their body with their hands. When a similar intrusion occurred in a familiar day-room area, hardly any patients fled. Felipe and Sommer (1966) did a second intrusion study in a university library. In this study, a female confederate invaded female students in one of several ways: (1) the confederate sat in an adjacent chair only a few inches away, (2) the confederate sat adjacent to a subject but at a distance of about 15 inches, (3) the confederate left a chair between herself and the subject, or (4) the confederate sat across from the subject. Within a half hour, only about one-third of the closely invaded subjects remained, compared with three-fourths of the distant-seating subjects and about nine-tenths of noninvaded control subjects. As in the study of mental patients, invaded subjects often moved or leaned away from the intruder, drew in their arms and heads, turned away, placed their faces on their hands, and sometimes used barriers such as books. Patterson, Mullens, and Romano (1971) found a similar pattern. Library invasions occurred in several ways: a confederate sat right next to a subject, two and three seats distant, or across from the subject. Twenty percent of the invaded people fled within a ten-minute period, especially those invaded most closely. Again, there were systematic nonverbal behaviors; for example, the closer the intrusion, the more often subjects glanced at the intruder. They also leaned or moved away,

Figure 6-1. © 1973 United Feature Syndicate, Inc. Reprinted by permission.

showed more blocking behavior (putting a hand or elbow between the intruder and the self), and often turned away from the invader. Similar results were obtained by McDowell (1972). In an interesting variant of this procedure, Barash (1973) manipulated the status of library invaders by having them wear either a suit or casual dress. Students intruded upon by the more formally dressed person fled more quickly.

Studies such as these and your own personal experience will readily confirm the idea that personal-space intrusion is a powerful event when it occurs inappropriately. Furthermore, people generally react to intrusions by re-establishing an appropriate boundary system. You might experiment by approaching strangers (or even acquaintances) very closely face to face on an escalator, in a line at a movie, or elsewhere, and observing their reactions. But do this cautiously; some people may react angrily to having someone "breathe down their neck"!

In addition to flight and nonverbal reactions there are a few studies that indicate physiological arousal to overly close distances. For example, McBride, King, and James (1965) found that subjects who were approached at 1, 3, and 9 feet showed lower galvanic skin responses (GSRs), which measure skin conductance in relation to arousal, at 9 feet. Also, lower GSRs, reflecting lower arousal, occurred when approaches by others were made from the side rather than from the front. Similar results were obtained by Bergman (1971) when chairs in discussion groups were separated by either 3 feet or 2 inches on each side. Those subjects sitting at closer distances showed higher degrees of palmar sweat and reported more feelings of stress.

All intrusions do not produce the same amount of threat. Invasions in some situations are reacted to more seriously than those in other settings. For example, Dabbs (1972) investigated intrusions at city street corners as pedestrians waited at traffic lights and at bus stops. Generally speaking, male intruders caused more people to move away, and females who were invaded tended to move away more often. However, there was less reaction to intrusion while waiting for a traffic light than there was at a bus stop, perhaps because it was a more temporary situation. People knew that close contact was only for a short time, often just a matter of seconds.

Our reaction often varies with different intruders. For example, Fry and Willis (1971) had 5-, 8-, and 10-year-old boys and girls intrude on adults in a public setting; they stood less than 6 inches behind adults in a theater line. Five-year-olds were often given a positive response when they invaded, as if they were cute; 8-year-olds were typically ignored; and 10-year-olds were responded to negatively, as if they were an adult who was inappropriately close. Thus there are probably developmental aspects to intrusion, with the expectation that by 10 years of age children should have learned to respect others' personal-space boundaries.

Another group of studies investigated intrusion from the perspective of the potential invader. A typical research procedure involves setting up opportunities for people to invade personal boundaries. The results generally indicate that people avoid intruding on others, act uncomfortably when they are forced to invade someone else, and show differences in probability of intrusion as a function of status, sex, and other factors. For example, Knowles (1973) had two- or four-person groups engage in conversation in a hallway, so that passersby could either go through and penetrate the group boundary or go around the group. Only 25% of the passersby intruded through the group. Seventy-five percent of the passersby intruded through a control group of trash barrels. Furthermore, fewer persons intruded on a four-person group than on a two-person group. Finally, manipulations of group members' status (as indicated by variations in age and dress) showed that low-status conversations were intruded on more frequently than high-status ones. Thus people avoid intruding on others, and they are particularly wary about going through large groups or groups with high-status persons.

A study by Cheyne and Efran (1972) used a similar procedure but varied the sex composition of the pairs and the degree to which pair members interacted. Again, most people did not penetrate conversing pairs. In addition, people were most reluctant to pass through male/female pairs, followed by female pairs and then male pairs, respectively. In the same study, people just standing around but not conversing were invaded very often. In a second experiment, conducted in a shopping center, distances between pair members were varied between 38 and 54 inches, the latter distance being at the edge of Hall's (1966) personal and social spatial zones. Intrusion increased when the members of the pair were more than 4 feet apart from each other; people perceived them as being in a less personal relationship. Again, mixed-sex groups were least susceptible to intrusion. Basically similar results were also obtained by Efran and Cheyne (1973). It was also observed in these studies that many intruders were apologetic. They often mumbled their apologies as they passed through, looked down at the floor, or lowered their heads in a deferential way as they penetrated the group boundary.

In a more systematic follow-up of the reactions of intruders, Efran and Cheyne (1973) tracked the nonverbal behavior, physiological responses, and subjective feelings of those who were put in situations where they could not avoid passing through a pair. Again, intruders in this situation often lowered their heads and gazed toward the floor, closed their eyes, and reported feelings of discomfort. Thus not only do people react to being intruded on themselves, but they are also sensitive to the personal-space boundaries of others; there is a strong feeling of discomfort when they are forced to intrude on others.[1]

In a somewhat different type of study, Knowles (1972) tried to intrude on pairs of people as they walked down a city street. Mixed-sex, male, and female pairs were approached head on, and it was quite clear that the confederate was going to go through the group. Over half the pairs moved together out of the intruder's path to avoid being split, supporting the idea that groups act to maintain their social boundary. Keeping the pair intact and moving away together was done more often by mixed-sex dyads (83% moved together) than by female (62% moved together) or by male pairs (38% moved together). Several pairs also verbally reprimanded the potential intruder. Thus groups and individuals attempt to maintain boundaries from others and use a variety of mechanisms to do so. And there is evidence that outsiders perceive, recognize, and respect boundary-maintenance attempts.

Several studies demonstrate that intrusion is an undesired state of affairs, and that too much distance from another person is also not ideal, especially if one has to deal with that person. These studies support the idea that too much closeness often results in negative reactions, a moderate degree

[1]Stanley Milgram, a social psychologist, recently reported his own extreme discomfort in an experiment he was conducting in the New York subways. In one condition, he was to approach seated passengers and say something like "Hello, may I have your seat?" Now in the crowded New York subways this is a rather extreme request and represents a dramatic intrusion. Milgram reported that he could barely fulfill his own experimental condition, since he felt extremely uncomfortable and quite anxious at even making the request. In my terms, he was apprehensive about violating another person's boundary in a situation in which boundary violation is a serious matter, especially in regard to a seat.

Figure 6–2. People are usually sensitive to others' personal-space zones. Reprinted from *National Enquirer.*

of closeness is facilitative of interpersonal relations, and too much distance sometimes has negative qualities. For example, Argyle and Dean (1965) found that, as subjects approached a photograph of a person or a real person who was looking at them, they gradually decreased their eye contact. At distances of 2 feet they exhibited less eye contact than at distances of 6 or 10 feet. Furthermore, at 2 feet they showed signs of tension, leaned backwards, faced away, scratched their heads, and squinted. While the 2-foot distance was too close, there was also a suggestion that 10 feet was too far; the subjects leaned forward, as if to reduce the distance. Similar results were obtained by Goldberg, Kiesler, and Collins (1969), Argyle and Ingham (1972), and Aiello (1972).

Patterson and Sechrest (1970) reported a curvilinear relationship between distance and liking of a confederate. Confederates were rated as most friendly when they engaged in conversation with a subject at 4 feet, with a drop in ratings at 2 and 6 feet. Again, when you expect to deal with another person, there may be an optimal contact distance; being closer than or farther than this distance is not desirable. Albert and Dabbs (1970) found persuasion to be most effective at intermediate distances. A hostile speaker who delivered persuasive messages was resisted most at distances of 1 to 2 feet versus 4 to 5 and 14 to 15 feet. Also, attention to the messages was generally greatest at the intermediate distances, and the speaker's expertise was rated highest when he was at the middle distance. In still a different setting Dinges and

Oetting (1972) asked subjects to rate the anxiety they would feel if they were in a series of situations (depicted in photographs of counselors and clients) in which the distance between figures ranged from 30 to 88 inches. The very near and very far distances received the highest ratings for anxiety, supporting again the idea that overly close and overly far distances are less satisfactory than intermediate distances.

But how can the results of the intrusion studies, some of which suggest a curvilinear relationship between reactions and distance (too close and too far being negative) be integrated with the studies in Chapter 5, in which closer distances were associated with friendship? Figure 6–3 outlines a hypothesized set of relationships that seem to tie together results from the intrusion and the liking-distance studies. The organizing feature of Figure 6–3 is the social relationship between people and the expectations they have about interacting with one another. Curve A portrays a hypothesized profile for good friends. Here data support the idea that personal-space zones of friends are smaller (they come closer to one another) than are those of casual acquaintances and strangers. Thus people in intimate or friendly relationships are more comfortable at closer distances and are predicted to be less comfortable at greater distances. This basic idea is strongly supported by the

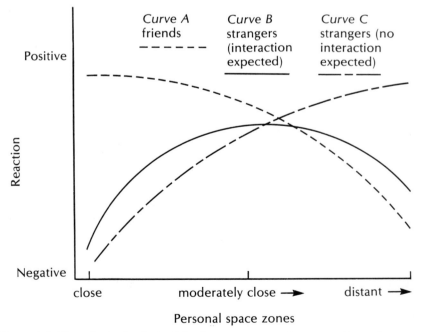

Figure 6–3. Hypothesized relationships between personal space and reactions as a function of social bonds.

research literature. In simulation, laboratory, and field studies, friends are consistently located closer to one another than acquaintances or strangers; people closer to one another are labeled as friendlier; and those with positive attributes are approached more closely. Moreover, positive experiences with others (praise, absence of stress) are typically associated with closer distances. I know of no literature, however, that deals with the impact of close friends interacting with larger personal-space distances. My prediction would be that such an arrangement would be undesirable.

Curve B describes social relationships between strangers (or perhaps between casual acquaintances) *in which there is an explicit expectation of interaction.* Here subjects are expected to work on a task or to socially interact with another person, often a stranger. One whole line of evidence supporting part of the curve includes those data just cited. Casual acquaintances or strangers are placed farther apart and approach one another less closely. Thus it is reasonable to infer that increased distances from strangers are positively viewed. But, as Curve B suggests, increased distances are acceptable only up to some intermediate point. That is, strangers who expect to deal with one another are likely to seek an optimum interaction distance; deviations from this distance (much closer or much farther) are unsatisfactory. The data generally support this idea. Sommer (1962) identified a comfortable distance for conversation; Kleck (1970) found that overly large distances were reacted to negatively; Haase (1970), Dinges and Oetting (1972), and Patterson and Sechrest (1970) all found results indicating that overly close and overly far distances produce less favorable reactions than intermediate distances.

The third curve describes another type of social relationship—a relationship that involves strangers and one *in which no social interaction is anticipated or expected.* The typical intrusion study is a violation of this expectation; someone often unknown to the person, with whom no contact is expected, moves overly close or intrudes in some way. As the curve and a large body of data indicate, reactions to intrusion are typically negative, and the research literature is consistent on the point that discomfort, physiological arousal, flight reactions, and a variety of nonverbal behaviors occur, all designed to re-establish acceptable distances. Furthermore, studies of group intrusion indicate that people avoid invading others, that groups protect themselves from intrusion by strangers, and so on. Thus, the closer a stranger (with whom one does not expect interaction) comes, the more uncomfortable the situation. To oversimplify this analysis: if you want to interact with a friend, being close is probably desirable. If you expect to deal with a stranger, there is probably an intermediate distance that is most comfortable, and being too close or too far from that person is not ideal. But for a stranger with whom you do not expect to interact, the greater the distance the better.

The intrusion studies are interesting in several respects. First, there is reasonable evidence that self/other boundaries are violated when certain others approach too closely, indicating a discrepancy between desired and achieved contact. Second, when boundary adjustments are made to bring desired and achieved privacy into congruence, flight, nonverbal behaviors, and other mechanisms are brought into play. Thus a whole system of responses is mobilized to reachieve a desired level of privacy. In addition, groups as well as individuals attempt to preserve and establish appropriate boundaries. Third, there is the idea that personal space and boundary regulation can be viewed as a "too-much" or "too-little" problem. The evidence indicates that the desire for contact with others varies as a function of the situation and who those others are. Thus optimal personal-space boundaries vary. Fourth, people are sensitive to one another's personal-space zones, and they seek to avoid inappropriate penetration of others' boundaries. And when inadvertent intrusion occurs, there are attempts to be apologetic, deferent, or submissive, as if to signal that the violation was not done maliciously.

Spatial Proximity

Most of the research I have discussed deals primarily with distance and does not examine more complex issues such as angle of orientation, role of barriers, and use of props such as desks, chairs, and seating configurations. There is a relatively large body of work on interaction in more molar spatial contexts—for example, friendship and residential proximity in neighborhoods and communities. Although these studies do not deal strictly with personal space, they support the idea that residential closeness facilitates interpersonal relationships; that is, people who live near one another tend to establish social ties. Between these larger-scale residential studies and the face-to-face personal-space studies falls a body of research termed "spatial proximity." This research deals with relatively middle-sized units of analysis—seating patterns, use of furniture, and the like. The studies involved are useful because of their position midway on a large scale/small scale continuum and because they use notions of angle of orientation and complex positioning arrangements between people and do not focus only on distance as the basic dimension of personal space.

There are several streams of research on spatial proximity that we should consider. One direction focuses on leaders and their location in small groups. Another line of analysis examines friendship and spatial locations. A third set of studies considers the dynamics of interaction in discussion groups as a function of locations of members.

One early line of investigation was on the spatial location of leaders in small groups. Several studies demonstrated that leaders occupied central positions—for example, at ends of tables or in otherwise prominent positions. For example, Bass and Klubeck (1952) found that persons who sat at end positions of a rectangular table emerged as leaders. Strodtbeck and Hook (1961) studied juries and observed that the foreman was typically selected from among those who occupied end seats. Sommer (1961) found that appointed leaders gravitated toward the ends of tables; Howells and Becker (1962) reported that emergent leaders sat in more prominent positions in a discussion situation; Lott and Sommer (1967) used a diagram approach and showed that people typically placed high-status persons at the ends of tables. In some research on family eating styles (Altman, Nelson, & Lett, 1972; Dreyer & Dreyer, 1973) it was found that fathers in American homes typically sit at the head of the dinner table, a sign of their symbolic, if not real, status in the family. Basically similar results on leadership and seating location were obtained by Ward (1968), Blood and Livant (1957), and Hare and Bales (1963).

In a historical analysis, Winick and Holt (1961) traced the use and positioning of room and furniture layouts and demonstrated that, historically, status and leadership are associated with spatial locations. For example, the ancients placed great value on chairs and thrones in which their political and religious leaders sat. With occasional exceptions, such as the legend of King Arthur's round table, kings and emperors usually sat at the ends of tables, often elevated above others. Furthermore, seating position is an important part of diplomatic protocol, with people often seated according to a complicated formula of rank and status. Hazard (1962) analyzed courtroom arrangements in different cultures and described how status was reflected in seating location. In Western courtrooms the judge and jury are separate from each other, to reflect their separate functions, and judges are often elevated above the whole courtroom. In other cultures the judge and jury are located closer to each other, since they deliberate jointly to determine guilt or innocence. Also, the witness in the Western world faces the audience and a jury, whereas in other systems he or she faces the judge.

A second line of research is on small-group interaction. In an early study Steinzor (1950) analyzed interaction in circular seating arrangements and found that people directed more comments to people they faced rather than to those in adjacent seats. Similar results were obtained by Hare and Bales (1963) and by Hearn (1957) in studies of problem-solving and discussion groups. In a related study, Sommer (1959) charted interactions of patients and staff in the cafeteria of a mental hospital. More interaction was observed among people seated corner to corner and face to face across the table than among those in a side-by-side arrangement. And schizophrenic patients often chose seating locations that did not facilitate interaction; they often sat side by side or at more distant locations. These data suggest distorted spatial habits by schizophrenics, corroborating personal-space studies described in Chapter 5. A questionnaire study by Russo (1967) confirmed these findings, with side-to-side and corner-to-corner seating associated with greater friendliness, interaction, and intimacy than more distant arrangements. Similar results were obtained by Mehrabian and Diamond (1971) in regard to closeness of seating and directness of body orientation. In another field study, in a university cafeteria and in a library, Sommer (1965) observed more corner-to-corner and across-the-table seating among conversant groups in a cafeteria and more distant arrangements in libraries, where, obviously, interaction is not a typical activity. In a related study Norum, Russo, and Sommer (1967) found that children and college students sat closer to one another when working cooperatively and sat at more distant locations when they believed they were competing with one another. Similar results were obtained by Sommer (1965), Batchelor and Goethals (1972), and Gardin, Kaplan, Firestone, and Cowan (1973).

With these data in mind, observe how headwaiters and hostesses seat people in restaurants. As often as not, I have noticed that people in pairs are located across from each other (even when other options exist), whereas the data I have reviewed suggest that their interaction would be facilitated if they sat corner to corner. It would be interesting to find out why restaurant hosts and hostesses choose the seats for people they do. Also, it is amazing to see how passive people are in such settings. It is rare that people will sit at a table location other than the one assigned to them by the restaurant "space manager." Even when other arrangements are possible, people are willing to sit with a flower pot blocking their view of each other, strong lights shining in their eyes, or passersby bumping them, or they are willing to sit facing a dreary blank wall—in spite of the fact that other alternatives exist. Try holding a personal and friendly conversation under such arrangements!

A third line of research deals with "liking" in different proximity arrangements. The results fit nicely with the earlier studies to the extent that closer proximity is maintained toward liked others or toward those with whom one is friendly and that close proximity is often a precondition for friendship formation. For example, Byrne and Buehler (1955) and Byrne (1961) showed relationships between seating proximity in a classroom and subsequent acquaintanceship; Byrne, Baskett, and Hodges (1971) and Allgeier and Byrne (1973) observed that people placed themselves closer to those with similar attitudes or to those they liked. Also, Almond and Esser (1965) reported cafeteria seating proximities to be associated with friendship patterns.

A related area of study concerns spatial proximity and feelings of comfort, ease, and relaxation. To identify the region of comfortable distance and conversational settings, Sommer (1961) systematically varied the distance between two sofas in a lounge and asked people to hold a discussion. When the sofas were 1 to 3 feet apart, people sat opposite and more or less facing one another (nose-to-nose distances were actually up to about 5½ feet). When the distance exceeded this range, side-by-side seating became prevalent, suggesting the people's attempt to be at an acceptable level of contact with one another. In a follow-up, Sommer (1962) used chairs to systematically vary side-by-side and face-to-face distances in all combinations. In general, people greatly preferred the face-to-face seating, and, when the chairs were 1 to 2 feet apart, people usually sat facing one another and continued to do so as long as the side-by-side distances were large. However, as face-to-face distances increased, people began sitting side-by-side. Thus subjects sought optimal seating arrangements in a combination of spatial locations.

Another cluster of studies tracked comfort, relaxation, and tension in various seating arrangements. Haase (1970) presented subjects with photographs of a counseling situation in which the distance between a counselor and client varied from 2½ to 8 feet (angle of seating was 45 degrees). Closer distances were rated as more comfortable, which was attributed to the counseling quality of the interaction and the presumed desire for more intimate contact. In a somewhat different procedure, Haase and DiMattia (1970) had clients, administrators, and counselors rate four seating arrangements: chairs side-by-side at a 45-degree angle, chairs opposite with a table alongside, two chairs at the corner of a table, and two chairs across the table. Counselors least preferred the intervening table, and administrators preferred it the most. In general, corner-to-corner seating was most preferred. In a similar study Widgery and Stackpole (1972) reported that subjects were more satisfied with same-side desk seating than across-desk seating in a counseling situation, especially anxious subjects. And Jourard (1970) found greater openness and self-disclosure as distance between an interviewer and subject decreased.

An interesting exercise is to see how different people arrange their offices. A formal arrangement with maximum distance and strong barriers involves across-the-desk seating of visitors. A less formal arrangement would be to have visitors seated at the side of the desk, and an even more informal arrangement would be to have visitors sit on the same side of the desk, at a neutral table, or around a coffee table. Thus it is possible to have a variety of seating configurations that can be suited to a particular relationship and to the expected nature of conversations. My own office has two such configurations—across the desk and around a coffee table. It is interesting to observe students who enter my office before I do. They are generally uncertain about where to sit. If I don't suggest where they should sit, they usually take the most formal and distant seat—across the desk, facing where they think I might sit. However, colleagues usually locate themselves in the least-formal seating arrangement. Thus spatial-proximity arrangements clearly reflect self/other boundaries from both parties' perspective.

In general, spatial-proximity studies fit with molecular personal-space studies, suggesting that closer proximity and more direct contact facilitates interpersonal exchange. But as the intrusion studies and some of the seating-position studies illustrate, the situation is not unequivocally simple. Sometimes, close proximity, especially among strangers, is less desirable. Equally important, these studies exemplify the complex nature of self/other boundary mechanisms; people use distance, angular locations, and barriers such as desks and tables as parts of a complex system to regulate contact with others.

Compensatory Aspects of Personal Space

One of the central themes of this book is that personal space is a mechanism designed to meet privacy needs—opening the self to others or reducing contact with others. But personal space does not operate alone; it is part of a system of responses that amplify, compensate, or work in concert with one another. Thus people can mobilize various behavioral resources and, depending on circumstances and others' responses, use different mixes of behaviors to achieve a desired level of interaction. Little is known about the rules by which these different behavioral mixes are used, especially in regard to amplification—whereby two or more behaviors intensify the meaning of a communication (for example, fist-shaking combined with a loud voice to express anger). However, there are more systematic analyses of so-called "compensatory reactions"—whereby one behavior replaces or substitutes for another (for example, fist-shaking as a substitute for a loud voice to express anger). Patterson (1973a) did an excellent review of this area, and I shall draw heavily on his analysis.

Table 6–1 is taken from Patterson's article and summarizes a variety of studies and behaviors concerned with compensatory processes. Many of these studies have already been reviewed in this and the preceding two chapters, and details of procedures and results will not be repeated. Several conclusions are suggested by Patterson's review. First, there is good support for a compensatory process involving distance/angle of orientation and other behaviors. Strong evidence comes from studies dealing with both distance and eye contact and distance and angle of orientation. As discussed earlier, a number of studies have repeatedly demonstrated the interplay of eye contact and distance. As people come closer to one another their eye contact decreases, and vice versa, presumably as they attempt to maintain a desired level of interaction. Both behaviors function as a system, working together in different mixes to maintain a desired level of intimacy. Furthermore, distance and angle of orientation are systematically related. Several studies consistently demonstrated that, as the distance between people decreased,

Table 6-1. Direction of Support for Compensation in Pairs of Immediacy Behaviors

	Eye Contact & Distance	Eye Contact & Orientation	Distance & Orientation	Distance & Lean	Miscellaneous[a]
Aiello (1972)	+, −	. .	. .	. .	. .
Aiello & Jones (1971)	. .	. .	+	. .	. .
Argyle & Dean (1965)	+	. .	. .	+	+
Clore (1969)	. .	. .	+	. .	. .
Ellsworth et al. (1972)	. .	. .	. .	. .	+
Felipe & Sommer (1966)	. .	. .	+	. .	+
Goldberg et al. (1969)	+	. .	. .	. .	. .
Jourard & Friedman (1970)	. .	. .	. .	. .	−
Kleck (1970)	. .	. .	. .	. .	+, −
McBride et al. (1965)	. .	. .	. .	. .	+
Mehrabian & Diamond (1971)	. .	. .	+	. .	+
Patterson (1973)	+, 0	+, 0	+	0	. .
Patterson et al. (1971)	−	. .	+	+	. .
Patterson & Sechrest (1970)	+	. .	+	. .	. .
Pellegrini & Empey (1970)	. .	. .	+	. .	. .
Sommer (1962)	. .	. .	+	. .	. .
Sommer (1968)	. .	. .	+	. .	. .
Stewart & Patterson (1973)	+	. .	. .	+	. .
Watson & Graves (1966)	+, 0	+, 0	+	. .	+

[a]Includes relationships between an immediacy behavior and another behavior which may be potentially relevant for compensation, e.g., distance and latency of flight reactions (Felipe and Sommer, 1966).

From "Compensation and Nonverbal Immediacy Behaviors: A Review," by M. L. Patterson, *Sociometry, 36*(2), 246. Copyright 1973 by the American Sociological Association. Reprinted by permission.

their angle of orientation toward each other became less direct. That is, the closer they came the more they began facing away from each other. Thus eye contact/distance and distance-orientation relationships support the idea of compensatory, system-like functioning of personal-space mechanisms.

Finally, there is some evidence for a compensatory relationship between distance and lean, with greater distance associated with more forward lean and overly close distances associated with a leaning away. In summary, while the volume of research is not great and only a few behavioral linkages have been tapped, the data provide reasonably good support for the idea that personal-space mechanisms fit with other levels of behavior to provide a person with a repertoire of responses that can be used to regulate social interaction.

Summary of Chapters 4 through 6

In Chapters 4 through 6 I described personal space as a behavioral mechanism that functions in the service of privacy goals to regulate interpersonal boundaries in accord with desired levels of social interaction. Other privacy mechanisms include verbal and paraverbal behavior, nonverbal bodily behavior, and environmentally related behaviors. It was also emphasized that personal space functions as part of a "system," sometimes substituting for, sometimes compensating for, and sometimes amplifying other behaviors.

Three general methodological strategies for studying personal space were described in Chapter 4. The most popular and earliest approach is a *simulation* strategy, whereby subjects are presented with dolls, cut-out figures, or symbols representing people and are asked to place or replace these in accordance with various instructions. *Laboratory* methods include measurement of subjects approaching others or being approached by others in a relatively artificial, obtrusive laboratory setting. *Field* methods include observations in natural settings in an unobtrusive fashion (for example, in schoolyards) and with no restrictions placed on the subjects' behavior. Simulation methods are the most frequently used techniques, followed by laboratory methods, and then field-based strategies. It is likely that these latter methods will become more popular in the coming years.

Chapter 4 also reviewed theoretical approaches to personal space. The dominant one, which has provided the most impetus for work in the field, was proposed by Edward Hall (1966), an anthropologist. He postulated four personal-distance zones and outlined a number of hypothesized differences among cultures in spacing behavior. Other approaches emphasized equilibrium processes whereby different levels of behavior acted together in a compensatory fashion, a social-learning approach linked to personality differences, and a perceptual-expectation model. Most of these approaches are only recent and not well-developed theoretical formulations. But they do hold promise, and further work investigating their ramifications should certainly be encouraged.

Chapter 5 reviewed research on personal space in terms of three classes of variables: personal/individual factors, interpersonal factors, and situational/setting factors. With regard to individual variables, research has emphasized such characteristics as sex, children's social development, personality characteristics (especially normal versus abnormal personalities), and cultural differences. Research on interpersonal factors has traditionally emphasized the effect of degree of acquaintanceship and liking on personal space. Finally, there are few analyses of the effects of settings or situations.

A number of propositions emerge from our review of research, although most require some qualification.

1. There are individual differences in use of personal space. People with diagnosed personality abnormalities often exhibit "mixed up" boundary-control mechanisms in regard to others—sometimes being overly close and sometimes being overly distant from others. It is as if their distorted psychological and social-emotional relationships are also reflected in their personal-space system.

2. The development of personal space is gradually learned by children. Learning occurs by early grade-school years in certain facets of boundary control, suggesting the pervasive quality of the phenomenon and its close ties with other social-development processes. Also, there seems to be sex-linked development of personal space, with girls developing adult-like management of personal space earlier than boys, which seems to parallel the earlier social maturation of girls.

3. Although sex differences in personal space are widely researched, simplistic conclusions are not justified. If any general statement is warranted, it is that males have less-permeable space boundaries than females. But the results are not unequivocal, since many studies show no differences between the sexes and others reflect complex sex-composition effects.

4. There is some evidence of cultural differences in personal space, but, once again, simple generalizations are not warranted. There is some support for the idea that Mediterranean and Latin American people—members of the so-called "contact" cultures—employ smaller space zones than other Western people, although the data are not unequivocal. Within the United States, there is some evidence of differences in distance zones of various ethnic groups, although recent studies suggest that any personal-space differences may also be related to socioeconomic factors.

5. With regard to interpersonal relationships, one line of research strongly indicates that friends or positively described persons are approached more closely than strangers or negative persons. Thus positive others are reacted to with more permeable, open, and accessible self-boundaries.

6. Relatively little research has been conducted on the impact of settings or situations, although the data suggest that interpersonal boundaries become more relaxed and permeable in informal settings.

Chapter 6 examined a number of special topics associated with personal space—personal-space intrusion, studies of more molar spatial proximity, and personal space as part of a complex system of responses.

A variety of personal-space invasion or intrusion studies indicate that overly close contact by others, especially strangers, is aversive and threatening and often results in flight, anxiety, and a variety of reponses designed to increase distance and to reduce interaction. In my terms, these invasions represent situations where the desired level of privacy is violated. There is also a smaller body of data indicating that overly large personal-space zones are also undesirable, especially when one is committed to contact with another person. Thus there are a variety of relationships between personal space and comfort. Overly close contact is undesirable when one is dealing with strangers who suddenly come close. Overly close and overly distant zones are also not desirable in situations where one is engaged in interaction with another person. Yet close contact is desired with those with whom one is intimate. Interpersonal-boundary permeability, therefore, interacts with the nature of an interpersonal relationship.

Spatial-proximity studies deal with more complex seating arrangements and other configurations compared with traditional personal-space studies. But they generally support the more molecular personal-space findings, with people who are attracted to one another adopting closer seating arrangments, interacting and cooperating more often. The chapter also discussed data on the compensatory nature of personal space, or its fit with other behaviors that function in the service of privacy regulation. As examples of the meshing of behaviors, several studies show how eye contact and distance work together and how angle of orientation between people and distance from others operate in a unified fashion.

Territorial
Behavior:
Conceptual
Issues

The idea of territory is present in everyday language; examples include "my turf," "my place," "keep out," "no trespassing," "members and guests only," and "a man's home is his castle." The fenced land or yard, the nameplate or sign on a door, the questioning look and cold stare given to strangers in a neighborhood bar, and the urban gang's respect for the turf of other groups are just a few examples of the intuitive validity of the idea of territory.

The concept of territory has its roots in the sociological analyses of urban life, beginning in the 1920s (Park, Burgess, & McKenzie, 1925; Thrasher, 1927; Whyte, 1943; Yablonsky, 1962; Zorbaugh, 1929). Participant observers and interviewers studied the functioning of social groups in places such as restaurants, bars, and neighborhoods. They consistently observed the presence of territories that were demarcated by streets, by places on a street, even by sides of the street, such that certain groups would rarely trespass into others' territory or turf. For example, Sommer (1969) reported a journalistic analysis of a neighborhood in Chicago where one street was populated solely by blacks and the adjacent street was populated by Irish whites. Each street was rarely used by the other group, and each was self-contained, with its own facilities, stores, and activities appropriate to the residents' cultures.

Early sociologists also described the territoriality of gangs. The gangs often had well-defined territories that were clearly recognized as owned by the occupants, and the territory was aggressively defended against intrusion. Yet these boundaries were not always rigid. Under certain circumstances passage through a turf was permissible, as long as it did not signify an

103

invasion and as long as it was done in a recognizably submissive fashion. I remember my own childhood street in New York City: one part of the street had Jewish residents, and the other section had Irish Catholic occupants. In the normal course of events the group of children from each area stayed in their own part of the street, but each day they had to travel through the other's turf, because the public school was on the other side of the Catholic area and the parochial school could only be reached by passing through the Jewish section. Each morning and afternoon a kind of armed truce existed. The children of each group passed as quickly as possible through the other's area, neither group being very comfortable, neither defacing the other's area, and both groups giving every conceivable signal that this was being done only because it was absolutely necessary. But when there was movement into the other group's area at other than school traveling times, the rules called for battle, for this was a territorial invasion. Thus while territories existed, they did not have inflexible boundaries but shifted with circumstances.

Suttles (1968) described an analogous situation in a Chicago neighborhood where the residents were black, Italian, Puerto Rican, and Mexican-American. While each group had its separate territory, they shared certain places in an agreed-upon fashion. For example, they literally took turns using the short-order restaurant, with each group avoiding entry when it was occupied by another group. Other places were "owned" by certain groups; outsiders could use them only until the primary occupants appeared, at which time the visitor had to vacate the territory. Many more examples of human territorial behavior illustrate that (1) territoriality involving ownership or possession and occasional active defense can be readily observed in human groups, and (2) territorial behavior is not a simple "It's mine—keep out" process. It is a complex process that changes with time and circumstances.

The study of animal territoriality has a long history. Scholarly reviews were done by Carpenter (1958), Nice (1941), and Eibl-Eibesfeldt (1970), and popularized analyses were done by Ardrey (1966, 1970), Tiger (1969), and others. Although Carpenter's analysis is over 15 years old, some basic themes are still appropriate. He says that the study of animal territoriality, despite its beginnings in the 1600s, is still at an early stage. It wasn't until Howard (1948) undertook systematic studies of birds that the properties, functions, and types of territorial behavior began to be identified. Since then much has been learned about territorial behavior in such animals as birds, fish, reptiles, seals, rodents, deer, and primates. Recently, Ardrey (1966, 1970) wrote a popularized account of territorial behavior that tried to link animal and human territoriality. He postulated an inherited, instinctive basis to human territoriality (an issue that we will discuss later). Ardrey and other popular writers have made topics of territory and crowding quite salient to lay persons and professionals alike. The mounting concern with ecology has meshed well with popularized writings about territorial behavior to create a vigorous interest in the topic. And while the volume of empirical research on human territorial behavior is small, it will surely increase in the future.

In the following chapters, I will first consider the meaning of the concept of territory and its relationship to privacy, personal space, and crowding. Then I will examine theoretical positions, methods used to study territoriality, and empirical knowledge in the field.

In my theoretical framework, territorial behavior is one of several interpersonal-boundary mechanisms that act as a *means* toward the *end* of some desired level of privacy. By regulating social interaction, territorial behavior also helps to smooth out contact between people and thereby avoids social conflict and miscommunication. Other mechanisms that assist in controlling social exchange include verbal and paraverbal behavior and personal space. Personal space, discussed in Chapters 4 through 6, is close to the self. Territory is more distant—somewhat removed from the immediate person—and involves use of places and objects in the environment. Like the other mechanisms, territorial behaviors are adjusted and readjusted over time and work jointly with other behaviors to yield complex behavioral profiles. These profiles shift and change, and which mix of territory, personal space, or verbal and nonverbal behavior is used depends on how successful the system is in regulating interaction.

A Definitional Analysis of Territory

In order to develop a shared meaning of the concept of territory, it is instructive to see how others use the term. Table 7-1 summarizes a few definitions of animal and human territoriality.

There are several common themes in these definitions. First, there are consistent references to places or geographical areas. Second, many definitions imply various needs or motives that territorial behavior serves—such as sex and mating, food gathering, child rearing, and the like. Third, all definitions convey the idea of ownership of a place. Fourth, territoriality seems to involve personalization of a place by some marking device—for instance, urination, glandular secretions, signs, or fences. In many respects, the process of personalization involves controlling of boundaries. People use fences, "keep-out" signs, and all manner of marking devices to point out to others that "their place" begins at such and such a point. Movement by outsiders across such boundaries is something special—to be done with caution or with permission only—and trespassing without the owner's agreement is an invasion. A fifth quality of territory is that it can be the domain of individuals or groups. Sometimes we speak of a person's place, such as a bedroom. At other times the term refers to a group's place, such as a family

Table 7-1.   Definitions of Territoriality

Animal Definitions

Burt (1943): Territory is the protective part of the home range or area around the home site over which the animal normally travels.

Hediger (1950, 1961): Territories are geographical areas where an animal lives and from which it prevents others of the same species from entering. Territorial areas are used for many functions, such as feeding, mating, and rearing of the young. They are often demarcated by optical, acoustical, and olfactory means. Thus they are areas that are rendered personally distinctive and that are defended against encroachment.

Carpenter (1958): Territoriality is conceptualized as a high-order, complex behavioral system expressed in spatial-temporal terms. It involves individuals or groups defending an area and ranges from preventive quasi-aggressive responses to actual fighting. It occurs in the service of some 30 functions including proper spacing of a population, breeding control, reduction of sexual fighting, security, and defense.

McBride (1964): Territories are fixed geographical areas that are maintained and defended against intrusion by other members of the same species and are important in mating, feeding, and nesting behavior. They may be permanent or seasonal, and they may change in size.

Human Definitions

Stea (1965): Territorial behavior reflects the desire to possess and occupy portions of space and, when necessary, to defend them against intrusion by others.

Sommer (1966): A territory is an area controlled by a person, family, or other face-to-face collectivity. Control is reflected in actual or potential possession rather than evidence of physical combat or aggression—at least at the human level.

Pastalan (1970): A territory is a delimited space that a person or group uses and defends as an exclusive preserve. It involves psychological identification with a place, symbolized by attitudes of possessiveness and arrangements of objects in the area.

Sommer (1969), *Sommer and Becker* (1969), *Becker* (1973), and *Becker and Mayo* (1971): Territories are geographical areas that are personalized or marked in some way and that are defended from encroachment.

Goffman (1963): Territories are areas controlled on the basis of ownership and exclusiveness of use—for example, "This is mine," and "You keep off."

Lyman and Scott (1967): Territoriality involves the attempt to control space. Territories can be public, home, interactional, and bodily. Encroachment can take the form of violation, invasion, or contamination, and defensive reactions can involve turf defense, insulation, or linguistic collusion.

Altman and Haythorn (1967), *Altman, Taylor, and Wheeler* (1971), and *Sundstrom and Altman* (1974): Territoriality involves the mutually exclusive use of areas and objects by persons or groups.

---

home. A sixth quality of many definitions concerns territorial intrusion and defense. Sometimes when a territory is trespassed upon, the occupant may warn or attack the invader, although I believe that aggressive defense is not that frequent in humans. Other reactions to intrusion may be discomfort, anger, or anxiety. One can also distinguish between preventive, marking behaviors, which are used to set up territories, and reactive or defensive behaviors, which occur in response to an actual or potential invasion. Reactive, defensive behaviors cover a wide swath from vocal threats, threatening movements, and aggressive gestures to overt attacks.

For working purposes I will use the definition of territorial behavior as follows:

> Territorial behavior is a self/other boundary-regulation mechanism that involves personalization of or marking of a place or object and communication that it is "owned" by a person or group. Personalization and ownership are designed to regulate social interaction and to help satisfy various social and physical motives. Defense responses may sometimes occur when territorial boundaries are violated.

Animal and Human Territoriality

In what ways are human and animal territorial behaviors similar and different? It is clear that animals and men consistently personalize and mark environments as a symbol of ownership and sometimes defend territories against encroachment. But are the governing mechanisms and manifestations of territorial behavior essentially the same in humans and animals? The weight of evidence suggests a "yes and no" answer.

Data and anecdotal observation indicate that both animals and humans show territoriality as individuals and as members of groups. For example, single individuals have places of their own, as do members of various groups (such as marital couples, families, or club groups). Also, citizens of large social units, such as nations, are often identified with geographical territories. Similarly, animals possess spatial territory as individuals, in mating pair bonds, and in troops or bands. However, animals do not typically possess territories on the scale of a nation or much beyond a relatively small social system.

Another distinction between animal and human territoriality concerns the relative diversity of group membership. Animals usually belong to only a small number of groups and have only a few social roles—mate, leader, or parent. Humans, on the other hand, belong to many groups and have a multitude of social roles at almost any point in time—mother or father, husband or wife, professional, social-club member, athletic teammate, and so on. And each of these roles may be associated with different spatial territories. Thus the complexity of social roles may make principles derived from animal territorial behavior not wholly applicable to humans.

Another comparison concerns needs or motives associated with territoriality. Most writers point to a number of functions that animal territories facilitate, such as food gathering, maternal care, mating, and reproduction. Such functions have strong biological underpinnings. There is little empirical evidence that similar basic needs are served by human territoriality. This is not to deny the possible role of territory in relation to human biological drives but only to point out the lack of research on the topic. Conversely, studies of human territorial behavior strongly suggest the social, learned quality of territoriality, the variety of socially significant markers used to demarcate places, and the general relationship of territorial behavior to social rather than biological motives.

Another issue concerns the geographical nature of territory. Animal territories typically involve restricted geographical areas, which naturally vary with the size of the animal, its capability for movement, its food supply, and other population characteristics. Human territories seem more variable in physical size, functional complexity, and location. For example, humans have territories in nonadjacent places such as homes and offices, and territory size varies from place to place and even from time to time. Perhaps more important, human territorial behavior seems applicable to a broader range of things—other people, objects, and ideas, as well as geographical places. While animals are territorial about geographical locales and perhaps about mates, their young, and members of a collective, human possessiveness for others is more durable over time and extends beyond the confines of a geographically present person or group. Parent-child and husband-wife ties exist far longer and transcend geographical boundaries to a greater extent than most animal associations; loyalties to a community and nation are far more abstract and diffuse than any comparable animal identification.

Human and animal territoriality also seem divergent in regard to objects and ideas. Human possessiveness for objects appears to be as salient as it is for places. Children not only possess a place at the dinner table or a bedroom of their own but continually accumulate "things." They collect rocks, stamps, baseball cards, and a host of seemingly useless junk, such as stones, pieces of wood, broken glass, and even supplies of candy and food. Possessiveness for objects also exists in adults. Not only is a person's home a "castle" but so is his or her automobile, pen, typewriter, clothing, watch, and book. Human object and idea territoriality also goes beyond fixed geographical areas. A family can move across the world but feel relatively "at home" after its furniture and possessions arrive; the ill person in a hospital is comforted by having a few personal objects and reminders of home. Of course, object territoriality does exist in animals, as in the case of house pets who often have a blanket or toy, but such behavior generally seems less pervasive in animals.

Idea or cognitive territoriality also seems to be a distinctly human property. In the sciences, arts, and many other fields, copyrights, patents, and possession of ideas are of great importance. In fact, this territoriality applies to most people, who spend considerable time developing and defending attitudes, opinions, values, and philosophies that identify them as unique beings.[1]

Another feature of territorial behavior is its *preventive* quality. For animals, behaviors in advance of contact with others typically involve marking an area and its boundaries by urination, defecation, release of glandular secretions, or vocal cues. Humans generally do not use such techniques, except perhaps verbal ones (because they are socialized out early in childhood; people learn to deposit bodily waste products in certain places and not to use them as markers!). Rather, they rely heavily on symbols, objects, and artifacts to mark territories and their boundaries—for example, insignias, fences, and nameplates.

Animals and humans also show *reactive* behaviors to territorial invasion. Animals exhibit vocal warnings, threatening movements, and actual aggressive behavior. For the most part these behaviors involve use of bodily resources rather than environmental objects, although certain primates will throw objects at intruders. Humans also show a broad array of responses to intrusion. However, people seem to place greater emphasis on verbal mechanisms such as argument, discussion, or pleading. Furthermore, while gestures, facial expressions, and body-posture changes may be used (many of which were reviewed in the context of personal-space intrusion in an earlier chapter), humans also extend their physical capabilities by all manner of objects, symbols, and signs. Thus human-response repertoires seem to be richer, more variable, and more complex than animal territorial responses.

A related area of comparison has not been empirically confirmed but seems nevertheless important. People seem to have a very subtle and sensitively graded response repertoire in relation to territory, involving complex blends of verbal, nonverbal, and environmentally related behaviors. The result is a rich and sensitive communication system that allows for a wide array of alternative responses of both a preventive and a reactive nature. While we often think of war and other forms of violent contact between people, the fact is that human territorial intrusion is probably quite infrequent on a day-to-day basis. And when it does occur, responses are so finely graded that aggression is rare and used only as a last resort. Thus full-scale aggressive defense reactions are probably atypical of humans.

The comparisons made between animal and human territoriality do not argue for a total discontinuity between humans and other species. There is sufficient overlap to suggest that comparative analysis is useful. But it is also

---

[1]It cannot be stated that all types of territorial behavior follow the same principles (the ownership of objects or ideas may serve different functions than place ownership) or that all may contribute directly or in the same way to the regulation of social interaction. We will deal with these aspects of the concept that bear most directly on regulation of social interaction.

the case that blind generalizations and assumptions of exact equality in territoriality across species are not sensible. It is useful to seek comparability, but it is also important to be alert to differences.

Territorial Behavior: Inborn or Learned?

Within the last ten years, several writers put forth the idea that certain aspects of human social behavior, especially aggression and territoriality, have a biological, inherited, or instinctive quality (Ardrey, 1966, 1970; Lorenz, 1966; Tiger, 1969). This is quite in opposition to the long-standing thesis in the behavioral and social sciences that social behavior is primarily learned and that humans are especially responsive to environmental and cultural influences.

Ardrey argues that humans are a product of biological evolution and are subject to the same principles of Darwinian evolutionary theory as any organism. He also states that modern social and behavioral scientists ignore this evolutionary link in studying phenomena such as territoriality. However, he states that territorial behavior is not totally governed by our biological heritage and that learning and culture have an increasing effect on territorial behavior as one proceeds up the evolutionary ladder, from less- to more-complex organisms. For Ardrey, territorial instincts are "open programs" of instinct. "The disposition to possess a territory is innate. The command to defend it is likewise innate. But its position and borders will be learned. And if one shares it with a mate or a group, one learns likewise whom to tolerate, whom to expel" (Ardrey, 1966, p. 24). Thus, in humans, culture and the environment play a role but only within the limits laid down by genetic factors.

In a popularized fashion, Ardrey reviewed studies of animal territorial behavior and drew analogies to human aggressiveness, wars, the psychological character of various nationalities, recent events in the mid-East, including the founding of the state of Israel, the Olympic games, and a variety of other historical incidents. Ardrey, Lorenz, Tiger, and others who have adopted an evolutionary perspective have been roundly criticized for oversimplification, overgeneralization, and a lack of scientific perspective (Elms, 1972; Klopfer, 1968). They have been taken to task for proposing untestable or as yet untested hypotheses, for overgeneralizing in inappropriate ways from animal to human behavior, and for ignoring studies that demonstrate how phenomena such as aggression and territoriality are substantially under the control of cultural or environmental conditions.

Esser (1971a, 1971b, 1972) and Greenbie (1973) offered a somewhat different analysis of territorial behavior, emphasizing its linkages to locations within the human brain. Esser noted that there are three levels of the human brain: (1) the biological brain (the reticular system, and the oldest part of the brain in evolutionary terms), which is concerned with elementary social behavior and basic self-preservation, (2) a social-emotional brain, which operates at the level of the limbic system and which deals with social life, and (3) an intellectual or prosthetic brain (the neocortex), which is concerned with use of environmental artifacts to extend ourselves into the environment and which relates to humans' ability to become part of social groups and to their capacity for expansion of intellectual and conceptual vistas about the world. Territory needs and dominance behavior are attached by Esser to brain activities at the reticular and limbic levels of functioning, which have strong evolutionary roots.

The whole issue of the biological roots of territorial behavior does not have any immediate impact on my analysis. It is presented here because there has been controversy and because it is a provocative topic. Furthermore, the question is by no means resolved, and it is not immediately evident how it can be resolved, except by the gradual weight of increased research knowledge. There are probably few who would disagree that most human social behaviors are an *interaction* of cultural-environmental and biological influences. The question is how much part each plays and how each operates. To me, territorial behavior is simply one of a series of mechanisms called into play in the service of privacy needs. As our knowledge base develops we may be able to assess better the differential contributions of heredity and environment to territorial behavior. At the moment, however, I am not convinced that an answer to the question is necessary in order to study the phenomenon and to learn about its functioning.

Types of Territories

From the preceding discussion it should be clear that the concept of territory is not a simple one. Territorial events can be related to (1) different motives or need states, such as mating or eating, (2) geographical features, such as size and location, (3) social units, such as individuals, groups, or large social systems, (4) temporal duration, with some territories temporary (such as a seat on a bus) and others relatively permanent (such as a home), and (5) response repertoires, or behaviors used to mark territories, and defensive reactions in response to intrusion. In the present section I describe three types of territories that capture some of these distinctions: *primary, secondary,* and *public.*

This classification refers, first, to how central a territory is to a person or group or how close it is to their everyday lives. One dimension is related to the sociological distinction between primary-, secondary-, and reference-group memberships. A primary group involves such groups as a husband-wife couple or a family. A secondary group usually refers to other groups with which a person is involved on a segmental basis—for example, a factory work team, an athletic team, or a social club. A public or reference group is a more diffuse social affiliation, like a professional-association membership or citizenship of a nation. Our typology reflects the idea that territories differ in terms of personal involvement, pervasiveness, and centrality to the everyday life of a person or group.

A second dimension in this classification is duration or permanence of territories. Several writers note that territories vary in the duration of their ownership—from short-term, transient occupancy to relatively long-term, consistent ownership. A family home or a bedroom is a long-term territory in primary groups, as is a country club in regard to secondary-group affiliation. However, a seat in a restaurant or a location on a beach is a relatively transient territory, often held only as long as the user is present. These two dimensions—centrality and temporal duration—are not comprehensive, but they provide a vehicle for translating between different types of human territoriality.

Primary Territories.   Primary territories are owned and used exclusively by individuals or groups, are clearly identified as theirs by others, are controlled on a relatively permanent basis, and are central to the day-to-day lives of the occupants. Brower (1965) referred to these as personal territories and used the home as an example. In such territories, the identity of the owner is salient, invasion or unpermitted entry by outsiders is a serious matter, and control over access is highly valued. Goffman (1961), in an analysis of life in a mental hospital, spoke of a variety of locales that fit roughly into this class of territory. For example, certain hospital areas were strictly and permanently off limits to patients, such as physicians' offices and nursing stations. From the patients' perspective these were personal territories of the staff. However, patients also occasionally had personal territories. A private sleeping room was a place like home, where the patient could be said to own the room—could decorate it with pictures and objects. And like a home or bedroom, the patient could control access of others (except perhaps hospital staff). In terms of my framework, primary territories are powerful privacy-regulation mechanisms, and, in Western culture at least, they are usually viewed in a sacrosanct fashion and are entered only after receiving permission from the owner.

The violation of a primary territory can be a serious affront to a person's self-identity, especially if the intrusion is repeated and if adjustment and readjustment of boundaries is unsuccessful. In fact, the absence of a primary territory or the inability to regulate others' access may well yield, in the long run, a lack of self-esteem and self-identity. In our culture the person who has

"Mr. Mitchell! You *know* you don't have kitchen privileges."

Figure 7–1. Kitchens, bedrooms, and homes are typical primary territories, where occupants have almost total control. Drawing by Chas. Addams. Copyright 1950 The New Yorker Magazine, Inc. Reprinted by permission.

"no place" is labeled a vagrant and is often a marginal member of the community. We intuitively place value on a family home or on a person or couple's bedroom as theirs to own, decorate, and use as a place of refuge. I have watched my two sons, each of whom has his own bedroom, gradually develop a sense of control over their "place." As they have grown older and entered the teen years, pictures of athletic stars, trophies, collections, and posters with vulgarisms (at least to my tender eye) have gradually taken the place of decorations my wife and I put up when they were younger. The rooms have gradually become less ours and more theirs and moved from being our territory to being their primary territory. Therefore, primary territories are important as boundary-regulation processes and illustrate the close linkage of privacy regulation, territorial mechanisms, and self-identity.

Secondary Territories. Secondary territories are less central, pervasive, and exclusive; the term parallels the sociological distinction between primary and secondary groups. Lyman and Scott (1967) identified two types of territories that roughly fit this category and that they termed "home" territories and "interactional" territories. In home territories regular users have relatively free access and some control over others' use of a place. For example, in neighborhood bars or social clubs there often is a restriction, formal or informal, on who can use the place. And ownership and possession sometimes extend to specific objects such as seats or tables. Cavan (1963, 1966) did a case study of neighborhood bars as secondary territories. She noted that there was a range of bar users—hard-core regulars, sporadic regulars, and different groups at different times of day as the neighborhood clientele shifted. The regulars often had certain seating locations and used the bar for a variety of functions, such as check cashing, receiving mail, handling of telephone calls, and even banking, with the bartender storing and disbursing funds. The neighborhood bar provided an intimate social life for its regulars and was considered by them as their personal domain, with outsiders often treated as intruders. A kind of physical perimeter of people was sometimes formed near the door, as if to prevent outsiders from entering. Long, hostile, or questioning looks were directed at outsiders, and insulting or mocking statements were occasionally made. At times, the regulars made downright offensive and baiting comments and kept recreational equipment from the outsider's use. Even the bartender sometimes entered in, making the situation extremely uncomfortable for the nonregular user.

Some secondary territories have a simultaneous blend of public or semipublic availability and control by regular occupants. Of course, some secondary territories (for example, private social clubs) have rules limiting occupants, but even within the membership there are often informal territories that are controlled by selective people. Secondary territories are the bridge, therefore, between the total and pervasive control allowed participants in primary territories and the almost-free use of public territories by all persons. As such, there may well be confusion regarding secondary-territory boundaries, and the possibility exists for considerable conflict as boundaries are established, tested, and violated.

A good example of the potential for conflict and miscommunication in secondary territories is illustrated in Newman's (1972) analysis of "defensible space." Newman examined crime in urban low-cost housing developments and observed that one of the key problems was the design of

Figure 7–2. In some secondary territories, outsiders are often made to feel uncomfortable. Drawing by Hans Moser. Copyright 1970 Hans Moser. Reprinted by permission.

semipublic areas—hallways, lounges, entranceways to buildings, and immediate street areas. In most instances of high crime rate, these places were not easily personalized, territorial, or under the control of residents. In addition, they could not be easily watched by occupants and were, in Newman's terms, nondefensible territories. Such areas are secondary territories in my taxonomy and have the distinct feature of not being controlled by occupants—resulting in public use and takeover by vandals and gangs. Put in other terms, there was no gradation of territories. Homes were primary territories, but the areas outside the door of one's house immediately became a public territory. There were no secondary territories or buffer zones under the partial control of residents.

Similar findings occurred in an analysis of vandalized cars in an inner-city area of Philadelphia (Ley & Cybriwsky, 1974). In this rather unique study, observations were made of where cars were stripped of various parts. Most stripping took place near abandoned houses, vacant lots, or institutional places such as factories, railroads, and schools. Also, there were more cases of automobile vandalism near street intersections. The authors concluded that lack of surveillance, territorial control, or evidence of territorial ownership of the place where cars were located led to greater vandalism, a conclusion quite similar to that reached by Newman.

Newman's solution to these crime problems is to convert such public areas into clearer secondary territories by a variety of architectural-design techniques. These include differentiating the grounds (creating subneighborhoods within a development), creating semiprivate entrance accessways, using symbolic territorial markers such as walls, stoops, hedges, and the like, using clusters of entranceways and stairways accessible to only small groups of residents, and arranging lighting and windows to permit better surveillance of streets and play areas.[2]

In summary, secondary territories, because of their semipublic quality, often have unclear rules regarding their use and are susceptible to en-

---

[2]Although Newman's thinking is provocative, his data and conclusions have come under considerable criticism (Adams, 1973; Hillier, 1973; Kaplan, 1973; Patterson, 1974). These criticisms cover the following points: (1) not only were there design differences between the low- and high-rise projects he studied, but there were also some socioeconomic differences that could have contaminated the results; (2) some of the data had errors in calculations; (3) there was no clear and specific quantification of the territorial design differences between projects; (4) in at least one case, neighboring high-rise projects also had very low crime rates, but they were not included in Newman's analyses; (5) the fact of a relationship between design and crime in no way ensures that design is a causative factor or the main factor associated with crime rates; and (6) police records and other archival data used to reflect crime rates are often subject to serious biases. These are serious criticisms, and Newman's conclusions should be treated cautiously. Nevertheless, his hypothesis is an intriguing one and is worth further analysis. It remains for those who pursue this line of research to take into account the criticisms cited here and to examine more clearly the relationship between territorial design features and social behavior. (I am indebted to Arthur Patterson for bringing these issues to my attention.)

croachment by a variety of users, sometimes inappropriately and sometimes predisposing to social conflict. For these reasons, it is important that a variety of techniques be used, as Newman suggested, to make clear the rules of use and ownership. Thus in community design it is not enough to provide people with good homes and plenty of space; the qualities of the space relating to distinctions among primary, secondary, and public territories must also be considered.

Another type of secondary territory is an *interactional territory* (Lyman & Scott, 1967)—that is, any geographical locale in which some type of inter-action occurs among a group of people (for example, clusters of people at a party). From my perspective, interactional territories are better classified as group personal spaces, because, in Lyman and Scott's own phraseology, such groups are surrounded by an "invisible membrane" rather than having boundaries associated with objects and areas.

Brower (1965) and Goffman (1961, 1971) used somewhat different terminology but seemed to agree that secondary territories lie somewhere between primary and public ones. That is, they have elements of public access but also a degree of control by occupants. *Community occupancy* (Brower, 1965) involves the restricted use of an area by individuals or groups within a certain framework of rules—for example, a private club. Goffman (1961) described *surveillance space* and *group territories* in a mental hospital, both of which have some of the elements of secondary territories. Surveillance space was freely available to patients, but they were still subject to observation, authority, and restrictions placed on them by the staff. There were also *group territories* for patients, which evolved informally and were often officially sanctioned by the hospital administration. For example, the patient newspaper office became a territory for the patient staff; in another case, patients who worked on janitorial tasks were free to use certain areas of the hospital after work. Similarly, Roos (1968) described different types of territoriality on a U.S. Navy warship. One form of territorial behavior cen-tered around work groups, each of which typically had an area in which they conducted their tasks and in which they spent their leisure time. Other crew members usually did not enter the territory, except on business or upon invitation. And when entering for business reasons, the visitors often were deferent, regardless of military rank, and did not linger unless invited to do so. Territory occupants further reflected their control and ownership by locking doors, storing personal belongings in the space, and decorating and keeping the area neat above and beyond military requirements. (Depending on how these spaces were used, one might consider some of them primary territories.)

In summary, secondary territories are places over which an individual or a group has some control, ownership, and regulatory power but not to the same degree as over a primary territory. In secondary territories, others often have access on an official or unofficial basis, the main users sometimes vary over time, and the area is not always or solely identified as belonging to a single set of users. Because of ambiguity of ownership and control, there is probably more miscommunication and more conflict associated with secondary territories. In addition, there is likely to be a greater mixture of use of privacy-regulation behaviors, as people constantly adjust and readjust to ensure adequate understanding of others' boundary processes and to ensure proper communication of their own. Thus as Cavan (1966) indicated, outsiders to a bar are presented with a variety of cues—verbal abuse, physical perimeters of people blocking off areas, nonverbal stares, and hostile intonations—all designed to communicate boundary violation by the outsider. Such a rich panoply of cues is probably not necessary in a primary territory, since the visitor is probably more tuned in to the ownership quality of the place.

Public Territories.   Public territories have a temporary quality, and almost anyone has free access and occupancy rights. Such territories have been termed free territories, public territories, temporary territories, and jurisdictions. For example, Brower (1965) described two types of public territories. *Occupancy by society* of places such as streets and parks is generally available without restrictions, as long as users respect certain rules. *Free occupancy* settings, such as deserted beaches, have even fewer restrictions and are open to almost anyone for a limited period of time. Lyman and Scott (1967) also spoke of public territories or "those areas where the individual has freedom of access, but not necessarily of action. . . . These territories are officially open to all, but certain images and expectations of appropriate behavior . . . modify freedom" (p. 237). Thus playgrounds, beaches, parks, and public facilities are available to a society's members, but their use is restricted by laws, customs, and regulations. And access and use are usually limited in time. One cannot legally sleep overnight on public beaches or set up residence in a park.

The idea of temporary access is evident in Roos's (1968) analysis of the difference between territories and jurisdictions on a U.S. Navy ship. As indicated earlier, work teams often had relatively permanent territories where outsiders' entry was restricted. Yet there were persons who could enter these areas under certain conditions and without permission. For example, in a combat-information-control center, technicians freely entered the territory to do maintenance or repair work. As another example, janitors often have access to almost any office in a building after work hours, and they sometimes even displace residents. If you have ever worked late in an office, you know that janitors often enter without knocking and either ask you to leave or literally clean right over you, as if you were nonexistent or no longer had any rights to the place. As Roos noted, however, jurisdictions do not usually

Figure 7–3. Janitors have jurisdictional rights in others' territories and often ignore the occupant as they go about their work. Drawing by Chas. Addams. Copyright 1942, 1970 The New Yorker Magazine, Inc. Reprinted by permission.

involve ownership or possession; they control only the right of access for a brief period of time and for a particular purpose.

In a study of a mental hospital, Goffman (1961) described *free spaces* —spaces that were public and accessible to all patients on a temporary basis. These were areas such as toilets, certain hallways, or places off main pathways where patients could go to be alone—free from surveillance and the presence of others.

In a broad analysis, Goffman (1971) described a variety of public territories. The *stall* is a public space to which individuals or groups can lay temporary claim (for example, tables and chairs in a restaurant, tennis courts, telephone booths, and bus seats). The stall is a temporary territory; if someone leaves for more than a short period of time, their claim to the stall is lost. The *turn* is another public territory. It is the typical "place in line" at the refreshment stand, the movie, the airline ticket counter, or the supermarket checkout lane—merely the order of access and claim to some resource or place. The turn is usually open to anyone, ownership is temporary, and users must follow certain rules and regulations. Another type of public territory is *use space*—that area around or in front of a person or group which is temporarily recognized as under their control; for example, the line of vision of an art-gallery visitor or window shopper is usually not obstructed by others or is done so in a deferential fashion. Other territories that Goffman described include *possessional territories* and *sheaths* or objects identified with a person, such as clothing, jackets, glasses, magazines, or eating utensils.

In general, public territories are relatively fragile mechanisms for control of self/other boundaries. They are heavily dependent on institutions, norms, and customs rather than on rules set down by an individual user. Thus restaurant tables are generally placed so that people don't disturb one another, bus seats are usually positioned a certain width apart so that people don't come into overly close physical contact with one another, and telephone booths have doors or acoustic material to prevent others from hearing one's conversation. But the occupant of a public territory is at the mercy of a culture or spatial designer. For example, the crowded elevator and the crowded subway or bus do not really allow very much space per person, crowd flows in public areas are often poorly planned, some telephone booths do not have good sound shielding, and restaurants sometimes seat different parties overly close to one another. Thus if the design of a public territory is bad, there may not be efficient boundary-control mechanisms. One might expect, therefore, that people will often have to rely heavily on other mechanisms, such as nonverbal and verbal behaviors, to assist in regulation of privacy in public settings.

To summarize, three types of territories seem to encompass the variety that appear in the literature. Distinctions among these types of territories are based on (1) degree of control and use by occupants and (2) relative duration of users' claims to the space. Primary territories are usually under relatively total control of occupants for long periods of time. In addition, they are usually quite central to the life of the occupant. Secondary territories also have a durable quality of ownership, but it is not wholly continuous or permanent and there is some access by others, so that occupancy is not totally exclusive. Public territories are relatively temporary and occupancy is public, as long as users follow some social rules and norms.

Territorial Encroachments

Lyman and Scott (1967) pointed to three types of territorial encroachments: violation, invasion, and contamination. *Violation* involves unwarranted use of or entry into a territory, such as a man's using the women's public restroom and vice versa. In this type of encroachment there does not appear to be a specific territory owner, only a culturally defined class of permissible users. *Invasion* involves bypassing boundaries and interrupting someone or taking over a territory, on either a temporary or an enduring basis. Although Lyman and Scott did not clearly distinguish between invasion and violation, invasion seems to suggest the encroachment on a specific person or group. In both cases the trespassing of a territorial boundary can be permanent or temporary and can be aimed at disrupting ongoing activities or literally conquering the place and changing its owner.

Goffman (1971) used the term *intrusion* (which encompasses both violation and invasion) to describe someone who uses and claims the place of another person or group. A second form of encroachment was termed *obtrusion* by Goffman and occurs when a claimant exhibits territorial demands in excess of what's socially acceptable. For example, the person who occupies two seats in a bus, the restaurant patron who speaks so loudly that others cannot avoid hearing, and the rowdy teenagers who take over a public park are examples of obtrusive encroachments, in that more territorial claims are made than are warranted by social custom.

In the most basic sense, any territorial encroachment involves unwarranted crossing of a self or a group boundary. Such boundary violations produce situations in which achieved privacy is less than desired privacy. However, there are different implications of territorial encroachment, depending on which types of territories have been trespassed. For example, violations of primary territories (home or bedrooms) are probably viewed quite seriously by the owner, since primary territories are central to a person's or a group's life and are expected to be under their total control. On the other hand, encroachments of public territories may not be viewed by the possessor as extremely threatening, although they may be annoying and yield less than desired levels of privacy. For example, the group who sets down a beach blanket and possessions close to an already situated group is likely to be seen as less serious violators of territory than the uninvited and unwanted visitor to one's home who moves in for a month. The extent of encroachment is different in these cases, as are the options for readjusting boundary systems. The unwanted visitor in the home is hard to avoid or adjust to, whereas one can simply move one's blanket farther away on the beach and restore a desired level of boundary control.

"Didn't you hear us ring?"

Figure 7–4. There are many forms of territorial encroachment. Reg Hider from *Ladies' Home Journal.* © 1963 by Downe Publishing, Inc. Reprinted by permission.

Another form of territorial encroachment described by Lyman and Scott (1967) and Goffman (1971) is *contamination,* or the rendering of a place impure. Spitting, urinating, or defecating on another person's things are vivid forms of territorial contamination. As a child, I participated in various forms of deliberate defilement of others' territory—for example, urinating on the sidewalk in front of a "mean" person's home because we weren't allowed to play there. Also, a common tactic used to take away someone else's candy was to spit on it and render it impure to the owner (or one could control one's own candy by quickly licking the whole surface to prevent having to share it with others).

Goffman (1971) outlined another property of territorial violation, termed *modalities of encroachment.* These include literal placement of one's body in another's place or glances or looks at others or at their property in an intrusive fashion. Goffman gave the example of teenage males who often felt it necessary to physically and verbally defend their girlfriends (a form of territory) from the overlong and seductive glances of their rivals—as if looks and stares were a territorial encroachment. Disruptive sounds and noisy

conversations were also considered by Goffman as modalities of encroachment, as were bodily defilement by excreta (spittle, perspiration, vomit,
urine), odors (flatus, heated breath, and body odors), body heat (on toilet
seats, used beds, and clothing), and food left on plates.

Whichever form of encroachment occurs, the basic process is a bypassing of self/other or group/other boundaries. The seriousness of the
violation depends on whether the territory is a primary, secondary, or public
one, how long and intense the encroachment is, and what mix of reactive and
adjustive mechanisms is available. Thus if a bedroom or home is permanently intruded upon, if the intruder is disliked and unwanted, and if the
owner has limited social skills and little understanding of the use of nonverbal, verbal, or personal-space mechanisms, the impact is apt to be very
serious and not easily handled. But if the encroachment occurs in a public
place where ownership is not permanent, such as in a restaurant, alternatives
are usually available to restore desired boundaries; for example, one can
change one's table. Thus all territorial violations do not have the same
meaning, nor are they responded to in the same way.

Responses to Territorial Encroachment

Territories are preventively marked in a variety of ways to indicate
ownership and to signal to outsiders that the place belongs to someone. When
encroachment occurs, reactive responses may result, ranging from repetition
of the markings to warnings and even to physical defense. Preventive markings and reactions to encroachments are not easily separable, since we are
dealing with a dynamic system in which beginnings and endings are not
easily distinguishable and in which markings often result from prior territorial violations as well as being preventive signals.

Markers can involve symbolic or actual physical barriers and boundaries. Fences, hedges, signs, controlled access pathways, and guards are
classic examples of preventive markers, which Lyman and Scott (1967)
termed *insulation* or "the placement of some sort of barrier between the
occupants of a territory and potential invaders." Insulating barriers can take
many forms beyond the examples just given. Homes are often designed and
sites planned to prevent physical and visual encroachment; uniforms are worn
by members of groups to signal and separate outsiders from insiders; and
objects are used to mark public territories (for example, books, sweaters, or
other clothing left behind to reserve spaces in libraries and dining areas). In
addition, verbal and nonverbal signals function as preventive mechanisms.
Hostile or questioning looks, glances, and facial expressions serve to warn
outsiders that they are about to intrude or are not welcome. Linguistic
collusion (for example, dialects and special languages) and the use of in-

group jargon by teenagers and professionals announce to outsiders that they are in fact outsiders and potential intruders.

These mechanisms are in advance of territorial violation and in response to boundary encroachment. They may be used in various mixes; sometimes one type of response is emphasized, and at other times a different profile of behavior is used. As the personal-space literature suggested, flight or re-establishment of distance also occurs in response to intrusion. While primary territories are probably not vacated that readily—that is, one doesn't leave a home when it is intruded upon—public territory may be given up in response to encroachment, especially if alternatives exist. Thus if more seats are available on a bus or if a public park is relatively empty, those who are encroached upon may simply move away and establish a new territory. Naturally, if this is not possible they may resort to any of the mechanisms described above. Reactions to encroachment may also take several other forms, varying in degree of aggressiveness. Through direct and indirect verbal insults, the territorial occupants may try to make the place unpleasant for outsiders. Or they may act in an obnoxious fashion and undertake reverse encroachment. For example, on a beach, the initial territory holders might signal the perimeter of their boundary by playing games or creating disturbances in the immediate locale of the new occupants, giving them hostile glances and signaling by nonverbal behaviors that the encroachers do not belong—much as the occupants of bars subtly and not so subtly inform outsiders that they are unwelcome.

Thus there is a gradated series of responses used to establish and maintain territorial boundaries, from mild warning signals to a variety of escalated responses that may result in actual aggression and fighting. While the principles are not yet known to specify which level of response will occur or which mix of preventive and reactive responses will be used, my framework suggests a few guidelines. For example, only a few preventive devices are probably necessary to mark primary territories, and a minimum level of response will be necessary to maintain those territories. People tend to be quite sensitive to others' primary territories and generally respect them. Thus we typically do not enter other people's homes without an invitation. If continuous or serious violation into primary territory does occur, one would expect rapid escalation of reactive responses, which could easily culminate in aggression. Not only is our home "us" in a personal-identity sense, but our legal system gives us the right to defend it against serious encroachment. Public territories, on the other hand, are open to almost everyone, and a greater mix of markers and reactive behaviors may be necessary to preserve ownership. And, generally speaking, most people will not immediately resort to aggressive physical acts to preserve territories (such as a bus seat) unless there is very little territory or unless the encroachment is deliberate and malicious. Thus territories may be established by several means and will be held onto differentially as a function of their role in the total privacy system.

This chapter described territorial behavior as one of a series of mechanisms used to regulate social interaction. Following an analysis of other definitions, human territoriality was defined as a self/other boundary-regulation mechanism involving personalization or marking of a geographical area or object and the communication of "ownership" by its users or occupants. A number of similarities and differences in animal and human territorial behavior were discussed, as well as the biological versus learned aspects of territorial behavior. Territories were classified as primary, secondary, or public, depending on their degree of importance and permanence of use by occupants, and forms of territorial encroachment and reactions to encroachment were described. The next chapter reviews empirical knowledge on territorial behavior.

Territorial Behavior: The State of Research Knowledge

Only about two dozen empirical-research studies on human territorial behavior have been done in the past ten years. As indicated earlier, urban and community sociologists of the 1920s and 1930s did descriptive analyses of urban gangs and street and neighborhood groups and compared various ethnic and immigrant groups with each other in a case-study fashion. For example, groups might have been studied intensively for months in an attempt to learn about their social structure—leadership, social organization, member roles, and role conflicts and how they fit into the larger neighborhood and community. In some of these analyses, groups were observed to have territories or places that they either used exclusively or shared with others. They sometimes defended these territories in hostile encounters; territories were often marked by natural boundaries such as streets, parks, or other indicators; and territories sometimes had overlapping users at different times of day. The early sociological tradition of naturalistic description has not completely disappeared. For example, Goffman (1961) and others (Roos, 1968; Cavan, 1966) have continued to analyze social settings such as mental hospitals, bars, and Navy ships. The early sociological analyses set the stage for recent research, pointing to the phenomenon of territoriality as worthy of study. However, early research did not particularly outline a direction of study or a theoretical framework that could be tested or used as a springboard for systematic research. As a result, work on territorial behavior lay fallow until the 1960s, and most empirical studies have been published within the last decade or so.

Methodological Strategies for Studying Territorial Behavior

There are three types of methodological strategies used in empirical studies of territorial behavior. One type of study is *observational*, whereby territorial behavior of intact social groups is examined in naturalistic real-world settings and in which the investigator does little manipulation or experimentation with a situation. For example, Esser, Chamberlain, Chapple, and Kline (1965) tracked the use of space by psychiatric patients in a hospital ward; Sundstrom and Altman (1974) observed how boys in a rehabilitation setting used cottage space; DeLong (1970, 1971, 1973) studied use of chair locations in a college seminar over a several-week period; and Edney (1972b) and Edney and Jordan-Edney (1974) studied uses of hedges, fences, and other markers in homes and the behavior of individuals and groups on a public beach.

A second approach uses an *experimental* strategy, whereby settings and social structures are manipulated or experimentally varied. For example, Altman and Haythorn (1967) and Altman, Taylor, and Wheeler (1971) observed socially isolated persons' use of chairs, beds, and areas in a small room over an eight-to-ten-day period, during which group composition, degree of contact with the outside, expected length of social isolation, and other factors were experimentally varied. Other studies systematically manipulated types of territorial markers in libraries and other settings to determine their effect on potential intruders (Hoppe, Greene, & Kenney, 1972; Becker, 1973). Becker and Mayo (1971) dealt with reactions to intrusion in cafeterias, and Sommer and Becker (1969) studied the role of neighbors in defending occupied spaces.

A third type of methodological strategy is analogous to personal-space simulation studies and involves questionnaire, interview, and other *self-report* techniques. For example, Sommer and Becker (1969) presented subjects with table-seating diagrams and asked them to select seats they would hypothetically choose if they were in the real situation. Or Becker (1973) used photographs of library tables that either had a book in one corner or were cluttered all over with books and papers. Subjects were asked questions about the occupants of the seats and their own hypothetical choice of seats for several seating configurations.

Several aspects of methodology used to study territoriality are worth noting. First, compared with personal space, the absolute volume of research on territorial behavior is quite small. The lack of research is probably related to the second point—namely, that simulation or laboratory studies of territorial behavior are quite infrequent, whereas personal-space research relies heavily on these methods. One possible reason for this difference in methodological strategy may be inherent in the phenomena themselves. By definition, personal space is an invisible boundary always carried around with a person. It may, therefore, be easier to study in a laboratory situation. Territories, on the other hand, necessarily include areas, objects, and places in the environment that exist only in real locations. Furthermore, it also takes time for many territories to develop, especially primary and secondary territories. In laboratory or simulation situations it is not easy to re-create or form such places. And there is usually not enough time for territories to develop—unless one adopts the strategy used by Altman and Haythorn (1967) and Altman, Taylor, and Wheeler (1971), who observed territoriality of groups living in laboratory environments for eight to ten days. Typically, it is not possible to create such simulations, and researchers have, therefore, tried to find naturalistic settings such as libraries or prisons where (1) people actually use environments as parts of their daily lives, (2) territories have time to develop, and (3) an aspect of the natural environment can be experimentally manipulated in a field setting.

If the preceding analysis is correct, it also accounts for the absence of studies between the descriptive observations of early sociologists and the present-day research of sociologists and social psychologists. The more recent vintage of social psychologist is very laboratory oriented and operates out of a philosophical system holding that scientific advances would best be made if phenomena were studied in the controlled and rigorous setting of laboratories. Because this philosophical model was so prevalent until the mid-1960s, it may have been that only behavior that could be scrutinized in the laboratory was studied. Therefore, phenomena like territoriality, which could not be readily translated into laboratory operations, were simply not conceived of as interesting problems. It wasn't until researchers became more tolerant of alternative methodological strategies that phenomena such as territorial behavior began to be studied. But the way is now open, and the study of territorial behavior will probably flourish in future years.

Empirical Studies of Human Territorial Behavior

Not only is there a small volume of research on territorial behavior, but there have also been only a few topics of investigation. These include (1) studies of how territorial markers are used and the effects of types of markers on potential intruders, (2) analyses of the relationship between the dominance, power, or status hierarchy of groups and members' use of territories, and (3) studies that investigate the general role of territories in stabilizing social systems and smoothing their operations. Subsequent sections review research in each of these areas.

The Role of Markers in Territories

As discussed earlier, one characteristic of animal territorial behavior is the use of markers. These markers serve a *preventive* function; they let others know who is the owner and occupier of a place. In my terms, markers are symbols that help define self/other boundaries. As such, they are direct mechanisms to regulate social interaction. Vocal sounds, glandular secretions, bodily excretions, and other forms of bodily-related activity serve as the main animal marking mechanisms, with markers located around the perimeter of and within geographical territories. From everyday knowledge it is also obvious that humans employ markers, although we noted that these often involve use of objects, symbols, and artifacts rather than direct bodily-related devices. Empirical research on human marking behavior has addressed some fairly simple but fundamental questions, such as "Do markers serve to protect territories against encroachment?" or "Are markers differentially effective in preserving a territory?"

An early analysis of marking was done by Sommer and Becker (1969) in a series of field experiments in a university library, a soda fountain, an eating place, and a dormitory study hall. In a baseline study, they determined whether or not a person occupying a place could keep others away, simply by virtue of his or her presence. In one condition, a student confederate sat in a room adjacent to a popular soda fountain on a college campus; in another condition no one occupied the room. The results were not statistically reliable but nevertheless suggested that entry by outsiders was much slower and less frequent in an occupied versus an empty room—a simple result that demonstrates the sensitivity of people to occupancy by others. Also, the table at which the confederate sat was rarely intruded upon, with newcomers typically seating themselves at other tables in the room. In a questionnaire analysis, they also found that people selected middle seats at a library table when under instructions to actively prevent others from intruding and chose end or corner seats in a passive-defense mode. Another study (which might be classified as a study of either territory or personal space) was done near a water fountain in a university (Barefoot, Hoople, & McClay, 1972). Confederates sat at varying distances of 1 to 10 feet from a water fountain and quietly read a book. Observations indicated that a smaller percentage of passersby used the fountain when a confederate sat at the closer distances. They also drank for a shorter time from the fountain when they did use it.

Figure 8-1. Fences and hedges are often used to mark territories and help regulate interaction. G. Mordillo. Reprinted by permission.

Thus people themselves serve as markers of occupancy, and other people are sensitive to their presence, even in a public place.

Sommer and Becker (1969) followed up their earlier work and investigated the effectiveness of different kinds of markers. In a university soda fountain, one of three types of markers was left at empty tables—a sandwich wrapped in cellophane, a sweater draped over a chair, and two paperback books. These markers not only protected the chair they were located near, but they also protected the whole table. That is, people avoided sitting at the marked tables to a greater extent than at unmarked tables. Similar results were obtained in a dormitory study hall and in a university library. Sommer and Becker also observed that personal markers, such as a jacket or notebook, were more effective than less personal markers, such as library-owned journals. In a follow-up study, Becker (1973) examined the impact of occupants versus markers on seating locations, occupancy, and seating time in a university library. The results paralleled the earlier study. Those who sat at occupied tables selected locations most distant from the original occupant to a greater extent than when only markers were on the table. And there was a greater tendency to sit at marker-only tables rather than occupant tables. Furthermore, the number of markers made a difference; tables having several markers were sat at much later than tables with fewer or no markers. Finally, people sat and remained at occupant-present tables for the shortest period of time, at no-occupant or no-marker tables for the longest time, and at marker-only tables for an intermediate period. Once again, the presence of a real person was the best signal of territory, but markers varying in quantity and quality also served as signals to potential users. This behavior pattern was also illustrated in another part of Becker's study, in which subjects were presented with photographs of library tables, some having just a few books and others having many books. People consistently indicated that they would not sit where books were located and that they were more willing to sit at tables with fewer books; they agreed that the books signified the presence of the owners.

Edney (1972b) examined home residents' use of markers. Homes with distinctive territorial markers such as fences, hedges, and signs indicating "private property" and "no trespassing" were compared with relatively unmarked homes. Interviews and unobtrusive observation indicated that residents of highly marked homes were longer-term occupants. Furthermore, occupants with more markers answered a doorbell ring more quickly than those without elaborate markers, which could reflect a greater sense of possessiveness, wariness about intrusion, and even a symbolic communication of more rapid defense of the territory. Thus those with a long-term commitment to a place had a more elaborate boundary-marking system and were more sensitive to potential territorial encroachments.

Another study by Edney and Jordan-Edney (1974) examined territorial behavior on a public beach in Connecticut. Observers interviewed different sex-composition groups (all male, all female, mixed) and different-sized groups in regard to biographical characteristics and perceptions, including what they considered to be "their space." The results indicated that territories were roughly circular; that is, groups perceived their space to be equivalent in all directions. In addition, female pairs had smaller territories than males (male-female pairs were intermediate), and the longer people were on the beach the larger their territories became. In addition, they found that larger groups had a greater number of markers (not per person, but overall), and mixed-sex groups had more markers the longer they were on the beach—a result similar to those of Edney's earlier study of length of residence and number of markers.[1]

While these studies do not have profound theoretical significance, they illustrate empirically that (1) humans employ various means to label territories, (2) others respond according to the quantity and nature of markers, and (3) markers serve to regulate social interaction.

Cooperative-group aspects of territorial control are reflected in several studies of the role of neighbors in protecting someone else's space. Sommer and Becker (1969) found that people who happened to be sitting near markers at a university library table sometimes served as defenders and interpreters, informing new arrivals that the space was occupied. But as time passed and the prior occupant did not return, neighbors began reinterpreting the situation, suggesting to new arrivals that the space was no longer occupied.

To examine the role of the neighbor as a marker, defender, or interpreter, Sommer and Becker conducted three studies. In one study, a confederate sat next to an occupant, left some books as markers, and departed after 15 minutes. Shortly thereafter, another confederate appeared, glanced at the neighbor and at the markers, and appeared to be questioning the neigh-

---

[1] A recent study of severely retarded adults may have implications for the nature and impact of territorial marking (Hereford, Cleland, & Fellner, 1973). Nine institutionalized retarded adults who had a long history of night bedwetting were placed in less dense sleeping arrangements; that is, a dormitory originally occupied by 25 people was shifted to a nine-person area, and then marking strips were placed on the floor to separate areas between beds. The results indicated a marked decline in bedwetting under the more spacious sleeping arrangements. (But, surprisingly, there was no return to original levels of bedwetting when territories were returned to their original size). The authors interpreted their results to mean that, under the close living arrangements where there were no real territories, bedwetting may have served a marking purpose analogous to what occurs in animals and that it was no longer necessary under the larger, clearly defined territorial layout. We are not completely sure what this study means since many factors in the new environment could have affected patients' behavior in addition to the marking strips. However, it is provocative to speculate about urination as a marking device in humans and the impact of changes in territorial arrangements on patients' behavior. Further work in this area certainly seems warranted.

bor. The results were negative; neighbors did little to protect the space. In a follow-up, they then varied the degree of contact between the original occupant and the neighbor by means of conversation, as if to establish a social bond between them. Again, neighbors would not protect the space. In the next study, the intruder directly questioned the neighbor concerning ownership of the space. This time the neighbor defended the seat and explained that it was occupied. A subsequent study yielded similar results and also demonstrated less neighbor involvement when occupants were gone for long periods of time (60 versus 15 minutes). In an analogous study, Hoppe, Greene, and Kenney (1972) found that neighbors often place their own marker in a place they have been asked to save. Thus under some conditions other people serve as markers, interpreters, or spatial defenders, but not always. Asking others to hold a place in line or to save a seat is a common practice. But we also know that neighborhoods vary in self/other responsibilities, with some neighbors developing agreements to watch one another's homes during vacation periods and other neighbors being totally oblivious to one another. In summary, people exhibit various marking techniques to identify their places; these markers serve as interaction-control mechanisms; and people respond to one another's markers in a variety of ways, such as respect, interpretation to others, and even surrogate defense.

Dominance and Territorial Behavior

One of the most popular research topics on territoriality deals with the question "What is the relationship between the influence or dominance hierarchy in a group and the tendency of individuals to possess territories?" The literature on animals seems fairly consistent and suggests that the powerful, influential, and strongest members of the group have control over spaces they wish to occupy—for food, mating, child rearing, and other functions.

Implicit in the early descriptive analyses of urban group behavior was the idea that the residents of an area were dominant in their own neighborhoods and thereby controlled the space. Thus, control of territory seemed to shift as the relationship between the person or group and the space changed. Recent studies have attempted to measure people's dominance or influence position in the group and then track their use of space. For example, in the earliest empirical study in this area, Esser, Chamberlain, Chapple, and Kline (1965) observed severely disturbed psychiatric patients in a mental-hospital ward. Dominance was defined in terms of social interaction—patient initiative in interaction and amount of social contact with the hospital staff and with other patients. Use of space was observed periodically over 16 weeks, with the floor of the ward marked off in 3-foot by 3-foot grids and territory defined as an area where patients were frequently located. The results suggested a *negative* relationship between dominance and territorial behavior. That is, highly dominant patients did not have territories. Rather, they were free to go wherever they chose and did not develop exclusive use of spaces. In a sense, the whole ward was their territory. Patients in middle parts of the social-contact hierarchy restricted their movements and had territories and spaces that optimized their chances for interaction (for example, in main traffic-flow areas). However, those at the bottom of the hierarchy often had secluded spaces in corners and in locations where the chance for social interaction was low. Thus when dominance was defined in terms of social initiative, it was not surprising (and perhaps almost inevitable) to find that use of space matched exactly such behavior. That is, high interactors did not restrict themselves to any space but circulated everywhere, as if to reach out socially to a large number of people.

In a second study, with hospitalized boys 6 to 10 years old who suffered from severe psychiatric disorders, Esser (1968) obtained basically similar results. Boys who rated high on dominance—again defined in terms of social contact with others—typically did not have fixed locations where they spent a great deal of time, whereas those at the bottom of the social-interaction hierarchy used space in a restrictive way. In this study Esser also ranked boys in regard to "pecking order," based on staff ratings of each boy's popularity and the respect shown him by the group. In some ways this measure is closer to the traditional meaning of dominance as involving influence and power. A comparison of the relationship between pecking order and territorial behavior suggested *no relationship* at all. The same number and proportion of boys at different pecking-order levels seemed to possess territories. Thus these results do not support a relationship between dominance and territorial behavior and run counter to traditional ecological notions.

In a more recent study, Esser (1973a) again tracked the locational behavior of institutionalized boys in a cottage setting. Using social contact as a measure of dominance, there was no indication that lower-ranked boys were more prone to have territories, contrary to earlier studies. And this time, ratings of pecking order by cottage supervisors yielded a *positive* relationship between dominance and territorial behavior. That is, boys ranked higher on dominance tended to be territory holders to a greater extent than lower-ranked boys. In summary, Esser's first and second studies (Esser et al., 1965; Esser, 1968) yielded a negative relationship between social contact and territorial behavior; that is, lower social contact was associated with territorial behavior. However, a third study (Esser, 1973a) suggested no relationship between social contact and territorial behavior. In two of these same studies, which related pecking order or status in the group to territorial behavior, one study showed no relationship (Esser, 1968) and the other suggested a positive relationship (Esser, 1973a): high-status boys were territorial owners.

Thus this series of studies provides equivocal results concerning the territory-dominance relationship in humans. The absence of consistent findings may be attributable to (1) the type of populations studied—that is, children and adults with psychiatric disorders—(2) the measures of dominance employed, which sometimes tapped interaction and sometimes measured influence, status, and popularity, and (3) the social dynamics of the groups. For example, Esser indicated that cottage supervisors had different power and behavior expectations in the different groups. Or Rosenblatt (personal communication) suggested that the dominance-territoriality relationship may be affected by the "worth" of territories. That is, if people want places because they are desirable or serve some purpose, then the dominance-territoriality relationship may be different from instances in which no one really cares about the place.

Several recent studies explored the dominance-territory question further. For example, DeLong (1970, 1971, 1973) observed a college seminar class during a 16-week semester. Territorial behavior involved a person's being seated in a particular location over successive class sessions, and peer rankings of "demonstrated leadership ability" served as the dominance indicator. The results of one analysis (DeLong, 1973) yielded a positive relationship between territoriality and dominance for the first 11 weeks of the semester.[2] Such results partially confirm one of Esser's studies on the relationship between pecking order and territoriality.

In further pursuit of the relationship, DeLong (1970, 1971) undertook other analyses of the same seminar group and found a positive dominance-territory relationship, which also occurred in subgroups of the whole class. When there was a change in leadership (that is, when the professor withdrew from an active role in the class), two subcliques developed, each with its own leader. Over successive weeks of the class, there gradually emerged a tendency for higher-status students to be more territorial but primarily within their subgroups. That is, each subgroup developed a positive dominance-territoriality relationship. If the Esser and DeLong analyses are pieced together, especially when dominance is measured by influence or power, results generally suggest that influential group members tend to have territories more often than do less-influential persons.

DeLong's results also indicate the dynamic quality of dominance-territorial relations as group composition shifts or as task demands change. Therefore, territorial behavior should not be considered as having unchanging relationships with such social factors as dominance. In my framework, territorial behavior is a mechanism that assists in the pacing and regulation of

---

[2]Subsequent analyses suggested that this relationship was primarily due to events in the sixth to eleventh weeks, when leadership and dominance struggles were salient, following a point where the professor withdrew from seminar leadership.

social interaction, and it ebbs and flows as desires for privacy shift from more to less and less to more needs for interaction. As group membership changes, disruption of group functioning may occur, and it is possible that the use of territories also shifts toward some new equilibrium point as individuals seek to readjust their boundary-control processes.

This theme is illustrated by a recent study of territorial behavior in a cottage at a boy's rehabilitation center (Sundstrom & Altman, 1974). Dominance was assessed on three occasions over a ten-week period by asking boys to privately rank 17 other cottage mates on influence and power. Territorial behavior was determined by daily mappings of where the boys were—in bedrooms, the dormitory area, the lounge and TV area, bathrooms, or throughout the cottage. In addition, boys rated various spaces for "desirability"; for example, in the TV area, the front and second rows of seats were rated as highly desirable, and halls and areas near the supervisor's desk were rated as undesirable.

The results showed a variety of relationships between dominance and territorial behavior, and this variety was linked to membership changes over time. During the first five weeks of observation, there was a positive relationship between dominance and territorial behavior. The more influential boys had areas in the cottage in which they spent large amounts of time, especially the desirable TV areas, whereas the less-powerful boys distributed themselves throughout the cottage. Furthermore, this was a period with no changes in the 17 members of the cottage. And supervisor records indicated that disruptive behaviors, such as disobedience, fighting, and stealing were low during this stable period.

During the second period of observation (weeks five through seven), the situation changed dramatically. Two dominant boys were removed from the cottage by the administration, and two subsequently dominant newcomers were placed in the group. Territorial behavior dropped sharply, and there was no longer a relationship with dominance. That is, all boys tended to be everywhere in the cottage, with almost no one having a frequently used location. And disruptions, in the form of fights, teasing, and misbehavior rose sharply, suggesting that the group was in turmoil. Thus, when group composition changed, the social system was upset.

During the third period (weeks seven through ten), there were fewer extreme changes in group composition (one high- and one medium-dominant boy were removed), and a third dominance-territoriality relationship emerged. There was a weak and not statistically reliable tendency for low-dominant boys to be more territorial than high-dominant boys. And disruption declined for low- and medium-dominant boys, suggesting that they had begun to return to a stable structure, while the high-dominant boys still exhibited much disruptive behavior. Analysis of the behavior of a subgroup of boys who were in the cottage throughout the ten weeks indicated a consistent dominance-territoriality relationship, with the more influential boys using desirable locations consistently more often than less influential boys. Thus in the stable subgroup there was an orderly relationship between dominance and space usage throughout the ten weeks.

This study reinforces the idea that we should view territoriality and its relationship to social factors as dynamic. If territoriality is one of several mechanisms designed to serve privacy goals, then its operation should be expected to shift over time as privacy needs change.

In summary, for studies that measure dominance in terms of influence or power, the weight of evidence is that group members who are more dominant possess territories to a greater extent than less prominent members. But this evidence occurs primarily under conditions of stable group structure. As group stability is upset, the dominance-territoriality relationship may also be less clear and only eventually re-established.

Another way of looking at the relationship between dominance and territoriality is how territory holders and visitors behave on their own and on someone else's turf. That is, does the home team win more often than the visitors? Do territory holders act more dominant or have more influence when they are at home rather than away? Several studies suggest that this behavior pattern is, in fact, true. For example, Esser (1970) demonstrated that psychotic patients had more success in influencing others when visitors came to their own territory; they were less influential when they were not in their own territories. Similar results were obtained by Martindale (1971), who reported that college-dormitory residents who worked on a negotiation task in their own room spoke more and won the negotiation more frequently than did visitors.

I looked at the records of the University of Utah football and basketball teams in their home and away games during the past three years. The results were striking, especially for basketball. Both teams won two-thirds of their home games, whereas the basketball team won only one-fourth of its away games and the football team won less than one-half of its away games. These results confirm the widespread belief that being on one's own turf is an advantage, partly because of crowd support and partly because of familiarity with the setting. And we have all heard stories of the small dog who chases the great dane off its yard, with the great dane walking slowly and deferentially away, exhibiting every submissive behavior it can muster.

Thus the thrust of current research evidence is that (1) high-dominant people tend to have territories to a greater extent than low-dominant people but that this can change as circumstances shift and (2) people tend to be more dominant and influential in their own territories. Obviously, research has only begun to tap the complexities of the relationship between dominance and territorial behavior. Of particular interest to my framework would be more precise analyses of conditions that alter social-structure/territoriality relationships and the ways in which territorial behavior meshes with other boundary-control mechanisms during periods of group stability and instability.

Territorial Behavior as a Social-Regulation Mechanism

A consistent theme among students of animal behavior is that territoriality helps stabilize and regulate social systems (Dubos, 1965, 1968; Eibl-Eibesfeldt, 1970). For example, Eibl-Eibesfeldt (1970) described how territories actually serve to prevent aggression and fighting once they are established and how they generally assist in maintaining stable social systems. Thus if everyone has a "place" to eat, mate, rear young, and perform other life functions and if these places are known and respected by others, much of life's potential frictions and conflicts will be reduced. Dubos (1965, 1968) also discussed how territoriality functions at all levels of the social system—at the level of the individual, the group, and the species—tend to yield a stable social structure and to play a role, however indirect, in evolutionary adaptation. In such a role, the healthier and more viable members of the species are the ones who gain territories and gradually, over generations, reproduce the most adaptive individuals and social systems. In this sense, territoriality may play a long-range role in the well-being of a whole species.

While all the relationships between territorial behavior and animal social systems have not been worked out, Ardrey (1966) hypothesized three essential functions of territorial behavior in animals and humans. First, territory serves as a *stimulator* in that defense and control of peripheral boundaries sharpen interactive and survival skills. Second, territories provide *security*, a place to perform certain functions in a locale where individuals or groups "know" (in a figurative sense) what is around and what belongs to them. Third, and most important, Ardrey proposed that territories contribute to a sense of *identity*, such that possession, ownership, and control of a geographical area help define concretely the person or group. This idea is compatible with my position; successful privacy regulation is hypothesized to contribute ultimately to self-definition and self-identity.

Edney (1975) described the role of territoriality as providing a stable social organization in humans as well as in animals. He stated that territories serve a stabilizing and regulatory role at individual, group, and community levels—to smooth social interaction, to provide a set of cues to others, and to make explicit role relationships and status hierarchies in a readily observable fashion. To carry this point to its logical extreme, it might even be said that the eventual necessity to defend and fight over territories is a *failure* of a social system. That is, having to resort to violence and even cause the death of an opponent in a territorial struggle suggests that the system is not working

Figure 8-2. Territories and the regulation of social interaction. (Photograph by Jim Pinckney.)

too well. In spite of the fact that wars are not uncommon among humans, overt aggression between individuals is a rather infrequent everyday event. And rarely does aggression occur in the context of territorial competition. As proposed earlier, communicative signaling among humans is so complex and well tuned, and societal norms operate so well to ensure adequate communication of territorial ownership, that the social order remains reasonably viable.

This stabilizing function of territories is evident in even the most nondescript, day-to-day activities of families. In a study of family-home environments (Altman, Nelson, & Lett, 1972), I discovered some simple facts reflecting how people use their homes in ways that ease and stabilize day-to-day activities. For example, people who share bedrooms—brothers, sisters, or parents—are generally territorial about space, in the sense that each person has his or her own closet or side of a closet and separate dresser or dresser drawers. Furthermore, people tend to respect one another's boundary markers in that closed bedroom doors, and especially bathroom doors, are usually not opened without knocking. Furthermore, seating patterns at mealtimes can be described as territorial, with most families having fixed seating arrangements for everyone, changed only when people eat alone or when guests are in the home. And roles affect seating arrangements. Fathers generally sit at the "head" or end of the table (a phenomenon also noted by Dreyer and Dreyer, 1973), and mothers sit either at the opposite end, or adjacent to the father, or at a center position.

In a sense, such spatial habits make life easier to live. With everyone having "places," there is no need to continually negotiate who belongs where or who has rights to what, so that day-to-day life smoothes out by virtue of territorial assignments or ownership. (I tremble thinking about the time when my second son becomes eligible to drive a car. There was a sufficient crisis with my oldest son, when I had to share "my" car with him. [He now calls it "our car!"] But when the third territory holder enters the scene, I fear there will be great disruption in our family social system, resulting in my losing most territorial rights to the vehicle and becoming the lowest-priority user. In fact, I may have to resort to walking, bike riding, or just staying at home!)

One could easily view all the research discussed thus far as support for how territorial behavior helps to stabilize social systems. The way in which people respond to and respect markers (Becker, 1973; Sommer & Becker, 1969), the elaborate use of markers with increased years of residence and ownership of a home (Edney, 1972b), and the relationships between dominance and territorial behavior, especially the shift as the social hierarchy is disturbed (Sundstrom & Altman, 1974), point to the role of territories contributing to a viable social system.

Several other studies examined this idea more directly. In two studies (Altman & Haythorn, 1967; Altman, Taylor, & Wheeler, 1971), strangers (U.S. Navy volunteers) were paired in two-person groups, lived together in socially isolated and confined quarters for 8 to 10 days, and had little contact with the outside world. (This was a relatively bare environment intended to simulate life in undersea situations.) In both studies, territorial and other forms of behavior were measured systematically over the whole period. Territorial behavior was defined according to the exclusive use of chairs, beds, and areas. For example, high territoriality occurred to the degree that one man exclusively used one chair and the other man used the other chair. In the first study, pairs were formed to be either compatible or incompatible, based on certain personality characteristics. For example, pairs in which both men were high on need dominance (desire to influence and control others) were hypothesized to be incompatible, since both members were interested in controlling the situation and each other. On several indicators of stress, task performance, emotional symptomatology, and ability to remain in the situation for the full term of the study, pairs in which both members were dominant were, in fact, incompatible and less effective. Members of such pairs also fought verbally and occasionally physically and generally exhibited less viability than compatible pairs. Compatible pairs were those in which one member was high in dominance needs and the other was low in dominance needs. Such pairs functioned best, as predicted.

Most important for our purposes, there were differences in territorial behavior in these two types of groups. Incompatible pairs had very *low* territorial behavior in the early days of isolation, which meant that neither man had a place of his own and that each used space and objects in an overlapping fashion. Only toward the end of their stay (which was often earlier than scheduled, since several groups refused to continue the experience) did they show increased territorial behavior. On the other hand, compatible groups had exactly the reverse pattern. They were quite territorial at first; each man used chairs, beds, and areas exclusively and encroached less on the other man's "places." However, later in their association, compatible pair members showed a decline in territorial behavior. It was as if viable group members established ground rules for space usage and for other facets of their lives early in their contact with each other and then gradually relaxed their boundaries once it was clear that they would be compatible. Thus early territorial behavior proved to be a good predictor of eventual social stability.

A second study (Altman, Taylor, & Wheeler, 1971) looked at the effect of opportunity to be away from the other man, expected length of isolation, and degree of outside contact. Again, several pairs were unsuccessful and did not complete the experience. In comparing groups, a pattern similar to the prior study emerged. Successful group members established territories early in their experience with each other, showed milder stress reactions, performed well on tasks, had levels of self-disclosure that were not overly high or overly withdrawn, and seemed to organize their lives according to eating and work schedules. Unsuccessful groups did not function as well and appeared to be disorganized, did not go about the job of group formation early enough or in a systematic way, and apparently had not prepared themselves for the isolation experience or for the difficult task of living for a long time with just one other person. Again, the territorial behavior of successful groups was highest in the early days and declined later on, whereas unsuccessful groups followed an opposite pattern.

The epitome of an "organized" and successful group was one pair of men who sat down early on the first day and decided where they would keep their clothes, who would have what space for storage, and what their eating schedule would be; they then laid out a schedule for exercising, sleeping, and general living. (For the most part, no such scheduling was imposed on groups.) This pair also built a chess set, a monopoly game, a checkers set, and a deck of cards out of paper towels, stored game materials for later use, and almost totally put their own organization on the bare unstructured environment. Thus territorial behavior meshes with other forms of behavior to generate a coherent life-style that reflects or contributes to a stable and viable social system.

Further evidence for the role of territoriality as a stabilizing device also comes from studies of more unusual populations. For example, O'Neill and Paluck (1973) demonstrated that the introduction of identifiable territories in a group of retarded boys (that is, each had a place of his own) was subsequently associated with a decrease in aggressive behavior. In another study, Paluck and Esser (1971a) found that retarded boys, aged 5 to 10, quickly established territories in a day room of a large institution and hung on with tenacity to these territories. These results were interpreted as illustrative of the role of territories in reducing the complexity of the world and allowing individuals to achieve some control and security over their lives. In a case-study analysis of the same group, Paluck and Esser (1971b) suggested that the ways in which boys used territories at two different times, separated by 20 months, reflected changes in their psychological health. If they moved from less to more favorable territories and showed more flexibility in territorial usage, they were also independently judged as having shown improvement in psychological functioning.

A study conducted within a totally different context also bears on territorial behavior as a reflection of a stable social system. Rosenblatt and Budd (in press) did a survey of married and unmarried cohabiting couples in relation to territorial behavior. They found that married persons, who might be more committed to a long-term social relationship, were more territorial than unmarried cohabiting couples. Territoriality was defined in terms of having separate beds or sides of the bed, separate areas of a closet, separate drawers for storage, separate portions of the bathroom for supplies, and separate chairs at the dinner table. When people are committed to a continuing relationship they may attempt to build regulatory patterns of behavior that will reduce conflict and increase the social order of their lives, much as did the successful sailor groups in the studies reported above. Unmarried couples in this study reported more tendency to have an area in the home to be alone. From these results it may be concluded that unmarried couples were less committed to the relationship, wanted to maintain their separateness by having places to be alone, but did not commit themselves to the detailed organization of space and living habits necessary for long-term group stability.

Another way to look at this issue is to study situations in which territories are absent or do not work well. Under such circumstances one may expect social disruption and poor group functioning. I already cited a study by Sundstrom and Altman (1974) of boys in a cottage situation where social disruption increased as the territorial structure of the group broke down. Also, Newman (1972) examined crime in low-cost urban housing developments in relationship to the presence or absence of "defensible space," in part determined by the existence of territories and the ability of people to monitor events in their neighborhoods. He found strong ties among the absence of territories, perceived control over space, and crime rates. When areas outside the apartment, such as hallways, elevators, entranceways to buildings, play areas, or streets were indistinguishable (that is, they had no clear boundaries or were not perceived by outsiders as linked to a building or cluster of buildings) and were not easily under the surveillance of residents, and when they had no natural or built boundaries such as fences, signs, or other symbols of ownership, then they were prey to crime by outsiders, gangs, and vandals. Thus when territories and their boundaries were not clear, there was a greater incidence of conflict, crime, and social disruption. Newman also provided examples from other housing developments that show the other side of the coin—that reduced crime and conflict occur when the territorial structure is more stable and visible.[3]

In summary, it seems reasonable to assume that territorial behavior has an important function in regulating social interaction, in easing the stresses of life, in clarifying roles, and in providing visible cues about social actors in groups. Furthermore, a number of studies suggest that territorial behavior is not rigid but changes over time and with shifting circumstances. This finding is not surprising in light of my conception of territorial behavior as one of a series of mechanisms used to service privacy desires. Because it is part of a complex network of mechanisms and because adjustments in self/other boundaries occur continuously, territorial behavior should blend in various mixes with other behaviors as circumstances change.

Summary of Chapters 7 and 8

Although empirical research on territorial behavior is not voluminous, human territoriality is a pervasive phenomenon and quite apparent in the everyday behavior of all types of groups—urban gangs, city dwellers, institutionalized patients, neighborhood-tavern users, home owners, bedroom occupants, and the like. Also, there is a large body of research that indicates the central role of territoriality in animal social systems.

Chapter 7 analyzed definitional and conceptual issues of territoriality. In the theoretical framework of this book, territorial behavior is one of a series of mechanisms that function in the service of desired levels of privacy. The territorial mechanism is at a more remote distance from the self compared with personal space, since it involves use of areas and objects. Territoriality refers to the personalization or marking of areas and objects and to the ownership of a place by a person or group.

The chapter considered similarities and differences between animal and human territoriality. Similarities included the idea of possession and ownership, demarcation of territories, individual and group territories, and

---

[3]See Chapter 7 for a critique of Newman's work.

levels of response to encroachment, including active defense. It was noted, however, that exact generalization from animal to human territorial behavior was probably unwarranted, since humans seem to have a greater variety of territories, exhibit a broader range of responses to encroachment, and mark territories differently. Finally, human territoriality seems to be related more strongly to social than to biological drives. We also considered the biological or innate versus socially learned or culturally determined aspects of human territorial behavior. It was concluded that the question cannot be answered at the present time, that there is probably some interaction of biological and cultural determinants of territorial behavior, but that research and theory can proceed productively without taking a firm position on the issue.

Different types of territoriality were also described in Chapter 7. *Primary territories* such as homes and bedrooms are central to a person or group's life, are typically under a high degree of control by the owner, and are clear-cut, powerful boundary-control mechanisms. *Secondary territories* may be attached to a person or group but may also have a public quality, in that others have limited access to the area (for example, a neighborhood bar). *Public territories* are temporary, accessibile to many people as long as certain basic norms are observed (for example, bus seats), and have little long-term boundary-control power.

Chapter 7 also considered territorial encroachments and reactions to encroachment. Various writers described *intrusions* and *violations*, which include trespassing and unwarranted use of or taking over of another's territory; *obtrusion*, or excessive use of an area, thus violating others in an indirect fashion (for example, a noisy theatergoer); and *contaminations*, or defiling of a territory by spitting, urinating, or in other ways contaminating a place belonging to others. In general, encroachments represent boundary violations in opposition to the interests and goals of the territorial occupant. Reactions to encroachment vary considerably, in an escalated fashion from preventive marking and nonverbal and verbal warnings to active defense and aggressive behavior. In some cases flight is the response to encroachment.

Chapter 8 reviewed empirical research on territoriality. It was noted that the number of empirical studies on territorial behavior is quite small, perhaps attributable to (1) the need for longitudinal studies, since territoriality takes time to develop and cannot be easily simulated in short-term laboratory studies, and (2) the fact that territorial phenomena involve objects and areas in the natural life of people, also not easily simulated in laboratories. For these reasons, most studies of territorial behavior are based on naturalistic observations and field experiments in such settings as cafeterias, libraries, and hospitals.

A reasonable amount of research has been conducted on the use of markers or objects to protect space. Findings generally indicate that (1) markers are effective in protecting rooms, tables, chairs, and seating locations; (2) the more personal the marker, the more effective the protective value; (3) the more permanent the occupancy of a territory, the more elaborate the marker system; and (4) under certain conditions, neighbors serve as territorial defenders in the absence of owners.

Another body of research investigated the relationship between position in a dominance hierarchy and territorial possession. The research results were not wholly clear but generally indicated that those in high-status positions were more territorial than low-status persons, especially in regard to desirable places. Yet under other circumstances this relationship did not hold—for example, when group composition changed or when other factors upset a stable social system. It was proposed that territoriality and dominance relationships might fluctuate as the total interpersonal boundary-control system shifted and adjusted to new circumstances. Other results support the idea that the "home team usually wins," in that territory holders tend to be more influential on their own turf.

Another body of research demonstrated how territorial behavior serves as a social-system regulator to help preserve a viable system and to assist in regulating interpersonal events. Several studies indicated that successful social systems had different developmental patterns and territorial behaviors from those of groups in a state of upheaval and deterioration.

The next two chapters turn to the topic of crowding, a situation in which boundary-control mechanisms such as territory and personal space do not function effectively.

Crowding: Meaning, Theory, and Methods

The topics of "crowding" and "overpopulation" are popular social issues and are as important as the energy crisis and environmental pollution. Some people fear physical, physiological, and psychological damage as a result of overcrowding, in the form of disease, aggression, suicide, crime, and other social pathologies. Some state that the negative effects of population growth are already here. There are those who are pessimistic about solutions, while others seek immediate and dramatic solutions. Still others do not view crowding as a problem of sheer number of people but as an interaction of population size and characteristics of social structures.

Regardless of one's philosophical stand, it is a fact that the world's population is growing rapidly. Ehrlich (1968) pointed out that from 6,000 B.C. to 1650 A.D. the world's population grew from 5 million to 500 million, doubling every thousand years or so. By 1850 it had reached one billion, doubling in 200 years. By 1930 the world's population had climbed to 2 billion, requiring only 80 years to double. As of a few years ago, doubling time was estimated at about 35 years.

In this chapter I will define "crowding" and how it differs from population density. Then, I will present a model of crowding derived from the framework of this book. The model links crowding to privacy through the mechanisms of personal space and territorial behavior. Briefly, crowding occurs when privacy mechanisms fail to function successfully, causing a person or group to have more interaction with others than is desired; that is, achieved privacy is less than desired privacy. The model considers factors that lead to boundary-control failure, coping responses used to correct the situation, and short- and long-range outcomes of poorly functioning boundary systems.

Following this analysis, I will present a historical overview of research strategies used to study crowding, including (1) correlational studies that relate population density to social pathology, such as crime, mental health, and physical disease, and (2) experimental laboratory research that examines social processes associated with density and crowding.

The Nature and Meaning of Crowding

What is meant by the term "crowding"? In everyday usage there are many situations in which people say "I am crowded" or "This place is crowded." For example,

> At a football game where the stands are filled or in a theater where there are no empty seats.
> As one squeezes into a packed elevator.
> A popular beer hall on Saturday night.
> The downtown area of a large city at lunchtime.
> A large family who lives in a small home or apartment.

In some of these examples crowding does not necessarily imply an undesirable or stressful situation. In fact, sometimes the presence of many people is expected or even sought. For example, as long as one has a seat, a crowd at a football game or at a theater adds to the pleasure of the event. A crowded party also provides an exciting atmosphere, with many interaction opportunities. And the visitor to a large city often feels the positive excitement of being with others. Even a crowded elevator is not always aversive, as long as one isn't in it too long. To press the point further, some of these examples demonstrate that *too little* crowding may be unpleasant. For example, who would want to be in an empty football stadium or theater or at a poorly attended party? Thus some degree of density or contact with others is often desirable. Yet other examples in the very same settings show how crowding can be negative:

> A theatergoer faces long lines trying to purchase refreshments at intermission.
> Football fans leaving the stadium are jostled, can move only slowly toward parking lots, and must inch their way home in bumper-to-bumper traffic.
> The packed elevator stops floor by floor, and people push their way on and off.
> People shove their way toward the bar in a crowded beer hall.
> The residents of an urban area wait to cross the street with droves of other people, struggle in lines to buy lunch, and are jostled in subways day by day and year after year.
> A member of a large family living in a small apartment must dress and undress in the presence of others, wait in line for the bathroom, and share a bed with others.

Figure 9–1a. Sometimes crowds are fun . . .

Figure 9–1b. . . . and sometimes they aren't. (Photographs by Howard E. Harrison. ©
1968 by Howard E. Harrison.)

These examples illustrate that crowding is not a simple concept. It has been applied to large populations, such as cities, and to relatively small groups at parties and in homes. It has even been used to portray a relationship between two persons, as captured by the phrase "You crowd me!" To understand crowding, therefore, requires an unraveling of its dimensions and a recognition that it is a complex idea. Moreover, the term is used in a variety of situations—where people want more physical space, where they are blocked from desired resources (for example, waiting in a long line for some service), where they are intruded on by others, and where they are in short- versus long-term situations of high density (for example, an elevator rather than a crowded ghetto or home). These examples point to a few dimensions of crowding, such as space availability, access to resources, intrusion, and duration of contact with others. In addition, our examples illustrate the optimization and dialectic qualities of crowding, discussed earlier in relation to privacy. The presence of others provides positive gratifications; yet there are circumstances in which the presence of others is negative. Furthermore, there is an interplay of forces in which other people can be simultaneously positively and negatively gratifying. For example, city life involves considerable positive stimulation—a variety of cultural, economic, and political resources that can be tapped, making life a rich experience. Yet these very qualities can be negative. People are subject to intrusion, noise, difficulty in gaining access to resources, and the impersonality of others (Simmel, 1950a; Wirth, 1938; Milgram, 1970).

At the root of my analysis lies a central theme—that crowding is an *interpersonal* process, at the level of people interacting with one another in pairs or in small groups. While it is proper and necessary to study crowding at the large-scale level of cities or nations, my emphasis is in understanding aspects of crowding that involve ongoing social interaction among people.

Some Distinctions between Crowding and Density

The differences between the terms "crowding" and "density" are not always made clear. Sometimes the terms are used synonymously, to reflect the physical idea of number of people per unit of space. And, even in that case, the unit of space is not always the same but covers the range from people per acre of land, people per census tract, people per room in homes, dwelling units per acre of land, and the like. As I shall discuss later, these different indicators of density may not yield identical effects on behavior.

Recently, Stokols (1972a, 1972b) brought the distinction between density and crowding into sharp focus. He limited density to a strictly physical

Figure 9–2. Sometimes even two can be a crowd. Drawing by F. B. Modell. Copyright 1950 The New Yorker Magazine, Inc. Reprinted by permission.

meaning—the number of people per unit of space. Crowding, on the other hand, is a psychological concept, with an experiential, motivational base. In his terms:

> The experience of crowding, thus, can be characterized as a motivational state directed toward the alleviation of perceived restriction and infringement, through the augmentation of one's space supply, or the adjustment of social and personal variables so as to minimize the inconveniences imposed by spatial limitation [p. 276].

Several points are worth highlighting about Stokols' approach. First, crowding is a personal, subjective reaction, not a physical variable. Second, it is a motivational state that often results in goal-directed behavior, to achieve some end or to relieve discomfort. Third, crowding centers around a feeling of too little space. Density, on the other hand, is strictly a physical quality with no inherent psychological meaning; it is merely a measure of people per unit of space.

Stokols stated that density is a necessary though not sufficient condition for the feeling of being crowded. That is, increased numbers of people per unit of space is an important prior condition for a feeling of crowding, but it is not always wholly sufficient to create that feeling. For example, one can be with a group of friends and not feel crowded, but can be with the same-size group of strangers and feel quite crowded. Thus certain other conditions such as amount and arrangement of space, noise, glare, and the like might interact with conditions of high density to trip off feelings of crowding. Similarly, social factors such as competition, interference from others, or power struggles can combine with density to affect feelings of crowding. Finally, personality and past experiences may interact with spatial density. As discussed later, my distinction between density and crowding is quite compatible with Stokols', although I will not emphasize feelings of spatial limitation as strongly.

Stokols also distinguished between *nonsocial crowding,* whereby physical factors alone generate feelings of inadequate space (for example, a space capsule), and *social crowding,* whereby the feeling of crowding comes primarily from the presence of too many other people. In addition, Stokols noted the difference in molecular and molar crowding. That is, feelings of crowding can be associated with large-scale, urban populations (molar crowding). But there is also a microlevel of analysis concerned with individual, small-group, and interpersonal events. The final distinction concerns subjective states of crowding and stress. Stokols observed that all feelings of crowding involve stress—either psychological or physiological. Psychological stress includes feelings of cognitive inconsistency (discrepancy between a person's desire for space and the amount of space actually available) and emotional imbalance (infringement, alienation from others). Physiological stress includes rises in blood pressure or hormone secretions.

Somewhat similar ideas have been offered by others. Esser (1971a, 1971b, 1972, 1973b) described crowding as a mental state with a stress component, and he also emphasized the link between psychological and physiological processes. He hypothesized that feelings of crowding stem from a disharmony between the central nervous system and stimulus conditions. For example, feelings of crowding can derive from novel or strange situations, which involve a link with the neocortex (the most evolutionarily advanced brain area) through perpetual information processing and expectancy judgments. Or crowding can involve the biologically older part of the brain, the reticular system, when basic needs for territory are frustrated by population concentration and density.

Desor (1972) also emphasized social aspects of crowding and defined it as "... receiving excess stimulation from social sources." Other writers also pointed to the stimulus overload aspect of crowding (Rapoport, 1972; Wohlwill, 1974; Milgram, 1970). Implicit in this approach is the idea that crowding represents more interaction than what was desired. In my terms, crowding exists when various privacy-regulation mechanisms fail to produce a match between desired and achieved levels of privacy, with less privacy resulting than was desired.

Varieties of Density

Relatively little attention has been given, until recently, to the concept of density (Michelson, 1970; Zlutnick & Altman, 1972; Day & Day, 1973). The most general meaning of the term has been number of people per unit of space. In sociological studies conducted since the 1920s, a variety of density indicators have been related to social behavior. These have included number of people per city, number of people per census tract, number of people per dwelling unit, number of rooms per dwelling unit, number of buildings per neighborhood, and so on. Several recent studies, to be described in more detail later, indicate quite clearly that these various indicators of density have very different relationships with crowding (Galle, Gove, & McPherson, 1972; Marsella, Escudero, & Gordon, 1970; Booth & Welch, 1973). In these studies little relationship existed between various measures of social pathology such as crime or mental health and the more molar indicators of density such as number of people per acre or per community. The main findings indicated that micromeasures of density (for example, high numbers of people in homes) were associated with various kinds of social problems. Thus being in a densely populated neighborhood has different implications than being in a home with many people. Not that one is more important than the other, only that they are different and cannot be lumped together and called the same thing—"high density."

A differentiated approach to density analysis is summarized in Figure 9–3. It combines two levels of density—inside housing-unit density and outside housing-unit density (Zlutnick & Altman, 1972). Inside density refers to the number of people per unit of space within a residence, whereas outside density refers to the number of people per unit of space in a larger spatial unit, such as a street or census tract. From this two-factor framework a variety of living situations can be identified. Typical suburban living involves a small number of people inside residences and a small number of people outside residences in the immediate community. At the other extreme is the big-city ghetto, which often has a high concentration of people both inside and outside homes. Rural areas are often characterized by high densities within a home (primarily among poor people) but few people immediately outside the home (neighbors are remote from one another). The east-side luxury area of New York, on the other hand, has apartments with relatively small numbers of people inside but high concentrations of people in the outside neighborhood and city. While one can speculate about the effects of such density profiles, I can illustrate here only that density is a complex concept that may require more than a unidimensional approach. Therefore, to speak of all "low-density" situations as similar is an oversimplification. Similar suggestions about the complex nature of density have been offered by Choldin (1972) and Carey (1972).

"Inside" density
(within residential units;
molecular,
people per room measures)

		low	high
	low	I. Suburbia	II. Rural area
"Outside" density (neighborhood and community; molar, people per census tract measures)	high	III. Urban luxury area	IV. Urban ghetto

Figure 9–3. Some Density Profiles. From "Crowding and Human Behavior," by S. Zlutnick & I. Altman, in J. F. Wohlwill & D. H. Carson (Eds.), *Environment and the Social Sciences: Perspectives and Applications.* Copyright 1972 by the American Psychological Association. Reprinted by permission.

Several writers distinguish between *social density* and *spatial density* (Hutt & McGrew, 1967; Hutt & Vaizey, 1966; Loo, 1973a, 1973b; McGrew, 1970). Spatial density involves comparisons of same-size groups in different-size spaces—for example, a six-person group in a large versus a small room. Social density involves constant-size space but different numbers of people—for example six- versus twelve-person groups in the same-size room. Loo (1973a) speculated that different outcomes might occur in social- and spatial-density conditions, particularly if group composition shifts, as when a group in a constant space adds new members (social density). She contended that this may introduce problems of absorbing newcomers, not merely problems of space limitations per person. Thus if you are in a stable social group and decide to add several new members, there is apt to be a period of adjustment, not only to absorb the newcomers physically and spatially but to weave them into the social fabric of the group. Growing organizations in a fixed space who must add employees may face problems of absorption in both physical and social terms. And the rate at which population density increases will also make a difference. One person added to a group at a time is a quite different matter from a large influx of new members added all at once. On the other hand, a group whose space becomes limited but whose membership is constant may perceive the high density to be due to an external source, and members may not react to the issue as a group problem. Thus if a fixed-sized office group is squeezed into a smaller space (spatial density increases), they may see the problem as one imposed on them by management and respond differently than if the increased spatial density were caused by their own actions.

Day and Day (1973) raised other considerations in relation to population density. They called for attention to such factors as geographical features of population distribution. For example, a "dispersed agricultural" arrangement, in which farm land is spread equally over a geographical area, is different from a "coastal" arrangement, in which the same number of farms are packed along a coastline and the interior is not used. And these arrangements are in turn different from a "strip" arrangement, in which farms center around one area (perhaps along a river), and other parts of the land are unused. In these examples, the same average population concentration can be very differentially dispersed over a fixed area, which will obviously have different implications for the lives of the people. Day and Day also argue that one must have an understanding of transportation systems in such areas, residential-commercial mixes of functions, and a host of other variables.

In summary, we must pay attention not only to differences between crowding and density but also to the potentially rich meaning of each of these concepts considered separately and to the possibility that varieties of each may have different relationships to social processes.

A Model of Crowding

Figure 9-4 summarizes how the concepts of density and crowding fit my framework. Crowding exists when the privacy-regulation system does not work effectively, causing more social contact to occur than is desired. As stated previously, my framework hypothesizes that persons or groups use various self/other mechanisms to produce desired levels of interaction. These mechanisms include verbal, paraverbal, nonverbal, personal-space, and territorial behaviors. When achieved outcomes match what was desired, we speak of a successful privacy system. When these mechanisms provide *less* contact with others than desired, social isolation exists. When a system permits *more* interaction than was originally desired, we speak of crowding. Thus crowding occurs when interpersonal-boundary regulation fails.

The model in Figure 9-4 outlines a network of events associated with the management and breakdown of interpersonal boundaries. It includes *antecedent factors*, which contribute to desired and achieved levels of privacy, *internal subjective responses*, which help monitor the situation, *overt coping behaviors*, designed to implement a desired level of privacy, and *psychological and physical costs*, which result from operation of the privacy system.

The chain of events begins on the left side of the figure, with a person or a group having some desired level of privacy (situation definition) that includes expectations about what is good, acceptable, or appropriate (Goffman, 1959). This desired level of privacy derives from a combination of personal, interpersonal, and situational factors. *Personal* factors include

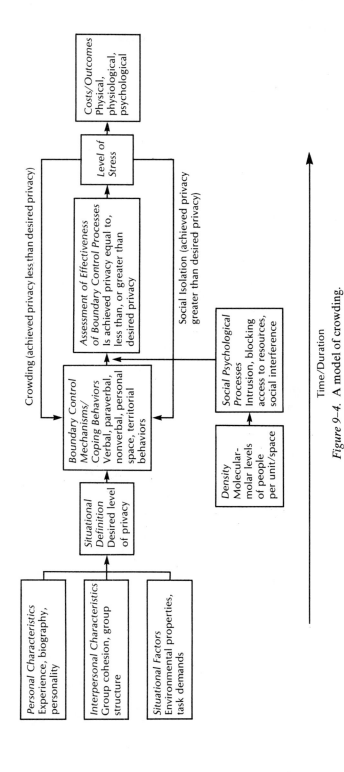

Figure 9–4. A model of crowding.

155

personality, past history, and momentary psychological and physiological states. Thus a withdrawn person, with a past history of little contact with others, who is in a depressed state or who is physiologically "down" from taking depressant drugs will probably not be interested in a high level of social interaction. In my terms, this person may desire impermeability of the self/other boundary, at least at that specific moment in time. *Interpersonal* factors include social factors such as liking or group cohesion. If a person likes someone with whom he or she is about to interact or feels a sense of identity with a group, receptivity to social contact will be high. *Situational* factors include physical features of the setting such as richness and articulation of the environment, furniture and decor, layout, and the task to be worked on. I hypothesize that these factors combine to yield a desired level of contact with others, labeled *situational definition.*

Various *boundary-regulation* or *coping mechanisms* of verbal, paraverbal, nonverbal, personal-space, and territorial behaviors are set in motion to achieve the desired goal (see middle of Figure 9-4). I have already described in previous chapters how people use different mixes of these mechanisms to regulate self/other boundaries. In the next step of the model, the person or group *assesses* how well the various mechanisms worked. Did what was desired by way of interaction actually occur? Did achieved privacy equal desired privacy? If so, the system worked, and everything is fine. If achieved privacy was *less* than desired privacy—that is, more interaction than desired —then *crowding* existed.

I would also hypothesize that a subjective, motivational state of *stress* accompanies over- or undershooting of the mark, along the lines postulated by Stokols (1972a, 1972b) and Esser (1970, 1972, 1973b). The stress state motivates the person or group to readjust boundary-control behaviors —that is, to take another try at realizing the original level of desired privacy (thus the feedback arrow in Figure 9-4 from *level of stress* back to *boundary-control mechanisms*). Such readjustments might involve the behaviors in greater numbers, more intense levels, or different combinations. For example, people may use more verbal and nonverbal behaviors to express displeasure at being intruded upon, may raise their voices or make dramatic body movements, may add door-slamming to the overall behavior profile, and so on. Thus the system is a *feedback system* that adjusts and readjusts itself as circumstances change. The process of assessment-stress-adjustment can cycle repeatedly until a desired outcome is achieved. Naturally, it is also possible that the ideal cannot be reached, so a person may eventually just accept an imbalance between desires and outcomes. Or it is possible that the desired level of privacy shifts along the way. Thus a previously undesirable outcome may eventually prove to be desirable, as when an originally unwanted person proves to be a pleasant companion after all.

The right-hand side of the figure indicates that some level of psychological and physiological "*costs*" results from efforts at establishing satisfactory self/other boundaries. These costs derive from the expenditure of physical, physiological, and psychological "energy." Sheer *physical* effort is often exerted to maintain a certain level of personal space from others, establish and protect a territory, or move away from or toward others. *Physiological* energy, such as adrenal functioning, cardiovascular activity, and overall bodily function is also a correlate of social exchange, as people strive to regulate their contact with others. *Psychological* energy is also often expended in monitoring the meaning of one's own and others' communications, in assessing whether contact is excessive, ideal, or insufficient, in being open and receptive to others, or in "tuning" others out. All these processes "cost" something to the organism; they require energy expenditure and may even lead to disease, higher death rates, physiological malfunctioning, or psychological stress and debilitation, such as mental-health disorders or psychosomatic illness. Or long-range social-system costs might involve crime and aggression, family disorganization, and other forms of social pathology.

As Figure 9-4 indicates, physical density is hypothesized to increase the possibility that *intrusion, social interference,* and *blocking of access to resources* may occur. Intrusion generally refers to a person or group's being approached too closely by others or to infringement on a territory without the owner's permission. Blocking access to resources occurs when someone is prevented from reaching a desired goal—for example, inability to purchase a hot dog at a football game because of the crowd. Rohe and Patterson (1974) studied this variable by allowing children to have access to many or to only a few toys in a playroom situation; sometimes there were enough toys for everyone, and sometimes there were too few toys. More aggression occurred when there were too few toys. Social interference is a catchall and occurs when an ongoing activity is interfered with by interruption. For example, Loo (1973a, 1973b) studied boys and girls in high- or low-density play situations and noted that there were more interruptions and other forms of social interference in high-density situations.

Thus physical density increases the probability that interpersonal contact will occur to an extent that may interfere with various boundary-control mechanisms. Furthermore, there is probably an interaction of density with interpersonal and situational factors; for instance, population concentration is apt to make a difference if one is with disliked others (interpersonal) in a barren space (situational) rather than with liked others in a comfortable and richly differentiated space. Thus two points are central. First, density has meaning only in relation to the interpersonal and psychological processes it sets in motion, not as a physical concept that has meaning in and of itself. Second, density can operate in interaction with other factors, especially those having some social importance.

Another factor to be added to the model is *duration* or *time*. Some of the anecdotal examples given at the beginning of the chapter suggested that short durations in dense conditions (for example, many people in an elevator) intuitively reflect a different degree of crowding than a long-term stay in the same situation (trapped in an elevator for a long time or raised in a small home with many people for several years). One would probably predict that stress, coping behaviors, and costs would be more extensive in long- versus short-term conditions.

Related Properties of the Model

There are a few other implicit features of the model. Beyond the description of crowding as a specific type of breakdown in privacy regulation, I would like to add the idea that crowding can exist even if there is successful maintenance of privacy. This situation occurs when extreme efforts are made to regulate interaction, the efforts are successful, but psychological, physiological, or physical costs are quite high. Other writers also (for example, Dubos, 1965, 1968; Cassel, 1971) noted that humans are quite adaptable to even the most severe conditions but may pay an extreme price for successful adaptation; that is, even though people may cope successfully with intrusion, goal blocking, and social interference, they may do so at some psychological or physical expense. My intent is, therefore, to broaden the use of the term crowding to include both successful management of interpersonal boundaries and successful coping, achieved at considerable expense.

It is important to note that this model views crowding as a *network*. Crowding is not density alone, stress alone, costs alone, or coping behaviors alone. It is a network of these and other factors that are associated with the failure of an interpersonal-boundary system or with an expensively maintained system..Put more specifically, a condition of *extreme* crowding exists when the following factors come together simultaneously, as a pattern:

1. A certain set of precipating conditions.
    a. *Situational factors,* which include high density of people per unit of space, for long periods of time, and in physical environments where resources are limited and where few behavioral options are provided.[1]
    b. *Personal factors,* such as inexperience and/or inability to deal with others in dense situations and low expectations and desire to interact with others, based on personal history, mood, and the like.

---

[1]A word is necessary concerning antecedent factors. First, the idea of density should be elaborated to include some of the distinctions described earlier—for example, high inside and outside density and high social and spatial density. Second, an important facet of situational factors concerns the richness of environmental settings. Two homes with equivalent space and density can differ enormously in how space is laid out, the interior decor, and the quality of facilities in general. A bare environment or one poor in resources might be more susceptible to loss of interpersonal-boundary control. For example, Desor (1972) demonstrated how walls and partitions, door locations, and other architectural features altered feelings of crowding, with more-differentiated space producing a feeling of less crowding.

   c. *Interpersonal conditions,* such as social interference, inability to obtain resources, and intrusion.
2. A set of *organismic, psychological factors,* such as feelings of stress, disruption, and malaise.
3. *Coping responses,* including verbal, paraverbal, nonverbal, and environmentally oriented behaviors that are ineffective in reducing stress or in achieving desired levels of interaction over lengthy periods of time.
4. Extreme *costs* in terms of physical, physiological, and psychological outcomes.

A key theme of my framework is that extreme crowding exists when all these factors occur in combination—that is, when a person is in a socially dense situation, in an impoverished and undifferentiated environment for long periods of time, does not desire interaction, and has feelings of stress associated with a variety of coping behaviors that do not work or are very costly. Since all these factors can occur in different amounts, the effects of crowding are a matter of degree.

This theme can be extended to say that crowding can exist even if certain variables, including density, are absent. For example, if two people are in a large spatial area but one intrudes on the other, does not allow the other person to "get away," creates stress, and prevents all coping responses from succeeding, high costs for the victim of intrusion will still be felt. Or a person raised in a heavily populated urban ghetto may not feel crowded on a regular basis yet may exhibit coping behaviors and incur costs of various types, from which one can infer that the person developed various means over time to achieve desired levels of social contact. Thus I believe that the concept of crowding should not necessarily be limited to situations involving high spatial density.[2]

Relationship of the Model to Other Approaches

My model draws on the thinking of many others who emphasize different parts of the chain of events. For example, my approach is compatible with Stokols' (1972a, 1972b) equilibrium model, described earlier, which also speaks of a network of factors associated with crowding—antecedent vari-

---

[2]Colleagues who commented on this model noted that I may have placed undue emphasis on interpersonal aspects of crowding, perhaps to the detriment of less personally directed events. Stokols (1975) has written recently of a distinction between "neutral crowding" and "personal crowding." Neutral crowding occurs when a person feels the stress of too little space but recognizes that it does not come directly from the intentional actions of another person; this crowding is recognized to be beyond the control of others. Personal crowding occurs when the closeness of others or their violation of one's boundaries are viewed as intentional and directed at that self. Thus, while both involve a boundary violation, the motives and direction of the violation are quite different.

ables, stress responses, and coping behaviors. In addition, I have relied on theoretical statements that portray crowding as a result of stimulus overload or too much interaction. For example, Wohlwill (1974) proposed a general equilibrium model in which people are hypothesized to function best within a limited range of stimulation. When there is deviation in either direction from the optimum, psychological and physiological stress may occur, which in turn trips off coping behaviors designed to achieve an acceptable level of stimulation. Crowding is one type of overload situation. Desor (1972) also focused on the overload idea and defined crowding as the receipt of excessive stimulation from social sources (which fits with my idea of crowding as involving less privacy than desired). Similarly, Simmel (1950a), Wirth (1938), and Milgram (1970) described the city dweller as someone who because of his or her exposure to unusual amounts of sensory stimulation gradually developed coping mechanisms of detachment, aloofness, and disregard of others as a way of achieving acceptable levels of stimulation.

There are also those researchers who focus on internal, subjective reactions associated with crowding. The earliest formulations concerning crowding emphasized psychological stress, mental strain, negativism, irritability, and psychological weariness (Plant, 1930, 1951). Stokols (1972a, 1972b) made stress in relation to feelings of space restriction central to his framework, and others also emphasized stress reactions to density (Freedman, Klevansky, & Ehrlich, 1971; Freedman, Levy, Buchanan, & Price, 1972; Baxter & Deanovich, 1970). And Esser (1971a, 1971b, 1972, 1973b) postulated links between psychological stress and nervous-system functioning.

Another compatible approach takes an ecological perspective (Wicker, 1968, 1969a, 1969b; Wicker & Mehler, 1971; Wicker, McGrath, & Armstrong, 1973). It deals with behavior settings, which are clusters of people, environments, and goals. Earlier work in this tradition (Barker & Gump, 1964) demonstrated that a greater proportion of people in small high schools became involved in activities than did those in large schools. Wicker and Mehler (1971) and Wicker (1968, 1969a, 1969b) obtained similar results in churches and schools. New members of small churches were more rapidly drawn into activities than were new members of larger churches, and members of small churches were more active on committees, donated more money, and were in leadership positions more often than those in larger churches.

Wicker, McGrath, and Armstrong (1973) offered a theoretical analysis of settings that included (1) *maintenance minimum,* or the minimum number of people necessary to maintain a setting or to do a job, (2) *capacity,* or the maximum number of persons a setting could accommodate, and (3) *applicants,* or the total number of persons who participate in a setting. Under-manning or undercrowding exists when applicants are fewer than the maintenance minimum; in other words, too few people are available to do a job. Adequate manning exists when the number of persons the setting can accommodate is close to what the setting needs, and there aren't more applicants than the setting can handle; that is, there are just enough people to do the job (analogous to desired interaction equaling achieved interaction). Overmanning, which Wicker believes to be related to crowding, occurs when the capacity is exceeded by applicants—there are more people than the setting can handle. The consequences of overmanning, in the form of adjustive coping behaviors, include pressure to reduce applicants, raise the standards for those admitted, or increase the setting capacity. These processes are analogous to establishing firmer boundaries around the person or group, and even changing system goals.

Historical Stages of Research on Crowding

Research on crowding began about five decades ago, as population in the Western world increased, as cities and technology grew, and as the social and behavioral sciences gained stature and turned toward the analysis of various social problems. Historically, two streams of research can be distinguished—one in sociology and the other in psychology. Within each tradition, there are some early-phase studies and some later-phase studies, distinguished by the sophistication of their methodological strategies.

Early Correlational-Sociological Studies

The earliest work on crowding was done by sociologists who, beginning in the 1920s, tried to identify social outcomes of population density and indicators of social pathology, such as mental health and disease, crime, and various forms of social disorganization. For example, Schmid (1969, 1970) found high population densities and high crime rates in ghettos and central-city areas of Minneapolis and Seattle and a progressive decrease in the less populated surrounding suburbs. In Honolulu, Schmitt (1957) found a high correlation between population density, juvenile delinquency, and adult crime. Many other studies confirmed this type of relationship in other cities (Bordua, 1958; Lander, 1954; Lottier, 1938; Shaw & McKay, 1942; Sorokin & Zimmerman, 1929; Watts, 1931; and White, 1931).

Correlational data for mental illness and density yielded similar results. Faris and Dunham (1965) reported a decreasing incidence of mental illness from city centers outward to suburbs. Lantz (1953) found a higher incidence of mental illness in military officers from densely populated areas. Supporting data along these lines have been found by Queen (1948), Schroeder (1942), Malzberg (1940), and Landis and Page (1938). Similar data on suicide were obtained by Cavan (1928), Schmid (1933, 1955), and Sainsbury (1956). Citation of additional studies could go on at length, but further examples can be obtained in a review by Michelson (1970).

Several characteristics of these earlier studies are worth noting. First, this research is correlational in methodological strategy. That is, studies examined statistical covariations between population density and social-pathology indicators, based on records and archives. While most of these investigations found moderate associations between density and social pathology, it cannot be concluded that density *caused* social disorganization. In many of these studies alternative explanations could have accounted for the correlations. For example, pure density is not the only variable that distinguishes the center of a city from its suburbs. Factors such as the inhabitants' physical well-being, economic status, health facilities, and education are only a few variables that often differ in central-city and suburban areas, and these factors might be related to social pathology. Thus the fact that two variables correlate in no way guarantees causation. Therefore, while these studies are suggestive, they do not justify hard conclusions about the effect of density on various social outcomes.

A second feature of early studies is that density was treated in a relatively undifferentiated fashion. Typical measures of density included people per acre, people per census tract, people per nation, and structures per acre or per census tract—all of which are relatively large geographical units. Only occasionally were measures based on people or families per dwelling unit or other small social units. And various measures of density were not compared systematically. Reading this literature gives the impression that researchers had a nontheoretical, pragmatic approach to density and crowding and explored such measures because they were available, quantitative, and seemingly rigorous.

A third feature of this early phase of research was its emphasis on social-system *outcomes* rather than on social *processes*. Crime rates, mental-health disorders, death, and disease are, in a sense, outcomes or final end products of a long history of social experience. Early studies did not examine what happened between people in high- and low-density situations on a day-to-day basis. They could only vaguely infer about ongoing social interaction as people coped with high and low density. Furthermore, their approach to crowding was to treat it as a broad social-system problem rather than as an individual or microinterpersonal phenomenon. Their interest seemed to be on how the whole society was affected by crowding, with only secondary concern for how individuals and families coped with and responded to population concentrations.

Later Correlational-Sociological Studies

Beginning in the 1960s sociological studies shifted their methodological strategy in several ways. A classic study was conducted by Galle, Gove, and McPherson (1972) in Chicago. They viewed population density in a more differentiated fashion than previously and studied how closely the density measure came to actual interpersonal processes. Their framework included (1) number of persons per room in a dwelling unit (the smallest and most directly interpersonal level of density), (2) number of rooms per housing unit, (3) number of housing units per structure (for example, apartments per apartment house), and (4) number of residential structures per acre (the least directly interpersonal measure). Thus they made different types of density indicators explicit, with the most microlevel one being relatively "close" to interpersonal relations. A second feature of their approach concerned the problem in prior research of the obscuring effects of ethnic background, socioeconomic status, and other variables on the relationship between density and social pathology. In this study, such factors were statistically controlled. Their results illustrate the value of a differentiated approach to density. The highest correlations occurred between *people per room* and social pathology indicators of mortality, fertility, public assistance, and juvenile delinquency. Thus the density measures that reflected social interaction most closely (people in a room) were the important ones. Galle and associates interpreted their results in terms of ongoing social processes that might have occurred in densely populated homes. For example, ill persons may not have obtained the quiet privacy they needed to recover, yielding higher mortality rates; higher fertility may have resulted, in part, from difficulties in using birth-control techniques in dense homes; and children may have received less attention in larger families and may have had to rely more on peers for guidance, thereby contributing to juvenile delinquency. While these were only post hoc interpretations, they reflect a focus on social processes that may have mediated density-pathology relationships. Thus this study attempted to get closer to ongoing social interaction rather than treat population concentration as a vague producer of ultimate outcomes.

Other recent studies also moved in these directions, giving more attention to different levels of analysis of population concentration. For example, Marsella, Escudero, and Gordon (1970) examined the impact of persons per dwelling unit in Manila on psychosomatic symptomatology; Mitchell (1971) analyzed the relationship between number of families per dwelling unit and marital satisfaction in Hong Kong; and Booth and Welch (1973) examined the relationship between density, health, and aggression in 65 countries.

In summary, recent sociological studies have taken a more sophisticated approach and emphasized (1) the differentiated analysis of density, with more attention given to the interpersonal, microlevel of density, (2) the interpersonal social processes that occur in high-density conditions rather than the broad social outcomes alone, and (3) the control of underlying variables that might account for density-pathology relationships.

Early Experimental-Psychological Studies

A second stream of research on crowding is different in several ways from the sociological approach. First, it is experimental and laboratory oriented, involving subjects who are often strangers and who enter social groups solely for the purpose of the study. Second, group members interact for relatively short periods of time compared with persons in sociological studies. Third, subjects in many experimental studies work on tasks developed for the specific setting, rather than those that are a part of the ongoing and natural aspects of their everyday lives. Fourth, this research style emphasizes manipulation and control of variables. An attempt is made to vary certain things, such as density, and to control other variables, such as sex, age, and testing conditions in order to permit reasonably strong inferences about cause-effect relationships.

Laboratory-oriented research on crowding began only in the last decade, with probably about two dozen studies reported at the time of this writing. Thus psychologists came late to the problem of crowding. There are two good examples of early experimental studies. Griffitt and Veitch (1971) gave subjects information about a stranger who presumably had attitudes similar to or different from their own. They were then placed in small or large groups. The room was an environmental chamber in which half the groups were in a cool, pleasant setting and the other half functioned in a hot, uncomfortable environment. The results indicated that people liked the hypothetical stranger more in the uncrowded and cooler environment, based on responses to a rating scale. Freedman and his associates (1971) examined the impact of room size and group size on individual performance on a variety of intellectual tasks, such as word formation, object use, memory, and concentration, and on a group-discussion task. There were no differences in performance as a function of density.

These and similar studies reflect early experimental approaches to the issue of crowding, comparable to the early phase of correlational research. In these studies, the concept of density was treated in a relatively undifferentiated fashion. Although the Freedman investigation varied both spatial and social density, many early studies did not. Moreover, many early experimental studies emphasized end products or outcomes, such as performance success, rather than social processes. For example, in the Freedman study, there was no analysis of how people attacked problems or how they gradually came to develop feelings about others. Rather, such studies examined only final performance or final liking of others.

Another feature of early experimental studies is the absence of social interaction among people. Both the Freedman and associates (1971) and the Griffitt and Veitch (1971) studies emphasized the effects of density on people who worked alone, not as members of an interacting group. If more recent sociological studies say anything, it is that we should try to understand interpersonal processes, not just individual effects of density.

Later Experimental-Psychological Studies

There are signs that a more advanced stage of research in the psychological, experimental tradition is beginning to emerge. For example, Hutt and Vaizey (1966) examined the impact of different group sizes on children's aggressive behavior in a playroom. The important element of this study was its focus on *ongoing social process* rather than on only the ultimate outcomes. This feature has become more prevalent in other research also. For example, Freedman, Levy, Buchanan, and Price (1972) examined the impact of density on performance of tasks involving cooperation or competition between people and on degree of social punitiveness in a mock-jury situation; Loo (1973b) studied aggression and dominance in children's groups; Stokols, Rall, Pinner, and Schopler (1973) tapped social behaviors of laughing, hostility, and so on in various density arrangements.

We can also now begin to see a richer conception of density. For example, a number of studies have varied *both* room and group size to get at spatial- and social-density effects (Freedman et al., 1971; Hutt & McGrew, 1967; McGrew, 1970). And there now are more attempts to study the richness, differentiation, and articulation of environment. For example, Desor (1972) examined the effects of wall partitions, room shapes, door placements, and other factors on willingness of subjects to place simulated figures in a room mock-up. Rohe and Patterson (1974) varied the richness of resources (number and variety of toys available to children) in different-size groups and studied the effect on aggressive behavior.

A recent program of research by Valins and Baum (1973) and Baum and Valins (1973) is important because it studied the longer-term implications of living in crowded environments on later social behavior. Dormitory residents who lived in a crowded corridor-room arrangement were compared with those in uncrowded suites. Residents in each living arrangement served as subjects and were directed to a waiting room where a confederate was seated. The results showed that crowded residents sat farther away from a confederate and spent less time looking at him or talking with him than did uncrowded residents, suggesting that dense living was associated with the mutual avoidance of social interaction—a kind of social-process cost. This type of study is important because it capitalizes on real-life crowding, it tracks effects on social process, and it works in a seminaturalistic situation.

An important issue concerns the relative strengths of correlational and experimental studies. Correlational studies have several advantages. They deal with factors such as mental health, mortality, and crime that involve the everyday lives of people. In addition, they reflect years of exposure to density, not minutes or hours. And the social groups are often real ones that have a long history and whose members are deeply involved with one another as families or neighbors. Such relationships are not easily produced in the laboratory.

On the other hand, experimental studies have several advantages not easily found elsewhere. The systematic manipulation and control of variables allows clearer inferences about cause-effect relationships involving density and behavior. By manipulating density directly and controlling other factors, it is easier to pinpoint ways in which behavioral changes are related to density. In correlational studies it is difficult to identify causal ties, and the possible contaminating role of unmeasured or unknown variables is greater. Another advantage of laboratory studies is that they allow *direct* examination of social processes. Because groups can be observed on the scene, measurement of aggression and other social behaviors is possible. This is not easily done in correlational studies. While these strategic approaches are not always categorically distinct, the strengths of the experimental laboratory study are generally the weaknesses of the correlational study, and vice versa. Elements of each strategy seem necessary to develop a full understanding of crowding, to generate and test out a range of hypotheses, to provide a kind of triangulation from different perspectives on the same issue, and to complement one another where questions cannot easily be dealt with in one setting or the other.

This chapter examined some conceptual and methodological issues on the topic of crowding. Distinctions were drawn between the terms "crowding" and "density," and a plea was made for more sophisticated analysis of each concept. Crowding was defined in terms of a network of antecedent, organismic, and behavioral variables and was described as a general failure of privacy-regulation mechanisms; more social interaction occurred than was desired. Density was conceptualized as a physicalistic concept (number of people per unit of space). I called for a more differentiated analysis of that concept, at several levels of molecularity-molarity, from people per unit of space in homes and dwelling units to indicators of population concentration at community, city, and national levels.

The chapter also presented a conceptual model of crowding that emphasized (1) how various privacy-regulation mechanisms come into play as a function of desired degrees of interaction, (2) assessment processes designed to track the effectiveness of these mechanisms, (3) subjective stress responses that occur when the self/other boundary system functions poorly, (4) adjustive, coping behaviors designed to achieve an acceptable level of interaction, and (5) long-term physical, physiological, and psychological costs that occur as a result of attempts to reduce crowding.

Research on crowding/density was also analyzed in terms of its sociological/correlational or psychological/experimental strategy. Early correlational research examined relationships between gross measures of population density and social pathology such as crime, juvenile delinquency, and mental and physical health. However, early conceptions of density were relatively undifferentiated, with little attention given to various levels of density, confounding variables, or ongoing social processes. Later studies have begun to attend to such factors. Experimental laboratory studies permit more direct observation of social processes and causal effects of density. However, early studies using this strategy did not examine different facets of density and ignored ongoing social processes. Later studies have moved in productive directions regarding these factors.

The next chapter examines research knowledge on crowding in terms of my conceptual model.

The Effects of Crowding and Density

This chapter reviews empirical research on crowding and density in terms of the theoretical framework outlined in the preceding chapter. We will first examine the relationship between population concentration and feelings of stress, anxiety, and other psychological reactions. Then, behavioral or coping responses to density will be discussed. These include culturally based behaviors, withdrawal and aggressive responses, and nonverbal compensatory behaviors. Finally, we will consider outcomes of density and crowding in the form of social pathologies such as physical and mental disorders, juvenile delinquency, crime, and harmful long-term effects on task performance.

A Brief Note on Studies of Crowding in Animals

The emphasis in this book is on the behavior of humans in relation to the physical environment. However, there is a body of knowledge on the behavior of animals in their environments, especially in regard to density and crowding. While we will not thoroughly review this area, there are some lines of thinking that may directly relate to crowding in humans.

The general thrust of much of this work is that animals show a variety of adverse reactions to extreme population concentration. Such reactions sometimes involve physiological malfunctioning of kidneys and glands, such as the adrenal glands; they sometimes involve excessive mortality rates, especially for female and young members of a species; reactions to density sometimes include breakdowns in social structures and behaviors, such as poor child rearing, aggression, and malfunctioning courtship and reproductive behaviors. Those who wish to delve further into this area should consult reviews by Davis (1971), Dubos (1965), Eibl-Eibesfeldt (1970), and Wynne-Edwards (1972).

A few dramatic studies illustrate typical findings in this area. For example, it is reasonably well established that many animal populations seem to rise and fall in a cyclical fashion, perhaps as a population-control mechanism. As one illustration, Dubos (1965) and others described the "march to the sea" of the Norwegian lemming, a small animal indigenous to Scandinavian mountain regions. Every three or four years the lemmings migrate en masse to the sea, and many drown, almost as if they are deliberately committing suicide. Although according to Scandinavian mythology they are seeking their ancestral home on the lost Atlantic continent, it appears that the migration is probably in response to overcrowding, since lemmings are prolific reproducers. Dubos noted that their movement is not an orderly march but a random frantic activity and that they exhibit metabolic malfunctions involving the adrenals and brain, which probably stem from the stress of extreme population concentration.

Another instance of natural population cycles is an isolated herd of deer that live on a small island in the Chesapeake Bay, off the Maryland coast (Christian, Flyger, & Davis, 1960). Many years ago a few deer were placed on the island and left to breed freely. The herd had grown to about 300 by the mid-1950s, at which time Christian and his associates began their study. Over the period of a few years there was a mass die-off, with the population eventually stabilizing at about 80. All along, Christian and his associates did histological examinations of various glands and organs of some of the dead animals—thymus, spleen, kidneys, heart, and adrenals. From these data it was concluded that infection, starvation, or illness was not the primary cause of death. Rather, the population crash seemed to be attributable to metabolic activity, particularly overactive adrenal functioning, which probably resulted from the stresses of crowding and confinement.

Another line of research on animal reactions to crowding is more experimentally oriented; groups of animals are studied in laboratory settings under different conditions of population concentration. The advantage of doing such work is that animals can be raised from birth in controlled environments, and long-term effects of population concentration can be readily studied. The results of many of these investigations are that severe disruptions occur in the physical well-being of animals and in their patterns of social behavior such as child rearing, mating, and social organization.

One of the most dramatic programs of research on this topic has been conducted by John Calhoun, who has studied crowding in rats and mice for two decades. In one of his most well-known studies (Calhoun, 1962a, 1962b), rats were placed in a crowded situation involving four pens arranged in a row, connected by openings. In a concentrated population of rats, it happened that dominant males took over the end pens, had a harem of females and young under their control, and lived in a rather spacious situation (about 30 animals altogether). The remaining rats (about 50 animals) were forced to live, eat, reproduce, and rear their young in the crowded center pens. Over time it became clear that those in the densely populated center pens—Calhoun called it a "behavioral sink"—began to show negative effects. For example, courting behavior deteriorated. Some male rats would attack females in groups, others would mount males and females indiscriminately, and others would not mate at all. Nest building, usually an elaborate process whereby mothers care for their young, was incomplete or poorly done, as was general care of the young. Mortality rates of females and young, as well as the rate of miscarriage, were quite high in the behavioral sink. Furthermore, Calhoun identified a number of physiological disorders in females that lived in the crowded areas, such as tumors of the sex glands and mammary glands and abnormal kidneys, livers, and adrenal glands. Calhoun has continued this and related work (a recent summary appears in Calhoun, 1971), and his studies, along with those of others, generally confirm the idea that excessive population concentration is associated with problems of social behavior and physiological malfunctioning in animals. The question for us is the extent to which similar problems occur in humans. As we have already indicated in the preceding chapter and in our discussion of territorial behavior, generalizing from animals to humans is difficult. Furthermore, the concept of crowding is so complex in humans that simplistic answers to causes and effects are often inappropriate. Nevertheless, these animal studies serve as a useful backdrop for our understanding of crowding in humans.

Psychological and Social Feeling States

Psychological Feelings Associated with Crowding/Density

This section examines people's feelings and attitudes about density or population concentration—ranging from mild feelings of being crowded to stronger stress and anxiety reactions.

Recent laboratory studies yield mixed results; some report feelings of crowding, discomfort, stress, and anxiety under conditions of high density, and other studies find no such reactions. For example, in a study described earlier, subjects were exposed to low-density situations (groups of three to five people with 13 square feet per person) or high-density situations (12-to-16-person groups with 4 square feet per person) under either cool or hot conditions (Griffitt & Veitch, 1971). Those in denser conditions reported more feelings of discomfort and more negative judgments of the situation. In another study, spatial density was varied for eight-person groups. In a high-density condition the groups worked in a 5-by-8-foot room, and in a low-density condition they worked in a 9-by-13-foot room (Stokols, Rall, Pinner, & Schopler, 1973). Self-reports of feeling crowded, confined, and restricted were greater in the small room. However, there were no strong effects of room size on anxiety or on more extreme feelings of stress. In one other supportive study, Baxter and Deanovich (1970) exposed subjects to doll figures that were placed in simulated crowded or uncrowded situations and that were portrayed as being in threatening or nonthreatening conditions. Moreover, subjects sat either very close to or at a distance from confederates. Anxiety attributed by the subjects to the dolls was greater when both dolls and subjects were crowded.

But a number of other studies did not show very strong personal reactions to crowding. For example, Freedman, Levy, Buchanan, and Price (1972) placed subjects in four-person groups in either a large room (8.5 feet square with 18 square feet per person) or a small room (5 feet square with 6 square feet per person), where they worked on tasks requiring cooperation and coordination. A questionnaire that measured enjoyment of the situation yielded no stress effects of density. In a second experiment, 6-to-7-person groups made judgments about a series of hypothetical court cases in either a dense room (100 square feet) or an uncrowded room (300 square feet) over a several-hour period. Once again, questionnaires showed hardly any stress effects. There was some indication, however, that females felt the crowded setting to be more pleasant than the uncrowded one, but there were no differences for males. Another recent study also demonstrated relatively weak effects of population density (Sundstrom, 1973). Three pairs of males worked on a self-disclosure task, in either a large room allowing 39 square feet per person or a small room permitting 6 square feet per person. The high-density condition was associated with feelings of crowding but not with other forms of stress. Finally, a study by Ross, Layton, Erickson, and Schopler (1973) yielded mixed results. Eight-person groups worked on a discussion task in a crowded room (6 by 8 feet with 5.8 square feet per person) or in an uncrowded room (12 by 13 feet with 16.8 square feet per person). Although there were greater feelings of crowding in the small room, there were only weak indications of personal upset, nervousness, or physical discomfort.

In summary, traditional laboratory studies have shown relatively weak or mixed stress reactions to high density. Several factors may have contributed to these results. For example, none of the situations ever lasted beyond a few hours, and subjects knew they were in time-limited experiments. In addition, participants typically were strangers and did not expect future contacts with one another, perhaps making the situation personally unimportant. There were also differences across studies in room size, area per person, and in group size. A final factor that may have contributed to weak results concerns the point at which stress measurements were taken. In most cases, reactions were assessed at the completion of the experiment. If my model is correct, stress reactions to density should precipitate coping responses designed to alleviate stress. Perhaps in the relatively mild conditions of these experiments, subjects *did* feel some slight initial stress but quickly used coping responses that reduced anxiety. Thus if measurements had been taken throughout these experiments, rather than only at the end, the *process* of adaptation to stress might have been observed.

Three recent studies bear on some of the issues raised above. Smith and Haythorn (1972) worked with two- and three-man U.S. Navy teams that were socially isolated for 21 days under either crowded or uncrowded living conditions (70 cubic feet per person versus 200 cubic feet per person).[1] Questionnaires measuring anxiety were administered over the 21-day period. Generally, most stress occurred in three-man crowded groups, and least stress occurred in three-man uncrowded groups, suggesting an interaction of group size and density. However, some measures of anxiety showed no effects. This is a particularly important study because it involved a 21-day period of isolation and crowding but still yielded only relatively weak effects of density—effects primarily in interaction with other variables.

An experiment by Sundstrom (1973), cited briefly in the preceding chapter, points to a potentially fruitful direction of laboratory research on crowding. He manipulated density, intrusion, and goal-blocking. Within each of three pairs, one member was a confederate. To vary density, pairs were placed in either a large room with great distances between pairs or a small room where pairs were side by side. The task was for pair members to take turns and disclose personal information about themselves. To vary intrusion, confederates either sat very near to the subject, leaning forward, touching his leg with theirs, and coming inappropriately close, or sat back and away. Goal-blocking was varied by having the confederate either ignore the subject when he was disclosing information (looking away, acting bored, or asking totally irrelevant questions) or be attentive and receptive.

A variety of questionnaire measures were taken, such as subjective feelings of mood (comfort, irritability, calmness, tension, and frustration), liking for the confederate, and willingness to disclose personal information. Measures were obtained on three occasions over the course of an hour. In addition, Sundstrom sampled nonverbal behaviors of self-manipulation

---

[1]Leadership structure was also varied. Some groups had a senior person, and others had a peer as leader. Moreover, group composition was manipulated according to compatibility on measures of achievement, dominance, and the like.

(hand rubbing, touching the face with the hands), postural changes (fidgeting, shifting of the body), object manipulation (tapping a pencil), head nodding, gesticulation with the hands, and looking at the confederate.

In general, there were hardly any density effects on stress, except for reports of feeling crowded. Furthermore, density did not interact very much with intrusion or goal-blocking to affect mood reactions. However, there were intrusion effects, to which subjects adapted over time. That is, they were less happy and less comfortable when the confederate came close early in the situation, but not later on, which suggests some adaptation. Nonverbal data suggested that subjects coped with intrusion by looking less at the confederate, which may have been successful in reducing stress. On the other hand, experiencing goal-blocking (when the confederate ignored them) generated stress reactions that remained the same or increased over time. Their response to being ignored was withdrawal, evidenced by lower self-disclosure and less head nodding and gesturing with the hands. But these reactions may not have adequately dealt with the confederate's ignoring of the subject, since the experimental task was to disclose; that is, one could not escape or adapt very well to being ignored by the other person when one was obliged to continue disclosing his self.

A second group of studies on the effects of dormitory crowding provides good support for a "stress-coping" sequence (Valins & Baum, 1973; Baum & Valins, 1973). Subjects in dense versus nondense dormitory living arrangements reported feeling crowded and having too much undesired contact with others. Crowded students also sat at greater distances from others in a waiting-room situation, suggesting that they had evolved a coping style that included avoiding contact with others. These studies emphasize the need to examine crowding in a longitudinal sense, to examine delayed and time-linked reactions to density.

In summary, laboratory-oriented studies yield inconsistent evidence of stress in reaction to density. Whether the results derive from the methodological issues raised earlier or from successful coping that reduces stress is a question for future research.

On the other hand, the older stream of sociological research is more affirmative in regard to psychological effects of density (although potentially confounding factors such as socioeconomic status often crowd the meaning of density-pathology correlations, as discussed earlier). The interested reader should see reviews of this work by Freedman (1972), Carson (1969), Schorr (1963), and Zlutnick and Altman (1972). These studies typically found moderate feelings of anxiety, stress and emotional symptomatology in densely populated environments. A psychiatrist, Plant (1930, 1951), speculated that crowded living interferes with children's mental health by dampening their sense of individuality and heightening mental strain, sexual maladjustment, negativism, irritability, and fatigue. Along with such armchair speculation, a number of empirical studies tracked the relationship betwen density and mental health. As an example of studies that have found stress effects, Marsella, Escudero, and Gordon (1970) investigated emotional symptomatology and psychological disorders in Filipino families and found more anxiety, nervousness, potentially eruptive violence, fear, and physical symptoms of stress among those in more crowded living spaces. However, there is some evidence that long-term crowding leads to only mild stress reactions. For example, Mitchell (1971) surveyed 4000 families in Hong Kong. Although he found complaints about lack of space and privacy and superficial feelings of strain in high-density situations, there were few indications of *severe* emotional symptomatology.

If the findings of experimental and correlational studies are pieced together, the results are not especially overwhelming. There is some evidence for the impact of density on stress, but in hardly any instance do the effects seem to be serious. However, several issues must be considered in reaching such a conclusion. A number of methodological factors described earlier are not common from study to study—for example, type and length of density and underlying variables. Furthermore, laboratory conditions may not be sufficiently prolonged or intense to generate crowding effects. Another possible issue derives from the framework of crowding presented. It was hypothesized that, if density and associated variables generate psychological stress, then people will exhibit coping behaviors to alleviate that stress. If such coping responses are successful, measurements might show no stress effects—not because stress didn't occur, but because it might have been measured at the wrong time or because it might have been dealt with successfully. Thus future research should (1) use repeated measures of stress and other psychological states and (2) link coping behaviors with psychological feeling states. In summary, the most legitimate conclusion is that population concentration has not yet been demonstrated to produce extreme psychological stress reactions.

Social Feelings Associated with Crowding/Density

Let's consider reactions toward others, especially liking and attraction, under various density conditions. Once again, research indicates rather mild negative social reactions under conditions of crowding.

Correlational sociological studies do not usually measure feelings toward others, although Mitchell's study (1971) of families in Hong Kong noted some minor marital unhappiness, feelings of lack of control over children, absence of privacy, and negative attitudes about entertaining neighbors or friends in homes in high-density situations. And Schorr (1963) referred to several studies that indicated lower family morale and greater interpersonal irritations in densely populated situations. These and similar correlational results do not indicate overpowering interpersonal hostility; they indicate only mild annoyances and frictions in crowded living situations.

Laboratory studies also yield mixed findings. For example, Griffitt and Veitch (1971), in a study described earlier, found that people in dense laboratory situations rated a hypothetical other person less favorably than did those in less crowded conditions. And Valins and Baum (1973) and Baum and Valins (1973) reported that dormitory residents in crowded living arrangements tended to feel more negative about having too much contact with others than did residents in less crowded conditions. Freedman and his associates (1972) obtained partly confirming and partly disconfirming results. Subjects in crowded situations felt their partners to be less cooperative, and they themselves acted more competitively in crowded situations (although they reported liking their partner *more* in a dense situation). In a setting where subjects were part of a mock jury analyzing criminal cases, the results were surprising; females gave *less* punitive jail sentences and were generally *more* positive to a hypothetical defendant in the crowded situation. They also had more positive feelings toward the group in crowded arrangements. Males reacted in an opposite fashion, although the data were not statistically reliable. Stokols and his associates (1973) also found that males in crowded environments felt more competitive and aggressive toward others (but no more hostile), with somewhat opposite results for females. Ross and his colleagues (1973) used a group-discussion task in crowded and uncrowded situations. Males rated themselves as less likable in the crowded rooms, but females rated others more positively in crowding—again a mixed set of results. In a long-term, 21-day social-isolation study, Smith and Haythorn (1972) reported little evidence of group members having hostility toward one another. In fact, they reported more hostile feelings in *less* crowded groups. And Sundstrom (1973), in a study described earlier, reported no differences in liking for others in dense versus uncrowded settings.

In summary, the results are mixed, although there is some inkling of feelings of anger, hostility, and lack of attraction toward others in densely populated environments. But, the results are not wholly in one direction; they often are opposite to expectations, and we are left with a conclusion of "crowding effects not clearly demonstrated." Once again, these ambiguous results may derive from the methodological issues raised earlier, or they may reflect successful coping processes whereby people had figured out ways to handle the situation by the time measurements were made.

Overt Coping Behaviors in Reaction to Crowding

I have hypothesized that people in groups manage social interaction by means of verbal, nonverbal, and environmental behavioral mechanisms. Crowding was said to exist when these regulatory mechanisms failed to operate effectively, with more social interaction resulting than desired. And people were predicted to react with stress, which in turn tripped off coping behaviors designed to provide a more acceptable level of contact with others. Here we will review research evidence on these coping responses. We will first consider some cross-cultural strategies for handling overcrowding and then examine more specific behavioral responses.

Culturally Based Coping Processes

Chapter 2 presented several examples of how different cultures achieve privacy. For example, the Tuareg use a veil and the Mehinacu expose their children to lengthy periods of social isolation.

Several writers feel that Japanese society illustrates the skillful management of crowded living (Hall, 1966; Canter & Canter, 1971; Michelson, 1970). For example, the Japanese have developed flexible use of their homes. With movable walls and separators, the same area can serve several functions, unlike the American tradition in which a room often has only one function. Thus a room can be an eating place, a recreation area, and perhaps even a sleeping place at different times. This arrangement has been described by Canter and Canter (1971) as a "metabolic" approach to design, which reflects a change-and-growth idea. In addition, the Japanese cope with limited space by miniaturizing parts of the environment and by fostering an attitude of pride in perfection of detail, as exemplified in their art and gardening practices—for example, bonsai plants. The Japanese also shut out the neighborhood and city, which are often noisy and unkempt, by means of walls, careful siting of homes, and arrangement of interior spaces. Thus a physical boundary is placed around a family group to literally wall off unwanted interaction, and the interior of the family environment is then richly differentiated by means of flexible use and decorative arrangements.

In related analyses, Michelson (1970) and Mitchell (1971) observed that a densely populated place such as Hong Kong had a relatively low incidence of social pathology, including disease, family disorganization, and the like, and a relatively low death rate. They attributed this to styles of family functioning, social organization, and other cultural mechanisms for coping with high density. Biderman (1963) made a historical, case-study analysis of various incidents of extreme overcrowding (slave ships, prisoner-of-war camps, immigrant ships, and the like) and concluded that disease and social pathology were lowest in those cases in which groups had a reasonable degree of social organization, often based on cultural practices.

Rogler (1967) and Lewis (1959, 1961) used an anthropological perspective to describe coping reactions in crowded Latin American and Mexican families. In city slum areas in Colombia and Peru, squatter families formed barrios (neighborhoods) by building shacks out of scrap metal and by pirating electricity from neighboring areas (Rogler, 1967). Although they did not have community-service facilities, or formal civic organizations, sewage or garbage-collection systems, or a governing structure, these small communities quickly developed their own social norms. Because these were densely populated areas, relationships among neighbors and matters of privacy became important. A norm of privacy gradually developed whereby people reacted strongly to others' noisiness or intrusion; in some instances children were kept inside, and families secluded themselves from others. Newcomers were received with extreme displeasure, often causing conflict and hostility even though no one had legal property rights. Lewis (1959) described a similar situation in a tenant community in Mexico, in which a norm developed that people did not visit one another's homes. This norm may have occurred because homes in the neighborhood were crowded or were not always nicely furnished. Or, the norm may have evolved as a vehicle to cope with high population concentration and to permit at least one place where members of the family could be alone and away from others. A similar practice exists in parts of India (Rosenberg, 1968), whereby small screened areas and corners are used by people who want to be alone.

Munroe and Munroe (1972) and Munroe, Munroe, Nerlove, and Daniels (1969) studied three East African societies that varied widely in population density. The Logali had a density of 1400 persons per square mile; the Gusii density was 700 people per square mile; in the least concentrated group, the Kipsigis, there were about 250 people per square mile. Data collected from questionnaires and psychological instruments revealed that the most densely populated group (1) had norms according to which holding hands with friends was avoided, (2) had the worst recall for interpersonal-affiliation words, and (3) tended to describe other family members in more negative terms, compared with persons from less densely concentrated groups. If one stretches the meaning of these data, the more crowded groups may have gradually developed cultural practices that involved avoidance of close contact with others, a devaluation of others, and a lowered desirability of affiliative activities—all of which reflect coping processes that may assist in controlling interpersonal boundaries, especially in response to heightened inputs from others.

Draper (1973) examined the effects of crowded living on the !Kung bushmen of Southwest Africa. This hunting-and-gathering culture lives in tribal groups of about 150 people, further divided into kinship groups. The typical !Kung settlement has less than 200 square feet of living space per person, well below the "desirable standard" of 350 square feet in the American culture. The group lives in village settings, and neighboring huts are so close that neighbors can literally touch one another. During the day about two-thirds of the people are in a small area, and social contact is quite high.

Yet the !Kung seem to enjoy touching, close physical contact, and extensive social interaction. And they don't seem to suffer physically or psychologically from this high-density life. Draper discovered that there is a norm among the !Kung that seems related to this issue. Individuals or families can leave the tribal group at any time to join another group or to establish a new group. The existence of social and family networks with distant groups permits easy withdrawal so that coming and going are not traumatic. Group affiliation is not necessarily a permanent thing; the norm for free departure makes the handling of social conflicts an easy matter and gives people a sense of interaction control whenever necessary. Thus interpersonal-boundary regulation seems to rely heavily on the literal moving in and out of contact with others.

Simmel (1950a), Wirth (1938), and, more recently, Milgram (1970) described protective coping responses used by city dwellers to deal with the large numbers of people they come into contact with on a daily basis. According to Simmel and Wirth, modern urban life involves a heightened level of stimulation from others, a rapid flow of interaction, and fragmentary social relationships with others—all of which have resulted in a need to protect the self from potentially overwhelming stimulation, contact, and demands from others. Protective mechanisms among city dwellers were described by Simmel as involving a blasé, distant, and detached attitude, which gave the impression of reserve, aloofness, coldness, and even lack of concern for others. Wirth amplified this theme and observed that urban people not only became less involved emotionally with others but also exhibited greater segregation among status levels in the society; they also came to value predictable routines, punctuality, and efficiency.

More recently, Milgram (1970) presented a theoretical analysis and some empirical data that extended this line of thinking. He theorized that city dwellers are essentially in a *stimulus-overload* situation, which involves more contact with others than they can handle or desire, and that a series of adaptive responses gradually develops to help them function in the face of many people and many social inputs. Such response mechanisms include (1) allocation of less time to each of the many inputs they face, often producing brusque contact with others; (2) disregard of low-priority inputs, which results in ignoring drunks or people who have fallen and giving attention only to those inputs that have direct personal meaning; (3) redrawing of boundaries and shifting of certain social transactions to others, such as the new procedure whereby bus drivers do not have to make change; (4) blocking of stimulus inputs by means of unlisted telephone numbers, doormen and guards who control entrances to buildings, and even an unfriendly countenance to discourage others; (5) reduction of intensity of inputs by filtering devices; and (6) creation of specialized institutions, such as welfare services, to handle inputs that might otherwise be directed toward individuals.

Figure 10–1. Low-cost government housing in Hong Kong—one family to a room. (Photograph by Gloria Altman.)

The person raised in a large city comes to use various combinations of these mechanisms, almost as a protection against the voluminous amount of social contact he or she is exposed to daily. We have all heard the story of the apartment neighbors who live next door to each other for years but who never exchange a word of greeting. Or there are the subway riders who see one another day after day and year after year but who never acknowledge one another's existence. "Not getting involved in other people's business" is a common big-city dictum that often occurs to the detriment of the victim of an accident or a robbery and serves to keep one's social interaction within bounds (although recent research on altruism and helping behavior suggests that some of these stereotypes do not always hold neatly). In general, however, the thrust of these ideas is that the resident of a densely populated area or culture learns to develop coping behaviors that are designed to regulate contact with others in accord with desired degrees of interaction.

Coping and Ongoing Social Interaction

In this section we will examine how people actually interact as they are exposed to densely populated situations. Do they become aggressive or withdrawn? What types of nonverbal and other behaviors do they exhibit as they struggle to regulate interaction with others?

One way to demonstrate basic behavioral reactions to density is in a minimal social situation, such as in congested public areas. Stilitz (1969, 1970) observed pedestrian flow in outdoor street settings, theater foyers, and subway stations in London. Pedestrians were observed to have stable behavior patterns, such as taking the shortest path between points, having preferred speeds, and being attracted to window displays. More important for our purposes is the fact that people had systematic transit rhythms; for example, they sped up and slowed down in anticipation of possible collisions. In theater foyers they distributed themselves evenly over the available space, avoided main flow paths, and occupied places where they could see others. Thus even the simple process of transit in densely populated places involved the use of implicitly agreed-upon coping processes. In a follow-up interview, pedestrians and theatergoers reported not minding crowds, except when flow patterns were complex, when they were jostled, or when they were prevented from obtaining a goal, such as purchasing a ticket. In a similar study, Bowerman (1973) observed people's walking speeds in downtown Boston. Under crowded conditions they walked more rapidly, which was attributed to the social and physical pressure of "... a large number of people who wished to use the same space within a short period of time" (p. 109).

Aggression and Withdrawal as Responses to Crowding

Several laboratory studies examined coping behaviors in high-density situations. One series of investigations dealt with the behavior of children in play situations; sometimes spatial density (amount of space in same-sized groups) was varied, and sometimes social density (number of group members in constant-sized spaces) was varied.

In an early study (Hutt & Vaizey, 1966), brain-damaged, autistic (severely withdrawn), and normal children were observed in a free-play situation in three different-sized groups: up to 6 children, 7 to 11 children, and more than 11 children. Autistic children showed almost no aggressive behavior in the three conditions and, if anything, withdrew toward the periphery as group size increased. Normal children showed increased aggression in the larger-sized groups and also spent less time in social contact as group size increased. Brain-damaged children showed the most aggression, especially as group size increased.

In another study, Hutt and McGrew (1967) varied spatial density and kept group size constant. Here, somewhat contrary to the preceding study, social interaction increased in smaller-sized rooms, whereas aggressive behavior did not show consistent trends. In another study, McGrew (1970) varied spatial and social density simultaneously. Children from 3 to 6 years of age were organized into 8-to-10- and 16-to-20-person groups and had either a whole playroom or parts of a playroom accessible to them, yielding all combinations of group size and space. Children in same-sized groups in spatially dense conditions were, not surprisingly, in closer social contact with one another than those in more spacious conditions. However, in larger groups, those in dense spaces were also more solitary, confirming the earlier Hutt and Vaizey findings. Considering the impact of social density, children in larger groups tended to spend more time in the presence of adults or showed more solitary behavior. Thus a relatively consistent pattern of coping behavior in these studies was for children to withdraw physically and socially as density increased, and only in some circumstances did aggressive behavior increase.

This pattern of withdrawal appears in several other studies. For example, Ittelson, Proshansky, and Rivlin (1970) examined the social behavior of patients in a psychiatric hospital ward as a function of the number of people in the ward. Observations over a three-week period indicated that people in single bedrooms were individually and socially active; they kept busy when they were alone, and they were also interested in socializing with others. Those in the more densely populated wards were more passive and withdrawn—sitting quietly, doing nothing—and were not so often engaged in social contact. Similar results were obtained by Loo (1973b), who observed 4- to 5-year-old boys and girls in six-person groups for which spatial density was varied to provide either 44 or 15 square feet per child. The results suggested less aggression and more withdrawal in dense conditions. There were also several acts of dominance and interruption, but these did not appear to fit into a strong pattern. Studies cited earlier by Valins and Baum (1973) and Baum and Valins (1973) also demonstrated social withdrawal and avoidance as a correlate of living in high-density dormitories. In one study, subjects from crowded and uncrowded residential living arrangements placed miniature figures in various simulated spaces. The results indicated greater sensitivity to crowding by those who lived in dense environments, as evidenced by smaller numbers of figures placed in settings representing bedrooms, waiting rooms, and the like. In another experiment, in which subjects were directed to a waiting room, residents from dense dormitories spent less time looking at a confederate in the room, talked less, and sat farther away from the confederate than did those from uncrowded dormitories. Thus in very different situations the pattern of social withdrawal and avoidance of others appears to be a characteristic coping response to high density.

An indirect type of social withdrawal, in the form of unwillingness to help others, was studied by Bickman, Teger, Gabriele, McLaughlin, Berger, and Sunaday (1973). College students who lived in high-density high-rise dormitories were compared with students who lived in small residential houses. Helping was measured by the "lost-letter" technique, in which an addressed, stamped letter was dropped in a public area, such as a hallway.

Willingness to help was determined by how many letters were picked up and mailed by passersby. The results of this study suggested that a smaller mailing rate occurred in the high-density dormitories, reflecting a lower willingness to help others (at least in relation to a task such as this). Similar results were obtained at another university on this measure and in a different helping situation in which students were asked to collect milk cartons for a classmate doing an art project. Again, those in high-density living arrangements were less responsive to even this direct request for assistance than were those who lived in smaller housing units.

In an attempt to unravel the circumstances under which aggression or withdrawal occurs in response to crowding, Rohe and Patterson (1974) hypothesized that a key factor leading to aggression is "competition for resources." Thus if desired resources are depleted as density is increased, we may see outcomes different from those occurring when resources are increased to match increases in group size. Rohe and Patterson (1974) examined this issue in children's play groups. They predicted that cutting back space (spatial density) and resources (number of available toys to play with) would produce different levels of aggression than would cutting back on space but *not* reducing resources. From analyses of films of children's reactions, they found that, when density increased and resources decreased, children showed the most negative social behavior (destructive play and aggressive behavior). A high-density/high-resource situation (crowded but with plenty of toys) did not produce especially strong negative behaviors. Thus this and other studies indicate that aggressiveness or withdrawal responses to crowding will depend on the composition of the group, the nature of the resources available to group members, group goals, and a number of other factors. It is simply not possible to make universal statements such as "Crowding produces aggression" or "Crowding produces social withdrawal." Both statements have some support from research, but which form of coping response will occur depends on a number of factors.

Other Coping Responses to Crowding

A recent study by Sundstrom (1973) undertook molecular analyses of nonverbal behavior as a reaction to density. As described earlier, he varied conditions of intrusion (close contact and inappropriate touching and intimacy by a confederate), goal-blocking (inattention by a confederate in a self-disclosure situation), and density (three interacting pairs in close and spacious quarters). Subjects generally found intrusion to be stressful at first, but they adapted over time. Stress reactions seemed to be consistent with nonverbal coping behaviors. For example, under intrusion conditions, when the confederate came inappropriately close, the subject's looking at the confederate's face decreased (perhaps a sufficient response to reduce the stress of too much intimacy). In the goal-blocking condition, when the confederate ignored the subject, stress did not decline over time, but there was less head nodding, less gesturing, more self-manipulation, and some drop in the subject's looking at the confederate—all responses reflecting either withdrawal or tension. High-density conditions did not produce feelings of more stress, although there was more object manipulation at first (such as pencil tapping), less nodding of the head, less willingness to disclose personal information, and less looking at the confederate—again reflecting tension and withdrawal.

Coping responses to density and intrusion may have been successful early in the experiment, and therefore subjects may have shown little stress in these conditions by the end of the experiment. Although similar coping occurred in response to goal-blocking (the confederate's acting rudely toward the subjects' disclosures), stress did not decline, perhaps because the situation required subjects to continue communicating with the inattentive confederate—a kind of double-bind situation in which withdrawal was contrary to the demands of the situation. However, some people attempted to withdraw nonverbally.

This study is particularly interesting in light of other research that showed only weak stress reactions to density. As proposed by my theoretical model and supported by the Sundstrom study, it seems quite possible that, in other research, stress was experienced *early* in crowding but was successfully coped with by means of nonverbal or other behaviors. By the time measurements were taken in these other studies, the interpersonal-boundary system could have been successfully readjusted, so that reactions to density were no longer evident.

A field study of married couples in crowded and uncrowded living conditions while in Peace Corps training demonstrates some interesting coping responses (MacDonald & Oden, 1973). Five couples who lived for 12 weeks in a single 30-by-20-foot room and who shared a single toilet were compared with others who lived in commercial hotels in private rooms with bathrooms. Among other findings, the authors reported that certain group norms developed in the crowded living arrangements that were designed to make life easier and to protect the privacy rights of everyone. For example, there was passive aggreement not to "peek" while others dressed and undressed, dirty jokes and vulgarisms were avoided, and intrusion into others' conversations was avoided. Thus people attempted not to violate others' self-boundaries. Couples also reported techniques they used to ensure control over their own dyadic boundary. They developed "code words" to communicate with each other in brief, private ways on topics of sex, others' behavior, and the like. And most crowded couples stated that they came to know their spouses better because of the experience. Thus, while the situation might have been initially stressful, couples in these crowded living arrangements developed a whole range of coping responses designed to regulate contact with others.

These studies fit the model presented in Chapter 9 reasonably well. As the self-boundary is violated and as more interaction occurs than is desired under increased density, people attempt to re-establish boundaries. One way to do so is to withdraw from others and thereby cut down on the amount of social contract. Other responses to density and boundary violation include aggression and other negative behaviors, as well as culturally based responses such as verbal and nonverbal behaviors.

Outcomes and Costs of Crowding

The chain of events in the model of crowding includes (1) stress reactions that result from an imbalance between desired and achieved levels of interaction, (2) behavioral coping responses, and (3) outcomes and costs of efforts to maintain self/other boundaries. The present section deals with these outcomes and costs. We will first discuss performance outcomes of density, based primarily on laboratory studies. Then we will examine longer-term outcomes of crowding, such as social pathologies of crime, juvenile delinquency, and physical and mental disorders.

Crowding and Task Performance

A number of writers have implied that work performance would be worse under crowded conditions. One group of studies searched for immediate, short-term impacts of density on performance and found essentially no effect. Other studies looked for longer-range, delayed effects and have uncovered some performance costs that can be indirectly associated with density and crowding.

Several studies focused on short-term performance effects in crowded and uncrowded laboratory settings. For example, Freedman, Klevansky, and Ehrlich (1971) had subjects work on simple and complex tasks, such as discussion in groups, crossing out individual letters from texts, forming words from letters, and identifying object uses. Results were totally negative, with no effects of density on task performance. A second series of studies, by Freedman, Levy, Buchanan, and Price (1972), also yielded no crowding effects on a discussion task or a psychomotor task. A study by Rawls, Trego, McGaffey, and Rawls (1972) did not change this conclusion. Subjects worked in two- or eight-person groups on a variety of psychomotor tasks—for example, eye/hand coordination and arithmetic reasoning tasks. Once again, there were practically no differences as a function of density or other factors.

A recent line of work on noise may be important to density-performance relationships, because it demonstrates delayed, long-term effects of noise on performance. Glass and Singer (1972) conducted an interesting series of studies on the impact of noise on performance and reported some important findings that have begun to be applied to the area of crowding: (1) they found differences in the effect of noise on simple and complex tasks, (2) they found differences in immediate versus delayed impact of noise on performance, (3) they identified differential impact of noise as a function of subjects' perception of ability to control or regulate noise, (4) they found that patterning and predictability of noise were important determinants of performance outcome, and (5) they hypothesized psychological and physiological adaptations and costs.

While their procedures varied from experiment to experiment, there were certain common elements. Noise levels were varied according to loudness and source; for example, noise stimuli included recordings of machinery, typewriters, and people speaking foreign languages that were played through headphones to subjects. A very important variable was whether noise was predictable (occurred at a fixed interval of time) or unpredictable (occurred at random time intervals). Another important variable was the degree of perceived control that subjects had to stop or to avoid the noise, with some subjects having control and others totally at the mercy of the situation. In these experiments, subjects worked on a variety of tasks, sometimes in the presence of noise and sometimes following the cessation of noise. Tasks also varied in complexity and included cognitive, reasoning, psychomotor, editorial, and number-comparison abilities.

It is not possible to summarize all the results, but there are certain findings that have considerable relevance to my analysis of crowding. In general, noise alone did not have any substantial effects on the performance of simple or complex tasks. However, performance did deteriorate when other factors came into play. For example, performance worsened when the work load was high and when the noise was experienced as uncontrollable or unpredictable. In my terms, when boundary-control mechanisms could not function and when people could not predict the kind of stimulation they would receive, detrimental effects were most serious—a result I would also expect in the context of crowding.

Another important set of findings bears on longer-term costs of adaptation to noise. Performance was negatively affected *after* the cessation of high-intensity noises (which had also been random and unpredictable) and when individuals felt they could not control the noise. That is, there were delayed noise effects. Glass and Singer concluded:

> ...we reasoned that inescapable and unpredictable noise confronts the individual with a situation in which he is at the mercy of his environment; that is, he is powerless to affect the occurrence of the stressor... in these

circumstances, we may describe the psychological state as one of helplessness [p. 157].

They went on to say that, while immediate psychological and physiological adaptation to noise seemed to occur, eventual costs of such adaptation were reflected in subsequent poorer performance.

Glass and Singer's work fits well within my framework of crowding and may account for the findings of the studies previously reported. Just as there was immediate adaptation to noise, crowding might also have resulted in short-term adaptation and satisfactory performance. If this line of reasoning is correct, there may have been no effects of crowding on performance because studies measured outcomes in too short a time frame. The studies may not have varied the key factors of perceived control over inputs and predictability of inputs. A recent study by Sherrod (1974) did exactly these things in an attempt to apply Glass and Singer's framework to the problem of crowding. Subjects worked in eight-person groups on a variety of tasks in either an uncrowded situation (150-square-foot room) or a crowded situation (37-square-foot room). Another crucial condition involved instructions to some groups of crowded subjects that they could leave the room any time they desired (perceived control). Following an hour of work, they were taken to an uncrowded room where they performed proofreading and frustration-tolerance puzzle tasks. There were *no* immediate effects of crowding on performance—a replication of earlier studies. However, delayed performance on the frustration task, measured in terms of persistence of attempts to solve insoluble problems, was *worst* among groups that came from highly crowded situations, was intermediate in the perceived-control/crowded conditions, and was best for those groups that had been in the uncrowded situation. Thus there were delayed effects of crowding on performance. Sherrod concluded that crowding is a form of social stress that does not necessarily impair short-term task performance, perhaps because of an adaptive process. However, costs may gradually accumulate and eventually affect subsequent functioning. And to the extent that a person perceives control over a situation, the effects of crowding may be somewhat alleviated. Thus the experiment by Sherrod, hopefully the first in a series of comparable studies, tapped crowding/density effects on a long-term basis and is important because of its sensitivity to the hypothesized stress→coping→cost/outcome chain of events.

Crime and Delinquency

One outcome of population concentration that has been of particular interest is antisocial behavior—crime and juvenile delinquency. Studies on this question have been correlational rather than laboratory oriented. A wide array of research over the years has shown moderate (but not overly strong) relationships between population density and crime, with high crime rates in heavily populated areas of cities and a decrease in crime toward suburbs (Schmid, 1969, 1970; Bordua, 1958; Lander, 1954; Lottier, 1938; Shaw & McKay, 1942; Sorokin & Zimmerman, 1929; Watts 1931; White, 1931; Schmitt, 1957, 1963, 1966). Several writers have noted, however, the difficulty in making inferences from such data, since ethnic background, occupational status, mobility, educational levels, and other factors are usually not equivalent in dense and nondense population areas. In addition, many of these studies treat density as a simple concept, with little regard to differences among types of density.

Recent studies by Galle, Gove, and McPherson (1972) and by Booth and Welch (1973) represent more sophisticated approaches to density analysis and to the role of mediating variables underlying crowding/crime relationships. As described earlier, Galle and his colleagues distinguished different types of density according to the relative closeness of the interacting people—for example, number of people per room in dwelling units (the most molecular and interpersonally relevant level of density), number of rooms per dwelling unit, dwelling units per structure (apartments), and building structures per acre (the most molar indicator of density). They also statistically controlled for differences in social class and ethnicity and thereby partialed out factors that might underlie density/pathology relationships. The highest correlations occurred between person-per-room density measures and juvenile delinquency, and successively lower correlations appeared for the grosser, less interpersonally oriented measures of density.

Their explanation of the results fits well with my model of crowding as a microinterpersonal boundary process. They hypothesized that as the number of persons within homes increases, the number of social contacts, lack of privacy, occurrence of intrusions, and heightened social interaction—all representing possible self/other boundary violations—will also increase. Furthermore, they speculated that the parents in homes with many people may have been unable to monitor closely their children's behavior, which could have resulted in a greater influence of peer groups and gangs, in turn yielding an increased likelihood of delinquent behavior. Thus in my terms, attempts to cope with difficult boundary-regulation conditions may have led eventually to socially deviant behaviors.

Booth and Welch (1973) obtained comparable results in regard to crimes of homicide and civil strife, such as riots. Data were examined from 65 nations for three indexes of crowding: average number of people per dwelling unit, number of dwelling units per acre, and number of people per acre. Again, homicide rates and civil riots were strongly related to person-per-room measures of density and less related to more molar indicators of population concentration (however, international aggression was more strongly related to person-per-acre population measures). Booth and Welch applied a frustration-stress-aggression conceptual analysis of these data and suggested that heightened interaction occurred in densely populated homes, where it was difficult to shield the self from undesired exchanges. In addition, basic aspects of life and access to simple goals (for example, eating or watching TV) can often be frustrating in crowded homes, and various activities (such as using the bathroom) must be closely coordinated with others. Booth and Welch hypothesized that such a situation can yield psychological frustration and stress. One outcome of such stress is aggressive behavior toward those interfering with one's boundary-control system. Booth and Welch also noted that homicide often involves family members acting against one another, presumably the most immediate source of boundary violation.

Thus, from most current studies, interpersonal factors related to population density seem to be associated with crime, juvenile delinquency, and violence. But as recent authors suggest, density alone, even at the social level, is probably not so much a "cause" as it is a medium within which interpersonal events occur. High density in face-to-face social situations probably makes for difficult self/other boundary management, with intrusions from others and access to desired goals and resources difficult and/or extremely costly. Interpersonal aggression, withdrawal from the family, ties with peer groups, and criminal activities may derive from long-term cumulative failures, frustrations, and costs associated with attempts to manage interaction with others.

Mental and Physical Disorders

Various indicators of physical and mental well-being have been examined in relation to population density—adult and infant mortality rates, disease, neuroses and psychoses, use of mental-health and welfare facilities, suicide rates, and the like.

With regard to mental illness, the data from early studies parallel the crime results. Weak to moderate correlations were obtained between various indicators of mental illness and population density. For example, Faris and Dunham (1965) found less mental illness in suburbs than in inner-city areas; Lantz (1953) obtained a similar relationship between mental illness and density in a military population; Cavan (1928), Schmid (1933, 1955), and Sainsbury (1956) obtained comparable data on suicide rates. Several studies also reported moderate relationships between density and diseases such as venereal disease and tuberculosis and between density and adult and infant mortality. Again, these data are not easily interpretable because of their noncomprehensive approach to density and because of the possibility of confounding variables.

More recently, Galle and his associates (1972) used more sensitive density indicators. Once again, an interpersonal measure of density (people per room in dwelling units) was the best predictor of mortality and fertility rates, and the next level of density (rooms per housing unit) best predicted mental-hospital admission rates. The researchers posited the obvious in regard to mortality—that is, that increased contact with others raised the possibility of infection and spread of contagious disease. However, they also hypothesized that social events were part of the picture. Sick persons may have been disturbed by the activities of others and may not have received the attention they required in crowded homes. Basically similar results were obtained by Marsella and his colleagues (1970), who found a higher incidence of psychosomatic illness, anxiety, and tension in crowded homes but weaker relationships when density was based on other indicators.

The complexity of the density/health relationship and of the role of social factors is evident from other studies. For example, Schwartz and Mintz (1963) found a *lower* incidence of schizophrenia and manic-depressive psychoses in *high-density* Italian neighborhoods in Boston than in less dense areas, suggesting the role of community structure and social-support systems. Schmitt (1963), Michelson (1970), and others noted that death, disease, and crime rates are quite low in Hong Kong as compared with other cities, in spite of the fact that it is a densely populated city. Winsborough and Davis (1963) and Winsborough (1965) also suggested that gross density was not necessarily associated with high rates of disease, death, and pathology, because public agencies often come into play to alleviate such problems. Loring (1956) and others proposed that more attention be given to the interior design of homes and to the use and nature of social structure in homes in tracking the density/health relationship.

Cassel (1970, 1971) has raised a number of questions about the relationships among density, social structure, and disease and has emphasized coping processes and costs involved in adaptation to crowding. In one analysis, Cassel (1971) observed that, historically, there are several sources of data relevant to the idea that density and disease are related: death and mortality rates in urban centers, industrialization and death/disease rates, and higher disease rates under crowded conditions such as military training camps. From an analysis of data in these areas, Cassel concluded that the relationships are very complicated and closely linked with social processes. For example, death rates (historically) have not risen with population concentration. Rural death rates have increased and even bypassed urban rates in the 1960s and beyond, in spite of increased population concentration in urban areas. Naturally, other factors are probably involved, such as emigration of younger people from rural areas, thus leaving an older population, and the greater availability of medical and health care in urban areas. For whatever reason, however, data do not support a simplistic density/mortality relationship.

Physical disease and urbanization are also not easily interpreted in a "density causes disease" paradigm. For example, Cassel noted that tuberculosis rates rose for almost 100 years following industrialization, then began to decline, and have continued to decline in the face of increasing population density. And he argues that improvements in medical care could not have accounted for the early decline, since antituberculosis programs did not begin until several decades after the initial decline. Recent studies of tuberculosis rates also suggest higher incidence of the disease among those who live alone and no relationship between tuberculosis and people-per-room ratios.

Furthermore, Cassel (1970) observed that diseases seem to wax and wane in popularity—to some extent independently of medical advances. For example, between World War I and World War II, ulcers seemed to be on the rise, but then heart disease, hypertension, cancer, and arthritis increased. Now these diseases appear to be on the decline. Therefore, Cassel feels that these patterns need to be understood in terms of social structure as well as population concentration. Some of his examples support my hypothesis that interpersonal events associated with density may be potentially critical factors in adaptation, outcomes, and costs. For example, he cited several studies indicating that people living in small cohesive societies had lower blood-pressure levels, which often rose for those who left the society.

The process of adaptation to social systems also seems important. One study reported by Cassel showed that death rates from lung cancer were higher in foreign-born workers living in cities than in lifetime urbanites, even when such factors as cigarette smoking were controlled. Also, second-generation rural mountaineers who migrated to industrial work settings had better health levels than first-generation migrants, suggesting a social-physical adaptation process. As a final example, Stewart and Voors (1968) examined cyclical rates of upper-respiratory infection among military recruits. Increased disease occurred in the early weeks of training, followed by a decline in the middle weeks and a rise in disease toward the completion of training. This pattern of illness is linked directly to the stress of a new and trying situation at the beginning of training, some stability in the middle of training, and uncertainty about one's future assignment toward the end of training. Patterns of health rates, therefore, seem to be associated with a blend of physical and social-stress factors.

A recent anthropological analysis confirms the idea that an understanding of population density must include attention to social processes and adaptation mechanisms. Draper (1973) observed the !Kung bushmen of Southwest Africa (described earlier), who live in small villages and whose living arrangements involve extremely close contact among neighbors and families—a situation that might be labeled "overcrowding." Yet Draper observed that the !Kung are quite free of biological stress indicators. Blood pressure is not especially high and does not rise with age, and blood-cholesterol levels are among the lowest in the world. Draper attributed the seemingly absent stress outcomes to the features of the social system. People are free to leave the community at any time to join other groups. Also, when the village reaches a population of about 150, people often leave to form new groups or to join other groups. Thus there is a general norm that leaving is acceptable to relieve tensions and conflicts. Excessive physical costs seem to be avoided because of a system that allows for the alleviation of boundary-control processes when social inputs are aversive or undesired.

Cassel did not offer a detailed theoretical model but suggested that an understanding of disease in relation to crowding must account for social structure, intervening psychological processes, and adaptive responses in order to establish a link between crowding and health. Furthermore, he argued that aspects of social structure may trip off physiological responses, which can result in increased susceptibility to illness. It is not merely the new or increased presence of disease agents or sheer physical density alone that creates the problem; it is the changed ability of the person to respond, cope, and adapt to those agents as the situation changes. In Cassel's terms (1970), "Disease should be viewed as occurring when the adaptive responses by the organism to stimuli are inappropriate in kind or amount or both" (p. 204).

René Dubos (1965, 1968) has dealt with some of the same themes in an eloquent fashion. For Dubos, as for Cassel, the issue of crowding does not so much concern the infectious spread of disease in dense populations; rather, it concerns the total interplay of social and physical factors and the way in which interpersonal stresses in dense environments upset the ecology of the organism and generate a stress syndrome, thereby heightening receptivity to disease. In my terms, Cassel and Dubos are speaking of a chain of events that involves: social stimulation→attempts at boundary control→psychological stress→coping behaviors→eventual costs.

One of Dubos' main theses is that people are capable of successful adaptation to even the most dire circumstances of climate, environment, and social situations, including extreme population concentration. Even more important, according to Dubos, are the long-term costs of adaptation. Glass and Singer (1972) demonstrated such costs in respect to delayed effects of noise, and Selye (1956) proposed a general stress syndrome involving psychological and physiological costs that result from successful coping with stressful events. As Dubos put it, the issue is not really one of survival; it is, rather, a question of whether such factors as population concentration will, over the long run, produce extreme cumulative costs and thereby degrade our "quality of life." Thus short-term adaptation may occur, but the long-term psychic and physical costs may be serious. As I have indicated, there is not much research on the delayed costs of crowding. However, the few studies I have cited indicate the importance of studying long-term and indirect effects of population density.

Summary of Chapters 9 and 10

In these chapters crowding was viewed as an outcome of an ineffective interpersonal-boundary system. In general, crowding exists when achieved privacy is less than desired privacy—when more social interaction occurs than is desired. Beyond this general statement, a number of dimensions of crowding were examined in Chapter 9, including: length of time in dense environments, richness of environments, interpersonal conditions involving social interference, intrusion and blocking of access to resources, and personal factors such as expectation and prior experiences in high-density settings. A distinction was also made between density and crowding. Density is a physicalistic concept, involving some measure of number of people per unit of space. The value of viewing density as a differentiated concept is also emphasized in relation to various levels of density such as people per room in dwelling units, dwelling units per housing structure, and people per acre.

A model of crowding was also proposed in Chapter 9, in terms of antecedent variables, organismic factors such as stress, behavioral coping responses, and consequent outcomes. It was hypothesized that boundary-regulation behaviors are set in motion in accord with desired levels of privacy, as described in earlier chapters. However, intrusion, blocking of access to various resources, and general social interference might occur under high population density and produce more interaction than desired. A resulting stress reaction was predicted to occur, which then set in motion coping behaviors designed to realign self/other boundaries and to provide a better match between desired and achieved levels of privacy. One result of these coping responses is physical and psychological costs of various types, including anxiety and stress, disease, and the social pathologies of aggression, crime, and mental disorders.

Chapter 9 also reviewed two strategies of research on crowding. One line of study, correlational-sociological research, has a long tradition in the area of relationships between density and social pathology. This early research used an overly simplistic approach to density and did not always partial out underlying factors such as education or economic opportunities, which may have accounted for the moderate relationship between density and social pathology. Later studies overcame some of these problems and demonstrated that negative effects of density are associated primarily with microlevels of population concentration (such as crowded homes) rather than with gross measures (such as people per acre of land). A second line of research, more recent in origin, is conducted in laboratory settings and attempts to track psychological correlates of density, such as interpersonal and individual feeling states, ongoing coping behaviors, and task performance.

A central theme of these chapters was that crowding and population concentration can be viewed according to a theoretical model that takes into account antecedent factors that interact with density, situations in which self/other boundaries are less effective than desired, and situations in which individual and interpersonal feeling states, including stress and anxiety, are generated. In turn, a variety of coping or readjustment behaviors are set in motion to re-establish desired levels of exchange. These behaviors can produce various costs, in the form of long-term stresses, mental and physical disease, or performance deterioration.

Research results were examined in Chapter 10 in relation to the model of crowding. Laboratory studies generally indicate only mild effects of density on individual or interpersonal feelings, such as anxiety, stress, and social feelings toward others. The absence of extreme effects was attributed to the short periods of density to which subjects were exposed, temporary group-member relationships, and the possibility that people were able to cope readily with the situation. Some research indicated the desirability of taking repeated measures of individual stress reactions—to track coping responses over time. Correlational studies, some based on longer-term exposure to population density, suggested the presence of individual feelings of stress and anxiety, especially in close microinterpersonal situations.

An analysis of coping mechanisms in reaction to crowding indicated a variety of culturally different response styles, varying from use of the physical environment to construct barriers to development of cultural norms and nonverbal behaviors that regulate interaction in high-density siuations. A few laboratory studies also examined nonverbal and other coping behaviors, such as physical and verbal withdrawal, aggressive behavior, eye contact, and the like. In general, research is only at its barest beginnings in the study of ongoing coping processes, and it is too early to state exactly what reactions will be used in various circumstances.

Another line of research examined physical and psychological costs of high-density situations, especially over long periods of time. In general, the results indicated few immediate effects on task performance, although recent work indicates delayed, postcrowding deterioration of task performance. Such results suggest that crowding may have cumulative, long-term costs that follow a period of successful coping. Longer-term, correlational studies of the relationship between population density and social pathology also indicate the need to consider cumulative, delayed effects of density.

Implications for Environmental Design

This chapter explores possibilities for translating into environmental-design principles our ideas about privacy, territoriality, personal space, and crowding. I will not specify detailed procedures or technical guidelines but only wish to point the way toward some general implications for design.

The first part of the chapter examines the history of contact between practitioners of environmental design—mostly from the fields of architecture, planning, and urban design—and researchers from the social and behavioral sciences. Practitioners and researchers have different orientations to environmental issues, and it is necessary for each to understand how the other thinks if there is to be any application of research to the solution of environmental problems. The middle part of the chapter summarizes a few ways of thinking about human behavior that are currently popular in the environment and behavior field. These represent "models of man," or philosophical views about human behavior that implicitly guide the activities of both researchers and designers. The final part of the chapter considers how ideas discussed throughout this book can be used as guiding principles in environmental design.

A Historical Perspective

Contact between environmental researchers and practitioners began on a large scale in the early 1960s. As their interactions grew, it became clear that they had different points of view on how to approach environmental problems. They defined problems in different ways, and they felt the need to do different things. By describing their separate orientations in a brief, historical perspective, I hope to set the stage for bridging between their viewpoints. In the preceding chapters I approached privacy, territory, personal space, and crowding from the perspective of the behavioral sciences. How is this view different from that of a practicing urban designer? What translation steps are necessary to make these ideas more practical?

In the late 1950s and early 1960s, many practitioners rebelled against a traditional norm that placed too much emphasis on aesthetics, form, and beauty as the primary criteria of design. The environmental needs of the consumer were foremost in the minds of the malcontents, even at the expense of abstract beauty and design. Thus alienated practitioners emphasized *people* in designed environments, and they reached out toward disciplines that presumably knew something about people's motivations and needs—sociology, psychology, political science, and anthropology.

During the same years a complementary discontent was building in the behavioral sciences (especially in psychology). Many scientists questioned the use of laboratory experiments on college sophomores as the *sole* approach to understanding behavior, and they called for the study of "real" people and groups in "real-world" settings. The hold of the laboratory as a setting for research was quite firm at the time, and it was not popular to conduct field research, so those who favored naturalistic studies often felt alienated from the mainstream of their field. In addition, a realization grew that some fields in the behavioral sciences had been studying human behavior without recognition of its link to the physical environment in which it occurs. If considered at all, aspects of the environment such as lighting, noise, and color were typically treated only as physical causes of responses. The environment was not conceived of as a social milieu or a social stimulus along the lines discussed in this book, or as a force that might modify social structures and social interaction. The efforts of early researchers in the social and behavioral sciences sensitized others to the role of the environment as a central feature in social behavior. The result was that a small group of scientists reached out toward disciplines that dealt with and knew about the environment—architecture, interior design, and urban planning—to learn concepts, methods, and perspectives. The object was to develop an interdisciplinary field that dealt with environment and behavior not as separate things but as a unified and holistic system.

During the initial period, there was a vigorous attempt to form a marriage between the behavioral-science and the practitioner disciplines. Spontaneous discussion groups formed, sometimes under the sponsorship of formal organizations and sometimes as ad hoc meetings. Soon more organization emerged; conferences and symposia were held, and newsletters and informal journals were started. Several such communication outlets still exist, as does a regularly published scholarly journal, *Environment and Be-*

havior. Another outgrowth was the establishment of formal interdisciplinary organizations, two notable ones being the Association for the Study of Man-Environment Relations (ASMER) and the Environmental Design Research Association (EDRA). Another development was academic programs, many with a multidisciplinary perspective, to train environment and behavior researchers and practitioners. Pennsylvania State University, City University of New York, Harvard School of Design, the University of California at Los Angeles, the University of Buffalo, and the University of California at Irvine are some schools with such programs.

During the late 1960s and early 1970s the honeymoon seemed to be over, as unfulfilled promises existed on both sides. What appeared to have happened was a clash in the basic value systems and styles of behavioral scientists and practitioners. The practitioner's need for solution-directed and problem-oriented information that could be readily translated into design decisions was not being satisfied by the researcher. From the practitioner's perspective, the researcher somehow could not provide answers to concrete questions about the necessary size of rooms, specific needs of different ethnic and socioeconomic groups for living and neighborhood arrangements, specific design configurations for homes, communities, and cities, or other questions that had to be answered with little delay. On the other hand, to the researcher, the practitioner seemed to phrase questions in an unanswerable form, or allowed insufficient time for careful research, or requested overly specific answers. By the time the researcher had barely formulated the problem, the practitioner was off and away on a new project with another impossible deadline.

Although this state of affairs still continues today, I have the impression that a new stage now exists. Both sides seem ready to make a more realistic assessment of each other's point of view and of mutual advantages and disadvantages. This readiness was illustrated at a conference arranged by Donald Conway, Director of Research at the American Institute of Architects, who asked four designers and four behavioral scientists to work together for several days in order to come up with a "model" by which teams of researchers and practitioners could collaborate on environmental-design problems (Conway, 1974). Here are some quotes that reflect recent thinking on the relationship between researchers and practitioners:

> One thing that interested me, which I had not anticipated, was the idea of you social scientists being in some sense programmers.[1] I don't know that I had a clear vision of what it was you could do or what form it would take. But what came out became very solid and something to grab hold of, a vehicle to start establishing your credibility. Clients can respond to the idea that architects can

[1]Programming refers to the establishment of goals and priorities that a designed environment is to satisfy.

do programming. But if, as you say, you can do programming too, but do it with a particular skill and depth that relates to your training and point of view, then it seems to me that you can opt for something more than just so many rooms and so many square feet to program. You are now saying that you can put in this other social science ingredient. In other words, you can literally make a commentary on these spaces and you can literally make a comment on them because you have these information gathering and social science theory skills [p. 65].

When we build buildings we want people to use them, hopefully, properly. The more they use it in the way that it is intended, or manipulate it, it becomes good, it becomes meaningful and useful and something for people to benefit by. We both (architects and social scientists) must have that as a common objective, and there has to be some way we can help relate this information to each other in order to build buildings that do a better job for people. It seems to me a building can be judged on how well it serves the people. If the building doesn't do that, we have failed somewhere [Appendix II, p. 7][2]

In many respects this chapter is directed toward furthering these goals of establishing realistic expectations between researchers and designers. If we do not make a concerted effort toward this end, then it is likely that the study of environment and behavior will fragment and once again be approached from the myopic view of separate disciplines.

Differing Approaches of Practitioners and Researchers

Figure 11-1 outlines a three-dimensional space that differentiates the approaches of researchers and practitioners. The first dimension, *unit of study,* refers to *places*, from small units, such as rooms or homes, to very large units, such as cities or communities. The second dimension refers to *behavioral processes,* such as privacy and territoriality. The combination of these two dimensions distinguishes sharply the approaches of behavioral scientists and practitioners. Practitioners usually focus on a particular unit or place—a home, a neighborhood, or a city. Their interest is in a specific environmental and social unit. In designing that place, practitioners deal with a variety of processes, such as the ones listed in the second dimension (privacy, territoriality), and with economic, political, and technological matters. In short, practitioners fix their attention at a particular level on the place dimension and scan across processes.

Behavioral scientists, on the other hand, are usually process-oriented. They are primarily interested in such things as privacy, territoriality, or crowding and are less concerned about specific places, except as qualifying

---

[2] From *Social Science and Design*, by D. Conway, 1974. Reprinted by permission of the American Institute of Architects.

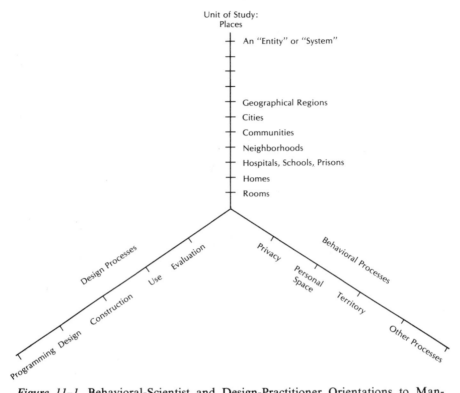

Figure 11-1. Behavioral-Scientist and Design-Practitioner Orientations to Man-Environment Issues. From "Some Perspectives on the Study of Man-Environment Phenomena," by I. Altman, *Representative Research in Social Psychology*, 1973, 4(1), 111. Reprinted by permission of *Representative Research in Social Psychology*.

factors. Thus the behavioral scientist often focuses on processes and scans across places. I must note that not all behavioral scientists take this approach. For example, some study a particular cell in the two-dimensional space of Figure 11-1, such as *privacy* in a *home*; others may examine a block of space, such as family *privacy* in the *home* and in the *community*. Nevertheless, it appears that the typical practitioner and the typical behavioral scientist place different emphasis on places versus processes.

The third dimension refers to the *design processes*, or the steps necessary to create a building, a home, or a city (Zeisel, 1974). Briefly, *programming* means identification of design criteria or the goals of the unit; *design* is a specific plan to achieve programming goals. *Construction* involves building a place; *use* refers to consumer activities and adaptations to the designed environment. *Evaluation* includes assessment of whether the completed unit satisfies original programming goals. Historically, researchers have not been involved very often in the process of environmental design. When they have participated, it has been largely in the evaluation stage, to pose such questions as: Does the place meet user needs? Is it doing what it was supposed to do? Does it have validity?

Although practitioners have occasionally sought the services of behavioral scientists in the design process, the two groups have not always worked successfully together. As I suggested earlier, behavioral scientists do not usually feel comfortable with such questions as: How can the cultural background of Group X be translated into the design of a home? What features should be built into the community that is designed specifically for poor people? Researchers do not typically pose questions in such specific place/locale form. The average scientist often replies that such problems can be researched but that answers will be tentative and that many studies will be necessary, along with long-term funding. The practitioner, caught in the bind of having to build a place immediately and operating with a fixed-dollar budget in an inflationary cycle, often throws up his or her hands in dismay and pleads that the design process must go on and that decisions must be made in spite of the lack of knowledge. The practitioner goes on to say that even educated guesses are acceptable, and the behavioral scientist must be willing to speculate about practical matters and not hide behind the purity of science. The researcher then often steps aside, unwilling to assume such responsibility, unwilling to be driven by schedules and dollar limitations, and unwilling to act in the absence of thorough documentation.

Implicit in this three-dimensional framework and in our paraphrased dialogue between practitioners and researchers are several differences in their approaches.

Criterion-Oriented versus Process-Oriented Approaches

So-called applied researchers who work on military, transportation, education, and health-care systems have much in common with environmental designers. The applied researcher and the practitioner are usually criterion- or problem-oriented in that they *begin* with a statement of real-life goals or end products to be achieved. They have a known observable criterion of tangible properties—for example, a building or community that is to house a certain number of people and to provide specific services or a transportation system that is to achieve a given flow of traffic in a specified period of time. The practitioner's job is to solve a tangible problem and to produce a workable product. In contrast, basic researchers generally proceed in the opposite direction. Although they are certainly interested in outcomes, their general strategy is first to pose the question "What are the major classes of predictor factors that affect Behavior X?" The next step, particularly if the researcher is experimentally oriented, is to design a multifactor study, with considerable attention given to features of the laboratory setting and to careful specification and manipulation of variables. And the traditional researcher is usually not concerned with a particular level of behavioral proficiency but wishes to demonstrate the effectiveness of certain independent predictor variables in producing differences in behavioral outcomes.

Analysis versus Synthesis

Implied in the preceding discussion is an issue that has been of long-standing philosophical interest. Practitioners often describe their job as "putting everything together." Not only must they worry about a host of technological questions—architectural design, plumbing, electricity, and materials—but they must also deal with sociological, psychological, economic, political, and other questions. Thus their job is to synthesize different areas of knowledge in order to create a viable entity. Furthermore, designers have many masters to serve (Zeisel, 1974; Conway, 1974). Years ago the architect, for example, worked face to face with the person whose home was to be built. Now there are massive construction projects whose ultimate users are not the ones who pay the designer. Housing-development investors contract with architects, and home buyers rarely have contact with designers. Furthermore, the designer has to be accountable to community building codes and laws, investment companies, and peers. In a word, the designer must be a *synthesizer* of knowledge, points of view, and practical demands.

On the other hand, implicit in many behavioral-science approaches is an *analytic* strategy—an attempt to dimensionalize phenomena and to discover the contribution of individual variables and clusters of variables to behavioral outcomes. Thus scientists usually focus on specific behaviors, settings, and causes. While their ultimate goal is generalization and synthesis, short-term goals usually involve partialing out of variables and detailed *analysis* of the impact of specific variables on specific behaviors. Or, to put it another way, the typical behavioral scientist is primarily interested in understanding *behavior*, and is only secondarily interested in putting together what is known to understand *whole people* or *whole groups* of people. So, when the practitioner poses the question "What does this particular cultural group need in the way of privacy, availability of transportation, or cultural centers?" the behavioral scientist may reply: "I'm a specialist in the religious institutions of rural members of that group, so I can only speculate about the many other parts of your question." The result is a mutual frustration.

Doing and Implementing versus Knowing and Understanding

Environmental practitioners are action-oriented and "doers," and their energies are directed toward achieving an end product within a specific time period. Behavioral scientists are usually less compelled to achieve a "real-world" product. Their accomplishments are generally published studies or a theory that analyzes a phenomenon in a relatively abstract fashion, with unknown or limited immediate application. Again, these differences can easily lead to an impasse. The practitioner, geared toward rebuilding a city or designing a low-cost housing project, must take immediate action. The behavioral scientist devotes energy to understanding rather than to direct action. The researcher is also generally less driven by professional needs or by other pressures to directly apply knowledge.

The distinctions posed here are not mutually exclusive, nor do they apply in all cases. However, they do illustrate a general pattern of differences in the approaches of behavioral scientists and practitioners. Of course, it may well be that the ideal relationship is not necessarily one of consensus or sameness of style. Divergencies in approach are probably healthy, for they bring to bear a variety of viewpoints to the same problem. Furthermore, the relationship will be particularly unhealthy if differences are seen as *inadequacies*, or if there is a refusal to translate between approaches. Practitioners and researchers can work a translation by shifting roles, with scientists stepping out of their roles occasionally and attempting to translate their work into the practitioner's framework, and vice versa. Only by trying to understand each other's styles, and accepting them as different, not deficient, can scientists and practitioners move toward an amalgamation of their separate contributions to environmental design.

A "Models of Man" View of the Field

So far I have described the struggles of researchers and practitioners to communicate with each other in order to weld their separate perspectives into a working strategy for dealing with environmental problems. One can also ask about underlying philosophical views of man that are present in the environment and behavior field and that implicitly guide the activities of researchers and practitioners. What assumptions are made about the "nature of man" in relationship to the environment? Is man to be viewed as a "machine," or as a sensing and perceiving organism, or as a strictly behaving organism, or what? The history of science, religion, and the arts shows that at different periods assumptions about man varied and that these different assumptions had a definite impact on thinking. Where does the environment and behavior field stand on this issue? Although this is not an easy question, it seems to me that there are, presently, a number of different "models of man" that have an important influence on present-day research and practice: (1) a mechanistic model, (2) a perceptual-cognitive-motivational behavioral model, and (4) a social-systems, ecological mode.

The Mechanistic Model of Man

The mechanistic-model perspective was one of the first the study of environment and behavior. It originated in th neering and hardware-oriented systems analysis of the 1950s a it was a maxim that the design of complex systems should in ations of the people who operated them. The "man-mac approach called for the design of equipment built arounc sensory, motor, and intellectual capabilities and limitations oi motto being "Fit the machine to man." The roots of this apprc back in industrial-psychology studies (in the 1920s and 193(motion, energy expenditure, and so on. In recent times thi been translated into environmental-layout analyses, traffic-fl lighting, color, and heating analyses of environments.

Several assumptions are implicit in this model. Man is v as a task-oriented, *performing* organism. As a result, emph: people's capabilities for sensing, processing, and interpretin; environment, and on skills to evaluate and select action alter this approach conceptualizes man as similar to a machine man-machine system, performance-related capabilities ar terest. Motivational and emotional feelings and interperso of secondary interest or are examined largely in terms of tl to performance effectiveness.

Another feature of this approach is its concern wi design, particularly the shaping of physical environments permit people to perform effectively. The goal is to er mance-related skills are optimized and that people's li exceeded or unduly stressed. Although training of employ effectiveness, emphasis is also placed on designing physic people. However, designs are often static and provide few to alter their environments or to function in them in a flex sense, people are merely one of several system componen degrees of operating freedom. This approach was popul early 1960s and still has relevance today, but current rese: not appear to be dominated by this model.

erceptual-Cognitive-Motivational Model of Man

st prevalent approach today conceives of man in terms of
al processes—*perceptual reactions* to the environment (how
re, organize, and respond to environmental stimuli), *motivational states* associated with environmental stimuli (stress and
sitive feelings), and *cognitive responses* to the environment
ie richness, complexity, and meaning of the environment).
ceives of man as an internal processing organism and is more
...n subjective psychological processes than with overt behavioral
responses.

Historically, psychology relied heavily on an "internal-state" or "inside-
the-head" model of man. This is especially true in clinical psychology,
which grew from the earlier Freudian tradition and emphasized people's
emotional and motivational states. This model is also prevalent in social
psychology, with its emphasis on attitudes, beliefs, personality-oriented social states (such as need achievement, need affiliation, and need dominance),
and interpersonal states (such as cooperation, competition, attraction, influence, and conformity).

Environmental researchers and practitioners were quick to adopt this
model, perhaps because there is a large body of theory and measurement
techniques available. Their goal has been to study how man *sees, perceives,
feels,* and *reacts* to the environment. Questionnaires and rating procedures
are used to measure these states. The semantic-differential method, for example, has people respond to environments on scales tapping *evaluation*
(good or bad characteristics of environments), *activity* (dynamic quality of
environments), and *potency* (impact characteristics of environments). Other
approaches employ "cognitive maps." People may be asked to literally draw
their neighborhoods, streets, and cities, or they may be interviewed as they
move through environments. The goal is to determine *subjective* perceptions
of an environment, not its *objective* characteristics. One of the earliest examples of this approach involved taking people on a walk and asking them to
give personal impressions as they moved about (Lynch & Rivkin, 1959). A
more structured approach developed by Ladd (1970) asked black children to
draw their neighborhoods and streets and then subjected the answers to
content-analysis techniques. Various aspects of cognitive-map research are
summarized in Downs and Stea (1973).

A large body of knowledge based on the perceptual-cognitive-motivational model is building, and it appears that this model of man dom-
inates thinking at the present time. It is also interesting to consider this
approach from an extended historical perspective. Early in the history of
modern psychology, during the last third of the 19th century, a substantial

aspect of research involved "introspection," or the systematic analysis and self-reporting of internal cognitive and psychological events. In fact, there was an attempt by Wilhelm Wundt to establish a "mental chemistry," whereby the workings of the mind would be understood in terms of its elements and combinations of elements. In many respects the cognitive-map movement is analogous to the introspectionist movement and also seeks to unravel how people cognize, perceive, and feel about their environments. It will be interesting to see how long this "inside-the-head" model of man remains prominent in the environment and behavior field.

The Behavioral Model of Man

Since the 1920s, psychology and other social and behavioral sciences have been dominated by a behavioral orientation that emphasizes the study of *overt* behavior. Man is viewed as a behaviorally functioning organism, and the study of what people *do* is stressed, rather than how they feel, perceive, or think. The work of Barker and his associates (Barker, 1968; Barker & Gump, 1964) is one type of behaviorally oriented approach, in which detailed observations are made of people's movements and activities in various natural-life environments. The operant or Skinnerian approach is another type of behavioral orientation. Here emphasis is placed on environmental contingencies or reinforcements as determinants of behavior, and the attempt is to track behavioral contingencies and weave these into environmental design (Studer, 1970, 1972, 1973).

Behavioral analyses are not restricted to naturalistic observation. Much of the work described in earlier chapters involves field and laboratory experiments coupled with behavioral measurement (for example, how people interact, protect spaces, occupy chairs, approach others at varying distances, and so on).

Certain behavioral approaches are beginning to have an impact on the field. Early multidisciplinary conferences were dominated by the cognitive approach, as attempts were made to better understand internal needs, perceptions, and motivational states. At one time, researchers and practitioners scampered about, armed with questionnaires, rating instruments, and interview schedules designed to tap all kinds of feelings and perceptions. More recently, however, Barker's ecological-psychological approach has begun to gain momentum. This work occupies more and more time at conferences in increasingly crowded sessions, people now talk about committing themselves to behavioral observation, and it is likely that the coming years will show a surge of energy in this direction. While the operant-oriented behavioral-contingency approach is not yet in vogue, it is likely that it too will become more popular.

From a broader historical perspective, the shift from a strictly internal approach to various behavioral ones is analogous to what happened in psychology when the introspectionist approach was replaced with the more current behavioristic approach. How far in this new direction the environment and behavior field will move is difficult to predict, although it is probably safe to say that *all* the preceding models will be used in varying degrees in the future.

The Social-Systems, Ecological Model of Man

The social-systems approach is not yet well established in the environment and behavior field, although it is a major theme of this book. As discussed in Chapter 1, this model has several features.

1. Environment and behavior are closely intertwined, almost to the point of being inseparable. Their inseparability says more than the traditional dictum that "environment affects behavior." It also states that behavior cannot be understood independent of its intrinsic relationship to the environment and that the very definition of behavior must be within an environmental context. This point is central to the approach of Barker (1968) and his followers (Willems, 1973, 1974). To a great extent the social and behavioral sciences have, historically, studied people almost as if they were separate from physical environments. What is now called for by Barker and others is recognition that the appropriate unit of study is a people-environment unit.

2. People-environment relations are best viewed as an ecological system, with mutual and dual impact between people and environments. Not only does the environment act on people, but they act on environments. The very term "ecology" involves a mutual and joint impact of environments on organisms and organisms on environments. Historically, the environment has been treated as an independent variable—as something that acts on, determines, or causes behavior. Thus one often encounters the idea that environments must be designed for people, to meet their needs and to satisfy their purposes. Implicit in this traditional notion is the idea that man's control over the environment is to be limited, that environments are to be tailored to people in a static, nonmodifiable form. More recently, however, emphasis has been given to the design of flexible, changing environments that can be manipulated, shaped, and altered. People become environmental change agents, not merely recipients of environmental influences. And, according to this new approach, the environment becomes an extension of

people's own beings and personalities. For example, the concepts of territory and personal space imply an *active, coping* use of the environment, not merely reactions by people to environmental stimuli.

3. This approach also assumes a dynamic, changing quality of people-environment relations. Territories shift, personal space expands and contracts, and people alter environments. Although this is a seemingly obvious truism, practitioners and researchers often act as if designed environments were fixed and unchanging through time. The fact is that social systems adapt and struggle, and this fact needs to be incorporated into environmental design.

4. A final theme is that people-environment relations occur at several levels of behavioral functioning and as a coherent system. The mechanistic, perceptual-cognitive-motivational, and behavioral models emphasize different facets of human functioning, and each model almost presumes that its use is sufficient to understand people-environment relationships. I have proposed in this book that *many* levels of behavior occur simultaneously and should be considered as a coherent system. Thus perceptions, cognitions, and feelings are internal forces that are translated into several levels of overt behavior: verbal content, paraverbal behaviors, nonverbal behaviors, and environmental behaviors, such as personal space and territory.

Also explicit in this theme is the idea that these different levels of behavior fit together as a "system," with various levels capable of substituting for, complementing, or amplifying one another. Although emphasis on one level of behavior may be necessary at a particular time, overemphasis on any level without integration can blind one to the system-like quality of environment-behavior relations.

I believe that the social-systems, ecological approach is the most potentially fruitful model of man. Although perhaps the most abstract and least readily translated into specific design solutions, it seems to fit well the complex nature of environment and behavior relationships. Another strength of this model is its potential for bridging the gap between the place-oriented approach of the practitioner and the process-oriented approach of the behavioral scientist. That is, a model based on multiple levels of behavior that function as a coherent system may permit a synthesis and re-creation of a total organism—a real person, group, or person-environment unit—as separate levels of behavior are pieced together to form a whole.

I have not done justice to all the varieties and subvarieties of "models of man" that exist in the environment and behavior field. But my intent was only to portray a broad grouping of approaches to provide a general perspective. A more detailed analysis of these and other approaches appears in Rapoport (1973) and Willems (1973). With these historical, comparative, and philosophical issues in mind, let us now be more concrete and examine some issues of environmental design.

Some Environmental-Design Guidelines

The remainder of this chapter considers three areas of design application that stem from my analysis: (1) the theoretical framework involving relationships among privacy, territoriality, personal space, and crowding, (2) the social-system or ecological approach, in which environment and behavior are viewed as a complex system, and (3) the time-linked nature of environment-behavior relationships and the short- and long-term consequences of coping with environmental events.

Derivations from Basic Concepts

Privacy.   I have treated privacy as a central concept and in a somewhat different way than it is used traditionally. Previously, privacy was viewed as an excluding process—as "being alone" or "getting away" from others. Practitioners often translate the traditional "keep-out" idea of privacy into the design of solitude areas in homes and other places. From the perspective of this book, privacy is better approached as a *changing self/other boundary-regulation process in which a person or a group sometimes wants to be separated from others and sometimes wants to be in contact with others.* Thus I have portrayed privacy as a dialectic process, in which forces to be with others and forces to be away from others are both present, with one force dominating at one time and the other being stronger at another time. As a corollary, being alone too often or for too long a period of time (isolation) and being with others too much for too long (crowding) are both undesirable states.

To translate this viewpoint into practical environmental designs is not easy. However, a general principle is that we should attempt to design *responsive environments,* which permit easy alternation between a state of separateness and a state of togetherness. If privacy has a shifting dialectic quality, then, ideally, we should offer people environments that can be responsive to their shifting desires for contact or absence of contact with others. Environments that emphasize only either very little interaction or a great deal of interaction are, to my way of thinking, too static and will not be responsive to changing privacy needs. Thus environmental designers should try to create environments that permit different degrees of control over contact with others. Such a philosophy is already used to some extent. For example, the door is a simple example of an environment-design feature that is responsive and that permits regulation of social interaction. Opening it signifies a desire for social stimulation, and closing it represents an impermeable self/other boundary. On the other hand, much environmental design does not have the flexible capability to meet changing privacy needs.

The "family room" in suburban American homes seems to be primarily a place for social interaction. It is hard to imagine someone using a family room as a place to be alone. In the American home, the den, the bedroom, and the bathroom are typically places to be alone and away from others. In fact, some people use the bathroom to read or think, since it is one of the few places in the home where people can be sure of maximum privacy. We seem to have a design mentality that thinks different places have single-minded functions—low or high interaction but not both. To achieve different privacy states requires, therefore, that we literally "go" to a different place. Why not think about having the same place serve different functions and have *it change* with our needs, rather than our changing needs requiring us to shift our location? This approach is used in certain other cultures—for example, by the Japanese. The interiors of their homes are flexible environments in which the same space is changed to reflect different social functions. In many Japanese homes, walls can be moved in or out of place; the same area may be used for eating, sleeping, and socializing at different times. The logic of our framework calls for more use of changeable environments so as to permit a greater responsiveness to changing needs for privacy.

Personal Space.   I have hypothesized that personal space and territorial behavior are mechanisms used to assist in the regulation of privacy. Personal space involves a combination of distance and angle of orientation from others. Research has indicated that personal-space behavior includes withdrawal and protective reactions to intrusion or overly close contact by strangers, and a desire to be close to liked others. The thrust of much of this research is that personal space is a dynamic, active process of moving toward and away from others, to make the self more or less accessible. Environmental designers have been intuitively sensitive to personal-space mechanisms in furniture design, layouts of office and living-room areas, and so on. For example, office desks and chairs usually place people about 4 feet from one another, within Hall's (1966) social-distance zone, which he described as an appropriate distance for strangers in public settings. Interior decorators, office-layout specialists, and others also arrange furniture to permit either "cozy" furniture arrangements or "formal" arrangements. But do these designers consciously use the concept of personal space in planning their layouts?

Research data also suggest that there are different personal-space mechanisms for men, for women, and for different social groups. To what extent are designed environments responsive to such different users? The literature could be examined to see how different groups employ personal space and how different settings elicit different personal-space relationships. Moreover, there are probably ways in which we can design environments so that personal space can shift with changing circumstances. One can pose the questions "To what extent do environments permit changes in personal spacing?" and "Are environments arranged so that when people are in them they are locked rigidly into personal-space relations?" For example, many offices have chairs in a fixed relationship, such as on either side of a desk, so that the occupant and visitor can assume only one type of seating position. A possible alternative would be to have an office arrangement with several optional configurations—chairs across the desk, chairs at the corner of the desk and behind the desk, or chairs on the same side of the desk. With such options, personal-space relationships between the occupant and different visitors could be adjusted in accord with desired levels of interaction. Another example is a social gathering at which furniture is arranged so that all participants sit in one group, often in a circle, and are literally forced to deal with one another as a group. An alternative arrangement would permit them to interact in subgroups and to shift their personal-space relationships as the party progressed in different directions. Once again, the concept of privacy and its associated mechanisms can be translated into design principles that reflect changing social interaction.

Territory. A distinction has been made among primary, secondary, and public territories in terms of degree of permanency of ownership and degree of control occupants have over use of a place. One issue concerns the design of territories to ensure that primary, secondary, and public territories are recognized as such and that users have appropriate degrees of control over spaces. As I noted in Chapters 7 and 8, territories serve the purpose of smoothing out social interaction and stabilizing social systems. Primary territories, such as homes, usually serve this function well, since people tend to respect them and since they are easily visible. But secondary and public territories are sometimes more difficult to recognize, and I suspect that environmental design needs to focus on ways to create and define secondary and public territories in clear terms. Thus we need to be sure that different levels of territory are viewed correctly by users and visitors and that they are clearly designated as to their degree and permanence of ownership. If this is not done, conflict is likely to occur, intrusions are more probable, and occupants must go to special, often expensive, lengths to define, manage, and even defend territories. In Chapters 7 and 8, I referred to Newman's (1972) work in urban housing developments, in which he noted problems of design of secondary and public territories, such as entranceways, play areas, and hallways.[3] When these places were not designed in a way that rendered them distinctive and under the control and surveillance of occupants of a building, crime was high and residents felt unsafe. It was, in my terms, a situation in which a secondary territory, presumably under the partial control of occu-

---

[3] See Chapter 7 for criticisms of this work.

pants, was actually a public territory and therefore inappropriately accessible to many people. Thus the design principle is that we must carefully attend to the nature of territories, and we must ensure that primary, public, and secondary territories, if they are to be included, actually permit appropriate levels of control over intended functions. A primary territory, such as a bedroom, that does not permit strong control by occupants because of a design feature will also increase the probability of stress, conflict, and discomfort. I recall my parents talking about the difficulties of living in "railroad flats" or apartments in the tenements of New York in the early 1900s. In these apartments, rooms were laid out in a single file from front to back. If you wanted to go to a back room from the front of the apartment, you had to pass through all the interior rooms, because there was no common hallway. Bedrooms, therefore, did not serve as effective primary territories, because everyone had the right to walk through. You felt that you had no place of your own and that anyone could intrude at any time. In summary, environmental design must consider the territorial functions of places and build into them appropriate mechanisms for making them usable as different types of territories.

A related issue concerns the way in which different people and groups use territories and the nature of their arrangement in space. Zeisel (1974) cited an example from Alexander (1969) of low-income families in Peru who had a systematic arrangement of territories in the home, especially with regard to visitors.

> As someone became increasingly a close family friend, he was allowed to come farther into the home. Boyfriends must stay at the front door; the minister is allowed to enter into the formal parlor or "sala"; close friends of the family can come into the informal living room and kitchen. Alexander's house plans for this group of people reflect this privacy gradient: a front porch with no view of the interior; a "sala" near the entry which one arrives at without passing through any other part of the house; and the family room and kitchen at the back of the house [p. 33].

This interior design represents a concept that meshes appropriate degrees of social interaction with the physical environment.

As another example of the need to design environments in terms of their territorial appropriateness, Zeisel (1973) described how Puerto Rican families in New York City treated their living rooms almost as sacred places. Their most expensive furniture was located there, along with pictures of political heroes and of family members holding diplomas and wearing graduation gowns. Zeisel stated that designing homes with a direct entry into the living room would be inappropriate for these people, since it was a special place not intended to be accessible to casual visitors. Again, we must be sensitive to the requirements of different people to ensure that their territories meet their particular social needs.

This is not to say that environmental designers are insensitive to the importance of creating environments in terms of the "functions" to be performed in them. Thus rooms in the home are designed to serve functions of eating, sleeping, or recreation. Office and factory designs are based on work flow and work relationships; community designers incorporate shopping areas, recreation facilities, and so on. What I speak of here is not only design for "task" or "resource" functions but design for *control over social interaction and stimulation.* If privacy and its associated mechanisms are ignored or rigidly incorporated into designs, or if the meaning of different levels of personal space and territory is not recognized, then people will have to struggle *against the environment* to achieve what they consider to be appropriate degrees of interaction. And, conflict, stress, and other costs are likely to the extent that people have to struggle with inappropriately designed environments. Thus the principle I am trying to state is that environmental design should take into account the dynamics of privacy as a changing process in which people open and close themselves to others, to different degrees at different times, using personal space, territorial behavior, and other mechanisms to achieve a desired degree of privacy.

Environment and Behavior as a Complex System

An important theme of this book is that various mechanisms for the regulation of privacy operate as a coherent *system.* These mechanisms include verbal behavior, paraverbal behavior, nonverbal behavior, personal space, and territorial behavior. These behaviors operate in different combinations, guided by needs and perceptions associated with desired levels of privacy. Thus we are dealing with a complex set of perceptual, motivational, and behavioral processes. I propose that environmental design deal with all these levels simultaneously, not one at a time. We should pose such questions as: To what extent is personal space a more dominant mechanism of privacy regulation by a particular person or family than other behaviors? Under what circumstances is territorial behavior combined with nonverbal behaviors? When territorial mechanisms cannot be employed, what combination of other behaviors is used by members of this group?

There are no simple answers to these questions, but they are intended to reflect the idea that environment design can involve more than only the *physical environment.* It is possible that we can design *environmental systems* in which the environment and various types of behavior are meshed together as a unity. But the designers, in collaboration with researchers, must become specialists in many levels of behavior, not merely those directly associated with the environment. The designers must become tuned in to the behavioral mechanisms for regulating privacy. If they can understand the regulation of privacy, designers may create extremely flexible and responsive environments, because a whole new set of resources will become part of the environmental-design package.

How can the designers get information about behavioral mechanisms? The designers can integrate information from researchers and clients, much as they do now. But other types of information also need to be gathered. The type of query I speak of is more expansive than the typical "user-need" and "user-want" questions that ask: What are the psychological needs of the user that should be satisfied by the environment? What do consumers *want* in the new environment? The direction I propose asks not only these questions but also additional ones. The designers need to deal with the *behaviors* that users employ in order to achieve desired levels of interaction. They should ask, for example, How are territories used? What mechanisms and combinations of mechanisms are employed to regulate social interaction? Is it important for this person, family, or culture to have systematic gradations of territory in homes, or are primary territories, for example, simply not congruent with their style of interaction? *These questions are behavioral and focus on the user as an active, coping organism that interacts with and employs the physical environment and other behaviors in various combinations.* Thus these design questions imply the theme of creating *responsive environments* that users can interact with and that become extensions of their behavioral repertoires. To gain such information may require direct observations, however informal, of user activities, in addition to interviews and questionnaires. People often cannot report accurately what they do or how they behave. It may be necessary to spend time watching them function in their actual environments to understand the total profile of their privacy-regulation system.

If profiles of user needs, desires, and behavioral styles can be determined, the environmental designer can then capitalize on both environmental and behavioral capabilities in an integrated fashion. Thus if one is designing an environment for a group that places considerable value on primary territories, then the design should build this style into the environment. But if a group uses territories in a more casual and changeable fashion, then the environmental design should permit such shifts to occur. Or if a group relies heavily on verbal and paraverbal mechanisms to control interaction, then the design should facilitate the operation of this coping style and not be so concerned with physical territories. So two areas of investigation seem important in environmental design: (1) What is the combination of mechanisms used by the consumer to regulate social interaction? Which behaviors are predominant? Which are unimportant? What seems to be the most appropriate combination most often used? (2) How stable or changeable does the environment need to be in regard to use of these mechanisms? Does the environment need to be a continually fluid one, or can it be relatively fixed, given the group's response profile?

In summary, I propose that environmental designers pay attention to *behavioral styles* of consumers, as well as to their perceptual-cognitive-motivational states. To focus on only one level of behavior misses the point that we are dealing with a complex system of needs, wants, and behavioral styles.

A dilemma arises, however, concerning this approach. Behavioral styles of an individual, a group, or a culture may have evolved because of the press and constraint of environments. For example, members of an inner-city, urban family may have developed other than territorial mechanisms simply because it is impossible to establish territories in densely populated homes. How can persons who sleep several to a room or to a bed use these places as primary territories? Should the practitioner, using my proposed strategy, then conclude that new environments should *not* include primary territories because the people did not use them in the earlier environment? If the answer is reached that no primary territories should be incorporated into the new environment, then the user is locked into a situation in which old environmental constraints are re-created and in which there is no opportunity to change his or her life-style. The path out of this dilemma is not totally clear, but at least two steps may be necessary:

1. *Maximize environmental capabilities.* Although people may not employ all mechanisms to the same degree, it may be wise to allow for the possibility that more than the current repertoire can be used. Thus, even though primary territories may not be a central concern, designs might allow for the possibility of their development in a flexible fashion at some future time. In this way, if people have inclinations toward territorial usage, or if a norm gradually develops that involves use of territories, then the environment will be sufficiently adaptive to permit that to happen. And, if they don't develop such mechanisms, then they at least are not locked into using them. Thus environments should not only be *responsive*, but they should also permit a degree of "evolutionary flexibility" and growth over time.

2. *Train people to use environments.* Sommer (1972) highlighted the idea that people often are overly passive and not willing to reshape environments, and they adapt too quickly to even the most undesirable places. For example, I have been in several conferences at which the arrangements of tables and chairs were simply not conducive to free discussion (they represented the janitor's idea of how our meeting should be organized!). Yet people hardly ever protest such arrangements or ask for a redesign of the place. They are willing to stretch their necks to see one another, speak to people sitting behind them by twisting around, fidget in uncomfortable chairs, and so on. We are simply unwilling to *act* on our environments to make them fit what we desire. Because of this problem, Sommer called for environmental workshops to sensitize people to possibilities for acting on and shaping environments. He described one such

workshop designed to make teachers more aware of their classroom environments. Discussions were held about seating arrangements, personal-space distances, and the effect of classroom configurations on student participation. Also, a series of awareness sessions was held in which teachers adopted the role of small children, sat in their chairs, and used the classroom environment much as children do to heighten their sensitivity to their environment from other than their own perspective.

In a different setting, Sommer held workshops with hospital staff members. Nurses and other personnel were placed in the role of patients as a way of giving them a different perspective on the hospital environment. In Sommer's words:

> As turn-on devices we used such prosthetic aids as crutches, wheelchairs, and gurneys. These produced some interesting perceptual experiences which were shared with the group at large. Distances seemed three times as long on crutches as they had previously. It took a very long time to go down the hallway in a wheelchair; when one person wheeled another, the speed of passage was very important. Wheeling a person at ordinary walking speed seemed much too fast; the person in the chair felt as if he were a bowling ball going down the alley. Tall men were particularly bothered by being looked down on as they sat in a wheelchair; this did not seem to bother short men, who apparently were used to being looked down on. Riding on the gurney, a long flat table with wheels, made a number of people nauseous; the ceiling became the visual environment and the overhead lights went flashing by *bang bang bang* in a very annoying manner [p. 44].[4]

But increasing environmental sensitivity is only a first step. One of our guiding themes is that people actively use and shape their environments, so that, ultimately, one goal of workshops should be to teach people how to use their environments more effectively. We might develop environmental user manuals, just as we use instruction books with new electric toasters and washing machines. More analogous would be learning how to use a stereo system, for the rules and procedures are less fixed, and the sound quality must be adapted to room and acoustic configurations, user preferences, specific mood states, nature and quality of the recording, and other factors. Many new stereo users simply do not appreciate the wide options available to help them create variety or the adjustments that are possible to fit changing personal moods, recording artists, and record quality. So it is with people and environments. Aside from stereotyped ideas we all have about the location of furniture, places for privacy, and kitchen layout, few people are really aware of possibilities for shaping our environments. Furthermore, only a few of us consciously see the complex interplay of environment with verbal, nonverbal, personal-space, and territorial behaviors. How many people are sensitive

[4] From *Design Awareness*, by R. Sommer, 1972. Reprinted by permission of Rinehart Press, a division of Holt, Rinehart and Winston, Inc.

to the fact that various personal distances change possibilities for nonverbal and other forms of communication, such as body heat, smell, and touch? How many people arrange their homes or offices in terms of personal-space concepts? How many families reshape their environmental life-style to match the different needs of growing children, or as they move from being middle aged to being elderly? Without setting down specific rules, I believe that environmental awareness and environmental-usage training might help people to better use, shape, and reshape their environments.

There is another feature of the environment as a complex system that needs to be considered, beyond the notion of many levels of behavior fitting together. Willems (1973, 1974) stressed the theme that a change in one part of the environmental system can have serious and reverberating effects, often unpredictable, on other parts of the system. It is easy to point to dramatic examples in the physical sphere. The increased use of detergent soaps often ends up with soapsuds in water supplies, insecticides sometimes speed up evolutionary processes and produce resistant strains of insects, and horrendous problems of disposal and pollution are sometimes created by new forms of wastes. But aren't such reverberations and ecological "stupidities" possible and even evident for social processes? Willems gave several examples of these social reverberations, one drawn from Turnbull (1972), who studied the impact of governmental relocation of the Ik tribal group in Uganda, Africa. The Ik lived a simple, cooperative life, hunted for their food, resided in small tribal bands, and were a kind and good-natured people. For a number of reasons, including conservation of land and wildlife, the Ugandan government declared their land a national park and forced them to live at the edges of the park. They were prevented from returning to their homes and were encouraged by the government to become farmers. Over time, Ik social life disintegrated. Willems' (1973) summary of Turnbull's account is vivid:

> The social and behavioral fabric of the Ik society fell apart completely. Malicious competition replaced cooperation. Hostility and treachery replaced kindness. Laughter became a raucous response to the misfortunes of people, rather than an expression of good will and humor. Members of the group were left to die and sometimes goaded to die instead of being nursed and helped. Strong isolation in booby-trapped enclaves replaced openness and companionship between people [p. 156].

Thus a seemingly simple relocation produced a change in one part of a complex system that reverberated throughout the group's total social life and disrupted a once stable system.

In a sense, much of what has been proposed really deals with interpersonal communication. The goals of the system for the regulation of privacy include management of interpersonal communication, regulation of self/other boundaries, and enhancement of people's responsiveness to one another. The use of the physical environment is part of a complex interpersonal-communication system. Applying environmental design and training people to use their environments really deal with effective social communication; that is, the physical environment becomes part of a complex behavioral repertoire that people use to deal with one another.

Evaluation of Environments

An important theme that I have dealt with is that privacy regulation is a dynamic and changing process. Different mechanisms to control interaction are used at different times, there is a continual monitoring of how well the system is working, and readjustments in behavior are made when necessary. These notions of monitoring, assessment, and readjustment are compatible with the increased call in recent years for the "evaluation" of environmental designs. Evaluators should pose the questions "Is the environment being used in the way it was intended?" "Does the environment satisfy user needs?" "Are there inefficiencies in the use of the environment?"

People realize that it is not enough to create new environments; we must also learn how well they work. Furthermore, designers and researchers have come to realize that people don't always use environments in predictable ways—sometimes because the environments don't fit their styles of life, and sometimes because environments give them opportunities that couldn't be predicted in advance. Therefore, if we are to learn how to design future environments better, then it is important that we see how people use places created for them.

Because we believe that the process of privacy regulation is an ongoing one that stretches over long periods of time, and that its immediate and long-term costs may be quite different (recall the absence of short-term crowding effects but the presence of longer-term ones), it seems sensible to build in a *continual and repeated evaluation* of designed environments. I propose that evaluation and assessment of how well environments are working be done *before* they are constructed, *soon after*, and over their *longer-term history*.

Design-Stage Evaluation of Environments. Zeisel (1974) described the first stages of environmental design as *programming* (during which design objectives, goals, and constraints are specified) and the next stages as *design* (during which specific decisions are made that satisfy the overall goals and criteria). The environmental designer can move, in these stages, toward incorporating knowledge about user privacy-regulation styles, needs, and desires. Even at this early point, it seems possible to *consciously, deliberately,* and *systematically* build in an evaluation process to deal with the question

"Does the proposed design look as if it will fit the projected social-regulation style of the users?" According to Conway (1974), it is possible to ask and answer such questions in advance of actual environmental construction. We can do it qualitatively and do our best to figure out whether or not the proposed system will work. In some instances, we may be able to simulate the system on a computer, if enough quantified information exists, and literally try out several variations—in much the same way as in aircraft design and in space-exploration programs, where simulations are done in advance of actual flights.

To give a concrete example, if an office team had operated for several years in a crowded, noisy, unpartitioned office with desks butted up against one another, and a new design was proposed for partitions to separate people, then several factors could be considered in advance of implementing the design. If co-workers had relied on close verbal contact to do business, to take informal breaks, to share monitoring of telephone calls, to gossip, and to help one another with work overloads, then a new design might be predicted to radically upset a stable privacy system that had developed over the years. With separate offices, more space, and lower noise levels, workers may not have been able to interact in the same way and may have had to struggle to eliminate physical barriers. In addition, their work patterns may have become more separate and less communal, and group feeling may not have been maintained because of newly imposed barriers between them. Now, I do not intend to prejudge the value of such changes for organizational efficiency, individual health, and other features of performance. I only wish to emphasize that changes in environmental design may have an impact on a total system and that some assessment of that impact might be made *in advance* of design changes, as long as one is sensitive to the privacy-regulation system used by people.

I do not necessarily suggest creating an exact match between behavioral styles and environmental design—only an analysis of possible discrepancies. To the extent that discrepancies exist, one might predict (1) a period of adaptation and adjustment by users and (2) possible long-term costs, as reflected in performance, illness, and psychological well-being. Thus one level of environmental evaluation can occur *prior* to implementation of a design.

Immediate Postdesign Evaluation of Environments.   Once an environment is created and has begun to be used by people, we can begin a short-term assessment process, in which we look at how the environment is used after a period of initial adaptation and adjustment. This short-term evaluation is analogous to a "shakedown cruise" of a ship (Conway, 1974), for we give the environment and its users a short period of time together and then assess the state of the system. For example, it may well be that our hypothetical office redesign showed problems of communication and performance very soon after the design was implemented. Or it might be that no such effects took place and that the goal of the environment was achieved. Again, the process of evaluation involves assessing the fit between what was intended and what resulted, as well as sensing unanticipated outcomes.

There has been a great interest in the environment and behavior field in postdesign evaluation, partly to correct flaws in the system and partly to gain information for future designs. But I also wish to emphasize that postdesign evaluation should not be just a one-shot, short-term process. It is equally important to look at the impact of a designed environment over a long-run time period.

Long-Term Evaluation of Environments.   Research that I reviewed in earlier chapters and my own theoretical framework suggest that there should be both short- and long-term environmental adaptations and costs. For example, research has indicated that there is short-term adaptation to noise and crowding but long-term negative outcomes (often of a delayed nature) in some circumstances. Thus short-term outcomes do not always predict long-term ones. Or, in our hypothetical office redesign, production may be enhanced by environmental changes, but we can also ask about what new modes of operating are called for by the new design, whether workers must develop new techniques for gaining or avoiding contact with others, whether they may have to rely more (or less) on verbal or nonverbal behavioral mechanisms, and so on. And, if there are dramatic changes in their behavioral styles, are there short- and long-term effects? Does workers' efficiency, health, or conflict rise and then fall over a period of time or gradually rise after an initially low level, and can shifts in attitude, morale, and efficiency be related to newly required coping mechanisms? Thus I propose a *continuing* evaluation of privacy-regulation systems on a longitudinal basis. Tapping into environmental systems at only a single point in time, no matter *when* it is, may mask important adjustment processes and thereby render an evaluation incomplete.

The strategy proposed here is not intended to rule out the ultimate criteria of productivity, efficiency, or health. Rather, I suggest that such criteria be linked with how people manage and pace their social interaction with one another. Naturally, this strategy is a large task, and practitioners may well see it as impractical. Although perhaps true at the level of detailed implementation, my position should be viewed as a point of departure and as a philosophy of environmental evaluation, not as a rigid prescription that must be followed in every case. What I am saying is that it is an oversimplification to state that the concept of "environmental evaluation" means only one thing. What is called for is an evaluation that (1) describes how people use various coping mechanisms to achieve control of interaction, (2) shows how environmental designs affect these mechanisms, and (3) tracks short- and long-term, direct and indirect effects of environments on these mechanisms and on various costs.

Studer (1970, 1973) offered a strategy within the spirit of my approach. Studer is a systems-oriented, environmental "interventionist" who believes that designers should take an active role in providing people with new, dynamic, and changeable environments. Environments should not, he says, be static and unchanging, but they should be continual and ongoing experiments that are modified according to their impact and how people cope with them. Studer recognized potential ecological dangers signaled by Willems (1973, 1974) and proposed a behavioral approach that minimizes the long-term effects of ecological stupidity by viewing environmental design as a dynamic process. His orientation is basically Skinnerian, and he attempts to find connections between behavior and environmental contingencies or reinforcements. Thus, for Studer, the goal of environmental design is to create reinforcing environments that are linked to the behavior of their users. To accomplish this connection, he proposed a series of design steps:

1. A baseline empirical analysis of environment-behavior-reinforcement linkages. (This involves a search for behavioral styles and environmental satisfactions and dissatisfactions that people have.)
2. Theoretical modeling of a relationship between these factors and computer simulation and testing of alternative design possibilities. (This represents a tryout of alternative environments, in simulated form, to discover the best possible fit of user styles and environmental factors that would maximize reinforcement outcomes.)
3. Actual design of environments.
4. Assessment of outcomes.
5. A continual recycling through earlier stages, gradually creating new environments that approach an optimal situation over time.

The last step—continued manipulation of environments and assessment of impacts—is critical, because it implies that environment-behavior relationships are dynamic and are not a static input-output process. In summary, Studer proposes continued approximation and shifting of environmental design as contingencies, circumstances, and group structure change. He also proposes repeated assessments of the state of the system and incorporation of new environmental contingencies as the people-environment system changes.

This chapter has not laid down a set of technical guidelines or "how to do it" procedures for using the concepts of privacy, territoriality, personal space, and crowding in environmental design. It has only attempted a preliminary translation of these concepts into real-world applications. And, this translation has been largely in terms of a point of view and a way of thinking about person-environment relationships. My main goal has been to provide a framework within which these basic concepts could be used in an integrated way. I hope that readers will see some value in what has been proposed and will use these ideas as a springboard to create better environments for more people.

References

Adams, J. R. Review of *Defensible space. Man Environment Systems,* 1973, *3*(4), 267–268.

Aiello, J. R. A test of equilibrium theory: Visual interaction in relation to orientation, distance and sex interactants. *Psychonomic Science,* 1972, *27*(6), 335–336.

Aiello, J. R., & Cooper, R. E. The use of personal space as a function of social affect. *Proceedings of the Annual Convention of the American Psychological Association,* 1972, *7*(Pt. 1), 207–208.

Aiello, J. R., & Jones, S. E. Field study of the proxemic behavior of young school children in three subcultural groups. *Journal of Personality and Social Psychology,* 1971, *19,* 351–356.

Albert, S., & Dabbs, J. M., Jr. Physical distance and persuasion. *Journal of Personality and Social Psychology,* 1970, *15,* 265–270,

Alexander, C. Houses generated by patterns. Center for Environmental Structure, Berkeley, 1969.

Allgeier, A. R., & Byrne, D. Attraction toward the opposite sex as a determinant of physical proximity. *Journal of Social Psychology,* 1973, *90,* 213–219.

Almond, R., & Esser, A. H. Tablemate choice of psychiatric patients: A technique for measuring social contact. *Journal of Nervous and Mental Disease,* 1965, *141,* 68–82.

Altman, I. Territorial behavior in humans: An analysis of the concept. In L. Pastalan and D. H. Carson (Eds.), *Spatial behavior of older people.* Ann Arbor: The University of Michigan-Wayne State University Press, 1970. Pp. 1–24.

Altman, I. Some perspectives on the study of man-environment phenomena. *Representative Research in Social Psychology,* 1973, *4*(1), 109–126.

Altman, I., & Haythorn, W. W. The ecology of isolated groups. *Behavioral Science,* 1967, *12,* 169–182.

Altman, I., Nelson, P. A., & Lett, E. E. The ecology of home environments. *Catalog of Selected Documents in Psychology.* Washington, D.C.: American Psychological Association, Spring 1972.

221

Altman, I., & Taylor, D. A. *Social penetration: The development of interpersonal relationships.* New York: Holt, Rinehart and Winston, 1973.

Altman, I., Taylor, D. A., & Wheeler, L. Ecological aspects of group behavior in social isolation. *Journal of Applied Social Psychology,* 1971, *1,* 76–100.

Ardrey, R. *The territorial imperative.* New York: Atheneum, 1966.

Ardrey, R. *The social contract.* New York: Atheneum, 1970.

Argyle, M., & Dean, J. Eye-contact, distance and affiliation. *Sociometry,* 1965, *28,* 289–304.

Argyle, M., & Ingham, R. Gaze, mutual gaze and proximity. *Semiotica,* 1972, *6*(1), 32–50.

Argyle, M., & Kendon, A. The experimental analysis of social performance. In L. Berkowitz (Ed.), *Advances in experimental social psychology.* New York: Academic Press, 1967. Pp. 55–91.

Bailey, K. G., Hartnett, J. J., & Gibson, S.W. Implied threat and the territorial factor in personal space. *Psychological Reports,* 1972, *30,* 263–270.

Barash, D. P. Human ethology: Personal space reiterated. *Environment and Behavior,* 1973, *5*(1), 67–73.

Barefoot, J. C., Hoople, H., & McClay, D. Avoidance of an act which would violate personal space. *Psychonomic Science,* 1972, *28,* 205–206.

Barker, R. G. *Ecological psychology.* Stanford: Stanford University Press, 1968.

Barker, R. G., & Gump, P. *Big school, small school.* Stanford: Stanford University Press, 1964.

Bass, B. M., & Klubeck, S. Effects of seating arrangement on leaderless group discussions. *Journal of Abnormal and Social Psychology,* 1952, *47,* 724–726.

Bass, M. H., & Weinstein, M. S. Early development of interpersonal distance in children. *Canadian Journal of Behavioral Science,* 1971, *3*(4), 368–376.

Batchelor, J. P., & Goethals, G. R. Spatial arrangements in freely formed groups. *Sociometry,* 1972, *35*(2), 270–279.

Bates, A. Privacy—A useful concept? *Social Forces,* 1964, *42,* 432.

Baum, A., & Valins, S. Residential environments, group size and crowding. *Proceedings, 81st Annual Convention, American Psychological Association,* 1973, 211–212.

Baxter, J. C. Interpersonal spacing in natural settings. *Sociometry,* 1970, *33,* 444–456.

Baxter, J. C., & Deanovich, B. S. Anxiety arousing effects of inappropriate crowding. *Journal of Consulting and Clinical Psychology,* 1970, *35,* 174–178.

Beardsley, E. L. Privacy: Autonomy and selective disclosure. In J. R. Pennock and J. W. Chapman (Eds.), *Privacy.* New York: Atherton Press, 1971. Pp. 56–70.

Becker, F. D. Study of spatial markers. *Journal of Personality and Social Psychology,* 1973, *26*(3), 439–445.

Becker, F. D., & Mayo, C. Delineating personal distance and territoriality. *Environment and Behavior,* 1971, *3,* 375–381.

Bergman, B. A. The effects of group size, personal space and success-failure on physiological arousal, test performance and questionnaire responses. Doctoral dissertation, Temple University, Philadelphia: University microfilm, 1971. No. 71–31072.

Bickman, L., Teger, A., Gabriele, T., McLaughlin, C., Berger, M., & Sunaday, E. Dormitory density and helping behavior. *Environment and Behavior,* 1973, *5*(4), 465–490.

Biderman, A., Louria, M., & Bacchus, J. *Historical incidents of extreme overcrowding.* Washington, D.C.: Bureau of Social Science, 1963.

Birdwhistell, R. L. *Kinesics and context.* Philadelphia: University of Pennsylvania Press, 1970.

Blood, R. O., & Livant, W. P. The use of space within the cabin group. *Journal of Social Issues,* 1957, *13,* 47–53.

Blumenthal, R., & Meltzoff, J. Social schemas and perceptual accuracy in schizophrenia. *British Journal of Social and Clinical Psychology,* 1967, *6,* 119–128.

Booth, A., & Welch, S. The effects of crowding: A cross-national study. Paper presented at American Psychological Association, Montreal, Canada, 1973.

Bordua, D. J. Juvenile delinquency and "anomie": An attempt at replication. *Social Problems,* 1958, *6,* 230–239.

Bossard, J. H. S., & Boll, E. S. *Ritual in family living.* Philadelphia: University of Pennsylvania Press, 1950.

Bowerman, W. R. Ambulatory velocity in crowded and uncrowded conditions. *Perceptual and Motor Skills,* 1973, *36*(1), 107–111.

Brower, S. N. Territoriality, the exterior spaces, the signs we learn to read. *Landscape,* 1965, *15,* 9–12.

Burt, W. H. Territoriality and home range concepts as applied to mammals. *Journal of Mammalogy,* 1943, *24,* 346–352.

Byrne, D. The influence of propinquity and opportunities for interaction on classroom relationships. *Human Relations,* 1961, *14,* 63–69.

Byrne, D., Baskett, D. G., & Hodges, L. Behavioral indicators of interpersonal attraction. *Journal of Applied Social Psychology,* 1971, *1,* 137–149.

Byrne, D., & Buehler, J. A. A note on the influence of propinquity upon acquaintanceships. *Journal of Abnormal and Social Psychology,* 1955, *51,* 147–148.

Calhoun, J. B. A behavioral sink. In E. L. Bliss (Ed.), *Roots of behavior.* New York: Harper & Row, 1962. Pp. 295–315. (a)

Calhoun, J. B. Population density and social pathology. *Scientific American,* 1962. Pp. 139–148. (b)

Calhoun, J. B. Space and the strategy of life. In A. H. Esser (Ed.), *Environment and behavior: The use of space by animals and men.* New York: Plenum, 1971. Pp. 329–387.

Canter, D., & Canter, S. Close together in Tokyo. *Design and Environment,* 1971, *2,* 60–63.

Carey, G. W. Density, crowding, stress and the ghetto. *American Behavioral Scientist,* 1972, *15,* 495–508.

Carpenter, C. R. Territoriality: A review of concepts and problems. In A. Roe and G. G. Simpson (Eds.), *Behavior and evolution.* New Haven: Yale University Press, 1958. Pp. 224–250.

Carson, D. Population concentration and human stress. In B. F. Rourke (Ed.), *Explorations in the psychology of stress and anxiety.* Ontario: Longmans Canada Limited, 1969.

Cassel, J. Physical illness in response to stress. In S. Levine and N. A. Scotch (Eds.), *Social stress.* Chicago: Aldine, 1970. Pp. 189–209.

Cassel, J. Health consequences of population density and crowding. In R. Revelle (Ed.), *Rapid population growth: Consequences and policy implications.* Baltimore: Johns Hopkins University Press, 1971.

Castell, R. Effect of familiar and unfamiliar environments on proximity behavior of young children. *Journal of Experimental Child Psychology,* 1970, *9*(3), 342–347.

Cavan, R. S. *Suicide.* Chicago: University of Chicago Press, 1928.

Cavan, S. Interaction in home territories. *Berkeley Journal of Sociology,* 1963, *8,* 17–32.

Cavan, S. *Liquor license.* Chicago: Aldine, 1966.

Chapin, F. S. Some housing factors related to mental hygiene. *Journal of Social Issues,* 1951, *7,* 164–171.

Chermayeff, S., & Alexander, N. Y. *Community and privacy: Toward a new architecture of humanism.* New York: Doubleday, 1963.

Cheyne, J. A., & Efran, M. G. The effect of spatial and interpersonal variables on the invasion of group control territories. *Sociometry,* 1972, *35*(3), 477–489.

Choldin, H. M. Population density and social relations. Paper presented at Population Association of America, Toronto, Canada, April 1972.

Christian, J. J., Flyger, V., and Davis, D. E. Factors in the mass mortality of a herd of Sika deer Cervus Nippon. *Chesapeake Science,* 1960, *1,* 79–95.

Comer, R. J., & Piliavin, J. A. The effects of physical deviance upon face-to-face interaction: The other side. *Journal of Personality and Social Psychology,* 1972, *23*(1), 33–39.

Conway, D. *Social science and design.* Washington, D.C.: American Institute of Architects, 1974.

Cook, M. Experiments on orientation and proxemics. *Human Relations,* 1970, *23*(1), 61–76.

Dabbs, J. M., Jr. Sex, setting, and reactions to crowding on sidewalks. *Proceedings, 80th Annual Convention, American Psychological Association,* 1972, 205–206.

Daves, W. F., & Swaffer, P. W. Effect of room size on critical interpersonal distance. *Perceptual and Motor Skills,* 1971, *33*(3 pt. 1), 926.

Davis, A., & Olesen, V. Communal work and living: Notes of the dynamics of social distance and social space. *Sociology and Social Research,* 1971, *55,* 191–202.

Davis, D. E. Physiological effects of continued crowding. In A. H. Esser (Ed.), *Behavior and environment: The use of space by animals and men.* New York: Plenum, 1971. Pp. 133–147.

Day, A. T., & Day, L. H. Cross-national comparison of population density. *Science,* 1973, *181,* 1016–1023.

DeLong, A. J. Dominance-territorial relations in a small group. *Environment and Behavior,* 1970, *2,* 190–191.

DeLong, A. J. Dominance-territorial criteria and small group structure. *Comparative Group Studies,* 1971, *2,* 235–265.

DeLong, A. J. Territorial stability and hierarchical formation. *Small Group Behavior,* 1973, *4*(1), 56–63.

Desor, J. A. Toward a psychological theory of crowding. *Journal of Personality and Social Psychology,* 1972, *21,* 79–83.

Dinges, N. G., & Oetting, E. R. Interaction distance anxiety in the counseling dyad. *Journal of Counseling Psychology,* 1972, *19*(2), 146–149.

Dosey, M. A., & Meisels, M. Personal space and self-protection. *Journal of Personality and Social Psychology,* 1969, *11,* 93–97.

Downs, R. M., & Stea, D. *Image and environment: Cognitive mapping and spatial behavior.* Chicago: Aldine, 1973.

Draper, P. Crowding among hunter-gatherers: The !Kung Bushmen. *Science,* 1973, *182,* 301–303.

Dreyer, C. A., & Dreyer, A. S. Family dinner time as a unique behavior habitat. *Family Process,* 1973, *12,* 291–301.

Dubos, R. *Man adapting.* New Haven, Conn.: Yale University Press, 1965.

Dubos, R. *So human an animal.* New York: Charles Scribner's Sons, 1968.

DuHamel, T. R., & Jarmon, H. Social schemata of emotionally disturbed boys and their male siblings. *Journal of Consulting and Clinical Psychology,* 1971, *36*(2), 281–285.

Duke, M. P., & Nowicki, S., Jr. A new measure and social learning model for interpersonal distance. *Journal of Experimental Research in Personality,* 1972, *6,* 1–16.

Duncan, S., Jr. Nonverbal communication. *Psychological Bulletin,* 1969, *72*(2), 118–137.

Edney, J. J. Place and space: The effects of experience with a physical locale. *Journal of Experimental Social Psychology,* 1972, *8,* 124–135. (a)

Edney, J. J. Property, possession and permanence: A field study in human territoriality. *Journal of Applied Social Psychology,* 1972, *3*(3), 275–282. (b)

Edney, J. J. Human territories as organizers: Some social and psychological consequences of attachment to place. *Environment and Behavior,* 1975. In press.

Edney, J. J., & Jordan-Edney, N. L. Territorial spacing on a beach. *Sociometry,* 1974, *37*(1), 92–103.

Edwards, D. J. A. Approaching the unfamiliar: A study of human interaction distances. *Journal of Behavioral Sciences,* 1972, *1*(4), 249–250.

Efran, M. G., & Cheyne, J. A. Shared space: The cooperative control of spatial areas by two interacting individuals. *Canadian Journal of Behavioral Science,* 1973, *5,* 201–210.

Efran, M. G., & Cheyne, J. A. Affective concomitants of the invasion of shared space: Behavioral, physiological and verbal indicators. *Journal of Personality and Social Psychology,* 1974, *29*(2), 219–226.

Ehrlich, P. *The population bomb.* New York: Ballantine, 1968.

Eibl-Eibesfeldt, I. *Ethology: The biology of behavior.* New York: Holt, Rinehart and Winston, 1970.

Ekman, P., Ellsworth, P., & Friesen, W. V. *The face and emotion: Guidelines for research and integration of findings.* New York: Pergamon Press, 1972.

Ekman, P., & Friesen, W. V. The repertoire of nonverbal behavior: Categories, origins, usage and codings. *Semiotica,* 1969, *1*(1), 49–97.

Ekman, P., & Friesen, W. V. Hand movements. *Journal of Communication,* 1972, *22,* 353–374.

Ekman, P., Friesen, W. V., & Tomkins, S. S. Facial affect scoring technique (FAST): A first validity study. *Semiotica,* 1971, *3,* 37–58.

Elms, A. Horoscopes and Ardrey. *Psychology Today,* 1972, *6,* 36.

Engebretson, D., & Fullmer, D. Cross-cultural differences in territoriality: Interaction distances of native Japanese, Hawaii-Japanese, and American Caucasians. *Journal of Cross-Cultural Psychology,* 1970, *1*(3), 261–269.

Esser, A. H. Dominance hierarchy and clinical course of psychiatrically hospitalized boys. *Child Development,* 1968, *39*(1), 147–157.

Esser, A. H. Interactional hierarchy and power structure on a psychiatric ward. In S. J. Hutt and C. Hutt (Eds.), *Behavior studies in psychiatry.* New York: Oxford University Press, 1970. Pp. 25–29.

Esser, A. H. Social pollution. *Social Education,* 1971, *35*(1), 10–18. (a)

Esser, A. H. The psychopathology of crowding in institutions for the mentally ill and retarded. Paper presented at Fifth World Congress of Psychiatry, Mexico City, 1971. (b)

Esser, A. H. A biosocial perspective on crowding. In J. F. Wohlwill and D. H. Carson (Eds.), *Environment and the social sciences: Perspectives and applications.* Washington, D.C.: American Psychological Association, 1972. Pp. 15–28.

Esser, A. H. Cottage fourteen: Dominance and territoriality in a group of institutionalized boys. *Small Group Behavior,* 1973, *4,* 131–146. (a)

Esser, A. H. Experiences of crowding: Illustration of a paradigm for man-environment relations. *Representative Research in Social Psychology,* 1973, *4,* 207–218. (b)

Esser, A. H., Chamberlain, A. S., Chapple, E. D., & Kline, N. S. Territoriality of patients on a research ward. In J. Wortis (Ed.), *Recent advances in biological psychiatry.* New York: Plenum, 1965. Pp. 37–44.

Estes, B. W., & Rush, D. Social schemas: A developmental study. *Journal of Psychology,* 1971, *78*(1), 119–123.

Evans, G. W., & Howard, R. B. Personal space. *Psychological Bulletin,* 1973, *80*(4), 334–344.

Exline, R., & Eldridge, C. Effects of two patterns of a speaker's visual behavior upon the perception of the authenticity of his verbal message. Paper presented at Eastern Psychological Association, Boston, 1967.

Exline, R., Gray, D., & Schuette, D. Visual behavior in a dyad as affected by interview content and sex of respondent. *Journal of Personality and Social Psychology,* 1965, *1*, 201–209.

Faris, R., & Dunham, H. W. *Mental disorders in urban areas* (2nd ed.). Chicago: Phoenix Books, 1965.

Felipe, N., & Sommer, R. Invasions of personal space. *Social Problems,* 1966, *14*, 206–214.

Festinger, L. A theory of social comparison processes. *Human Relations,* 1954, *7*, 117–140.

Fisher, R. L. Social schema of normal and disturbed school children. *Journal of Educational Psychology,* 1967, *58*, 88–92.

Forston, R. F., & Larson, C. U. The dynamics of space. *Journal of Communication,* 1968, *18*, 109–116.

Frankel, A. S., & Barrett, J. Variations in personal space as a function of authoritarianism, self-esteem and racial characteristics of a stimulus situation. *Journal of Consulting and Clinical Psychology,* 1971, *37*(1), 95–98.

Frede, M. C., Gautney, D. B., & Baxter, J. C. Relationships between body image boundary and interaction patterns on the Maps Test. *Journal of Consulting and Clinical Psychology,* 1968, *32*, 575–578.

Freedman, J. L. The effects of population density on humans. In J. Fawcett (Ed.), *Psychological perspectives on population.* New York: Basic Books, 1972.

Freedman, J. L., Klevansky, S., & Ehrlich, P. I. The effect of crowding on human task performance. *Journal of Applied Social Psychology,* 1971, *1*, 7–26.

Freedman, J. L., Levy, A. S., Buchanan, R. W., & Price, J. Crowding and human aggressiveness. *Journal of Experimental Social Psychology,* 1972, *8*, 528–548.

Fry, A. M., & Willis, F. N. Invasion of personal space as a function of the age of the invader. *Psychological Record,* 1971, *2*(3), 385–389.

Galle, O. R., Gove, W. R., & McPherson, J. M. Population density and pathology: What are the relationships for man? *Science,* 1972, *176*, 23–30.

Gardin, H., Kaplan, C. J., Firestone, I. J., & Cowan, G. A. Proxemic effects on cooperation, attitude, and approach-avoidance in a prisoner's dilemma game. *Journal of Personality and Social Psychology,* 1973, *27*, 13–19.

Garfinkel, H. Studies of the routine grounds of everyday activities. *Social Problems,* 1964, *11*, 225–250.

Glass, D. C., & Singer, J. E. *Urban stress.* New York: Academic Press, 1972.

Goffman, E. *The presentation of self in everyday life.* New York: Doubleday, Anchor Books, 1959.

Goffman, E. *Asylums.* New York: Doubleday, 1961.

Goffman, E. *Behavior in public places.* New York: The Free Press, 1963.

Goffman, E. *Relations in public.* New York: Basic Books, 1971.

Goldberg, G. N., Kiesler, C. A., & Collins, B. E. Visual behavior and face-to-face distance during interaction. *Sociometry,* 1969, *32*, 43–53.

Goldring, P. Role of distance and posture in the evaluation of interactions. *Proceedings of the 75th Annual Convention, American Psychological Association,* 1967.

Greenbie, B. B. A tale of two worlds: Group territory and social space. *Man-Environment Systems*, 1973, *2*, 365–369.

Griffitt, W., & Veitch, R. Hot and crowded: Influence of population density and temperature on interpersonal affective behavior. *Journal of Personality and Social Psychology*, 1971, *17*, 92–98.

Gross, H. Privacy and autonomy. In J. R. Pennock and J. W. Chapman (Eds.), *Privacy*. New York: Atherton Press, 1971. Pp. 169–181.

Guardo, C. J., & Meisels, M. Child-parent spatial patterns under praise and reproof. *Developmental Psychology*, 1971, *5*(2), 365. (a)

Guardo, C. J., & Meisels, M. Factor structure of children's personal space schemata. *Child Development*, 1971, *42*, 1307–1312. (b)

Haase, R. F. The relationship of sex and instructional set to the regulation of interpersonal interaction distance in a counseling analogue. *Journal of Counseling Psychology*, 1970, *17*, 233–236.

Haase, R. F., & DiMattia, D. J. Proxemic behavior: Counselor, administrator, and client preference for seating arrangement in dyadic interaction. *Journal of Counseling Psychology*, 1970, *17*(4), 319–325.

Haase, R. F., & Pepper, D. T., Jr. Nonverbal components of empathic communication. *Journal of Counseling Psychology*, 1972, *19*(5), 417–424.

Hall, E. T. *The silent language.* New York: Doubleday, 1959.

Hall, E. T. *The hidden dimension.* New York: Doubleday, 1966.

Hamid, P. N. Birth order and family schemata. *Perceptual and Motor Skills*, 1970, *31*(3), 807–810.

Hare, A. P., & Bales, R. F. Seating position and small group interaction. *Sociometry*, 1963, *26*, 480–486.

Hartnett, J. J., Bailey, F., & Gibson, W. Personal space as influenced by sex and type of movement. *Journal of Psychology*, 1970, *76*(2), 139–144.

Haythorn, W. W., & Altman, I. Together in isolation. *Transaction*, 1967, *4*, 18–22.

Hazard, J. N. Furniture arrangement as a symbol of judicial roles. *A Review of General Semantics*, 1962, *19*(2), 181–188.

Hearn, G. Leadership and the spatial factor in small groups. *Journal of Abnormal and Social Psychology*, 1957, *54*, 269–272.

Hediger, H. *Wild animals in captivity.* London: Butterworth and Co., 1950.

Hediger, H. P. The evolution of territorial behavior. In S. L. Washburn (Ed.), *Social life of early man.* New York: Wennergren Foundation, 1961.

Helson, H. *Adaptation level theory.* New York: Harper & Row, 1964.

Henderson, E. H., Long, B. H., & Ziller, R. C. Self-social constructs of achieving and non-achieving readers. *The Reading Teacher*, 1965, Autumn, 114–118.

Hereford, S. M., Cleland, C. C., & Fellner, M. Territoriality and scent-marking: A study of profoundly retarded enuretics and encopretics. *American Journal of Mental Deficiency*, 1973, *77*(4), 426–430.

Hildreth, A. M., Derogatis, L. R., & McCusker, K. Body buffer zone and violence: A reassessment and confirmation. *American Journal of Psychiatry*, 1971, *127*, 1641–1645.

Hill, A. R. Visibility and privacy. In D. V. Canter (Ed.), *Architectural psychology.* London: RIBA Publications, 1969, Pp. 39–43.

Hillier, W. In defence of space. *RIBA Journal*, 1973, November.

Hoppe, R. A., Greene, M. S., & Kenney, J. W. Territorial markers: Additional findings. *Journal of Social Psychology*, 1972, *88*, 305–306.

Horowitz, M. J. Spatial behavior and psychopathology. *The Journal of Nervous and Mental Disease*, 1968, *146*, 24–35.

Horowitz, M. J., Duff, D. F., & Stratton, L. O. Body-buffer zone. *Archives of General Psychiatry*, 1964, *11*, 651–656.

Howard, D. *Territory and bird life.* London: Collins Publication Co., 1948.

Howells, L. T., & Becker, S. W. Seating arrangement and leadership emergence. *Journal of Abnormal and Social Psychology*, 1962, *64*, 148–150.

Hutt, C., & McGrew, W. C. Effects of group density on social behavior in humans. Paper presented at Association for the Study of Animal Behavior, Symposium on Changes in Behavior with Population Density, Oxford, England, July 1967.

Hutt, C., & Vaizey, J. J. Differential effects of group density on social behavior. *Nature*, 1966, *209*, 1371–1372.

Hutton, G. Assertions, barriers and objects: A conceptual scheme for the personal implications of environmental texture. *Journal for the Theory of Social Behavior*, 1972, *2*(1), 83–98.

Ittelson, W. H., Proshansky, H. M., & Rivlin, L. G. A study of bedroom use on two psychiatric wards. *Hospital and Community Psychiatry*, 1970, *21*(6), 177–180.

Jacobs, J. *The life and death of great American cities.* New York: Random House, 1961.

Johnson, C. A. Privacy as personal control. Paper presented at Environmental Design Research Association, Milwaukee, 1974.

Jones, S. E. A comparative proxemics analysis of dyadic interaction in selected subcultures of New York City. *Journal of Social Psychology*, 1971, *84*, 35–44.

Jones, S. E., & Aiello, J. R. Proxemic behavior of black and white first, third, and fifth grade children. *Journal of Personality and Social Psychology*, 1973, *25*(1), 21–27.

Jourard, S. M. An exploratory study of body accessibility. *British Journal of Social and Clinical Psychology*, 1966, *5*, 221–231. (a)

Jourard, S. M. Some psychological aspects of privacy. *Law and Contemporary Problems*, 1966, *31*, 307–318. (b)

Jourard, S. M. Experimenter-subject "distance" and self-disclosure. *Journal of Personality and Social Psychology*, 1970, *15*, 278–282.

Jourard, S. M. The need for privacy. In S. M. Jourard (Ed.), *The transparent self.* New York: Van Nostrand Reinhold, 1971 (rev.). (a)

Jourard, S. M. *Self-disclosure.* New York: Wiley, 1971. (b)

Jourard, S. M. *The transparent self.* New York: Van Nostrand Reinhold, 1971 (rev.). (c)

Kaplan, S. Review of *Defensible space. Architectural Forum*, 1973, May, 98.

Karabenick, S., & Meisels, M. Effects of performance evaluation on interpersonal distance. *Journal of Personality*, 1972, *40*(2), 275–286.

Kelly, F. D. Communicational significance of therapist proxemic cues. *Journal of Consulting and Clinical Psychology*, 1972, *39*(2), 345.

Kelvin, P. A social psychological examination of privacy. *British Journal of Social and Clinical Psychology*, 1973, *12*, 248–261.

King, M. G. Interpersonal relations in preschool children and average approach distance. *The Journal of Genetic Psychology*, 1966, *109*, 109–116.

Kinzel, A. S. Body buffer zone in violent prisoners. *American Journal of Psychiatry*, 1970, *127*, 59–64.

Kira, A. *The bathroom.* Ithaca, N.Y.: Cornell University Center for Housing and Environmental Studies, 1966. (Also in H. M. Proshansky, W. H. Ittelson, and L. G. Rivlin (Eds.), *Environmental psychology.* New York: Holt, Rinehart and Winston, 1970. Pp. 269–275.)

Kleck, R. E. The effects of interpersonal affect on errors made when reconstructing a stimulus display. *Psychonomic Science*, 1967, *9*, 449–450.

Kleck, R. E. Interaction distance and non-verbal agreeing responses. *British Journal of Social and Clinical Psychology,* 1970, *9,* 180–182.

Kleck, R. E., Buck, P. L., Goller, W. C., London, R. S., Pfeiffer, J. R., & Vukcevic, D. P. Effect of stigmatizing conditions on the use of personal space. *Psychological Reports,* 1968, *23,* 111–118.

Klopfer, P. H. From Ardrey to altruism: A discourse on the biological basis of human behavior. *Behavioral Science,* 1968, *13,* 399–401.

Knowles, E. S. Boundaries around social space: Dyadic responses to an invader. *Environment and Behavior,* 1972, *4*(4), 437–447.

Knowles, E. S. Boundaries around group interaction: The effect of group size and member status on boundary permeability. *Journal of Personality and Social Psychology,* 1973, *26*(3), 327–332.

Korner, I. N., & Misra, R. K. Perception of human relationship as a function of inter-individual distance. *Journal of Psychological Researches,* 1967, *11,* 129–132.

Koslin, S., Koslin, B., Pargament, R., & Bird, H. Children's social distance constructs: A developmental study. *Proceedings of the Annual Convention of the American Psychological Association,* 1971, *6*(1), 151–152.

Kuethe, J. L. Social schemas. *Journal of Abnormal and Social Psychology,* 1962, *64,* 31–38. (a)

Kuethe, J. L. Social schemas and the reconstruction of social object displays from memory. *Journal of Abnormal and Social Psychology,* 1962, *65,* 71–74. (b)

Kuethe, J. L. Prejudice and aggression: A study of specific social schemata. *Perceptual and Motor Skills,* 1964, *18,* 107–115.

Kuethe, J. L., & Stricker, G. Man and woman: Social schemata of males and females. *Pscyhological Reports,* 1963, *13,* 655–661.

Kuethe, J. L., & Weingartner, H. Male-female schemata of homosexual and non-homosexual penitentiary inmates. *Journal of Personality,* 1964, *32,* 23–31.

Kuper, L. Neighbour on the hearth. From L. Kuper (Ed.), *Living in towns.* London: The Cresset Press, 1953. (Also in H. M. Proshansky, W. H. Ittelson, and L. G. Rivlin (Eds.), *Environmental psychology.* New York: Holt, Rinehart and Winston, 1970. Pp. 246–255.)

Ladd, F. Black youths view their environments. *Environment and Behavior,* 1970, *2*(1), 74–99.

Lander, B. *Toward an understanding of juvenile delinquency.* New York: Columbia University Press, 1954.

Landis, C., & Page, J. D. *Modern society and mental disease.* New York: Farrar and Rinehart, 1938.

Lantz, H. R. Population density and psychiatric diagnosis. *Sociology and Social Research,* 1953, *37,* 322–326.

Laufer, R. S., Proshansky, H. M., & Wolfe, M. Some analytic dimensions of privacy. Paper presented at the Third International Architectural Psychology Conference, Lund, Sweden, 1973.

Lee, D. *Freedom and culture.* Englewood Cliffs, N.J.: Prentice-Hall, 1959.

Leibman, M. The effects of sex and race norms on personal space. *Environment and Behavior,* 1970, *2,* 208–246.

Lerea, J., & Ward, B. The social schema of normal and speech-defective children. *Journal of Social Psychology,* 1966, *69,* 87–94.

Lerner, R. M. The development of personal space schemata toward body build. *Journal of Psychology,* 1973, *84*(2), 229–235.

Lewis, O. *Five families.* New York: Mentor Books, 1959.

Lewis, O. *The children of Sanchez.* New York: Random House, 1961.

Lewit, D. W., & Joy, V. Kinetic versus social schemas in figure grouping. *Journal of Personality and Social Psychology,* 1967, *7,* 63–72.

Ley, D., & Cybriwsky, R. The spatial ecology of stripped cars. *Environment and Behavior,* 1974, *6*(1), 53–68.

Little, K. B. Personal space. *Journal of Experimental Social Psychology,* 1965, *1,* 237–247.

Little, K. B. Cultural variations in social schemata. *Journal of Personality and Social Psychology,* 1968, *10,* 1–7.

Little, K. B., Ulehla, F. J., & Henderson, C. Value congruence and interaction distance. *Journal of Social Psychology,* 1968, *75,* 249–253.

Long, B. H., & Henderson, E. H. Self-social concepts of disadvantaged school beginners. *Journal of Genetic Psychology,* 1968, *113,* 41–51.

Long, B. H., Henderson, E. H., & Ziller, R. C. Self-social correlates of originality in children. *Journal of Genetic Psychology,* 1967, *111,* 47–57. (a)

Long, B. H., Henderson, E. H., & Ziller, R. C. Developmental changes in the self-concept during middle childhood. *Merrill-Palmer Quarterly,* 1967, *3,* 201–214. (b)

Long, B. H., Ziller, R. C., & Bankes, J. Self-other orientations of institutionalized behavior-problem adolescents. *Journal of Consulting and Clinical Psychology,* 1970, *34,* 43–47.

Loo, C. M. Important issues in researching the effects of crowding on humans. *Representative Research in Social Psychology,* 1973, *4*(1), 219–227. (a)

Loo, C. M. The effect of spatial density on the social behavior of children. *Journal of Applied Social Psychology,* 1973, *2*(4), 372–381. (b)

Lorenz, K. *On aggression.* New York: Harcourt Brace Jovanovich, 1966.

Loring, W. C. Housing characteristics and social disorganization. *Social Problems,* 1956, *3,* 160–168.

Lott, B. S., & Sommer, R. Seating arrangements and status. *Journal of Personality and Social Psychology,* 1967, *7,* 90–95.

Lottier, S. Distribution of criminal offenses in metropolitan regions. *Journal of Criminal Law and Criminology,* 1938, *29,* 39–45.

Luft, J. On nonverbal interaction. *Journal of Psychology,* 1966, *63,* 261–268.

Lyman, S. M., & Scott, M. B. Territoriality: A neglected sociological dimension. *Social Problems,* 1967, *15,* 235–249.

Lynch, U., & Rivkin, M. A walk around the block. *Landscape,* 1959, *8,* 24–34.

MacDonald, W. S., & Oden, C. W. Effects of extreme crowding on the performance of five married couples during 12 weeks of intensive training. *Proceedings of the 81st Annual Convention of the American Psychological Association,* Montreal, Canada, 1973, *8,* 209–210.

Mahl, G. F., & Schultze, G. Psychological research in the extralinguistic area. In T. A. Seboek, A. S. Hayes, and M. C. Bateson (Eds.), *Approaches to semiotics.* The Hague, Netherlands: Moulton, 1964. Pp. 51–124.

Malzberg, B. *Social and biological aspects of mental disease.* Utica, New York: State Hospital Press, 1940.

Margulis, S. T. Privacy as a behavioral phenomenon: Coming of age. Paper presented at Environmental Design Research Association, Milwaukee, Wis., 1974.

Marsella, A. J., Escudero, M., & Gordon, P. The effects of dwelling density on mental disorders in Filipino men. *Journal of Health and Social Behavior,* 1970, *11*(4), 288–294.

Martindale, D. A. Territorial dominance behavior in dyadic verbal interactions. *Proceedings of the Annual Convention of the American Psychological Association,* 1971, *6,* 305–306.

McBride, G. *A general theory of social organization of behavior.* St. Lucia, Queensland, Australia: University of Queensland Papers, 1964, *1,* 75–110.

McBride, G., King, M. G., & James, J. W. Social proximity effects on galvanic skin responses in adult humans. *Journal of Psychology,* 1965, *61,* 153–157.

McDowell, K. V. Violations of personal space. *Canadian Journal of Behavioral Science,* 1972, *4*(3), 210–217.

McGinley, P. *Province of the heart.* New York: Viking Press, 1959.

McGrew, P. L. Social and spatial density effects on spacing behavior in preschool children. *Journal of Child Psychology and Psychiatry,* 1970, *11,* 197–205.

Mehrabian, A. Attitudes inferred from neutral nonverbal communications. *Journal of Consulting Psychology,* 1967, *31*(4), 414–417. (a)

Mehrabian, A. Orientation behaviors and nonverbal attitude communications. *Journal of Communications,* 1967, *17,* 324–332. (b)

Mehrabian, A. Inference of attitudes from the posture, orientation and distance of a communicator. *Journal of Consulting and Clinical Psychology,* 1968, *32,* 296–308. (a)

Mehrabian, A. Relationships of attitude to seated posture, orientation and distance. *Journal of Personality and Social Psychology,* 1968, *10,* 26–30. (b)

Mehrabian, A. Significance of posture and position in the communication of attitude and status relationships. *Psychological Bulletin,* 1969, *71*(5), 359–373.

Mehrabian, A. *Silent messages.* Belmont, Calif.: Wadsworth, 1971.

Mehrabian, A., & Diamond, S. G. Seating arrangement and conversation. *Sociometry,* 1970, *34*(2), 281–289.

Mehrabian, A., & Diamond, S. G. Effects of furniture arrangement, props, and personality on social interaction. *Journal of Personality and Social Psychology,* 1971, *20,* 18–30.

Mehrabian, A., & Ferris, S. R. Inference on attitude from nonverbal communications in two channels. *Journal of Consulting Psychology,* 1967, *31*(3), 420–425.

Mehrabian, A., & Weiner, M. Non-immediacy between communicator and object of communications in a verbal message: Application to the inference of attitudes. *Journal of Consulting Psychology,* 1966, *30,* 420–425.

Mehrabian, A., & Williams, M. Nonverbal concomitants of perceived and intended persuasiveness. *Journal of Personality and Social Psychology,* 1969, *13*(1), 37–58.

Meisels, M., & Canter, F. M. Personal space and personality characteristics: A non-confirmation. *Psychological Reports,* 1970, *27,* 287–290.

Meisels, M., & Dosey, M. A. Personal space, anger arousal, and psychological defense. *Journal of Personality,* 1971, *39*(3), 333–334.

Meisels, M., & Guardo, C. J. Development of personal space schemata. *Child Development,* 1969, *49,* 1167–1178.

Michelson, W. *Man and his urban environment: A sociological approach.* Reading, Mass.: Addison-Wesley, 1970.

Milgram, S. The experience of living in cities. *Science,* 1970, *167,* 1461–1468.

Mitchell, R. Some social implications of higher density housing. *American Sociological Review,* 1971, *36,* 18–29.

Munroe, R. L., & Munroe, R. H. Population density and affective relationships in three East African societies. *Journal of Social Psychology,* 1972, *88,* 15–20.

Munroe, R. L., Munroe, R. H., Nerlove, S. B., & Daniels, R. E. Effects of population density on food concern in three East African societies. *Journal of Health and Social Behavior,* 1969, *10,* 161–171.

Murphy, R. F. Social distance and the veil. *American Anthropologist,* 1964, *66,* 1257–1274.

Newman, O. *Defensible space.* New York: Macmillan, 1972.

Newman, R. C., & Pollack, D. Proxemics in deviant adolescents. *Journal of Consulting and Clinical Psychology,* 1973, *40*(1), 6–8.

Nice, M. M. The role of territory in bird life. *American Midland Naturalist,* 1941, *26,* 441–487.

Norum, G. A., Russo, N. F., & Sommer, R. Seating patterns and group task. *Psychology in the Schools,* 1967, *4,* 276–280.

O'Neill, S. M., & Paluck, R. J. Altering territoriality through reinforcement. *Proceedings of the 81st Annual Convention of the American Psychological Association,* Montreal, Canada, 1973, *8,* 901–902.

Osmond, H. Function as the basis of psychiatric ward design. *Mental Hospitals,* 1957, *8,* 23–30.

Paluck, R. J., & Esser, A. H. Controlled experimental modification of aggressive behavioral condition of severely retarded boys. *American Journal of Mental Defi-Deficiency,* 1971, *76*(1), 23–29. (a)

Paluck, R. J., & Esser, A. H. Territorial behavior as an indicator of changes in clinical behavior condition of severely retarded boys. *American Journal of Mental Deficiency,* 1971, *76*(3), 284–290. (b)

Park, R. E., Burgess, E. W., & McKenzie, R. D. *The city, Chicago.* Chicago: University of Chicago Press, 1925.

Pastalan, L. A. Privacy as an expression of human territoriality. In L. A. Pastalan and D. H. Carson (Eds.), *Spatial behavior of older people.* Ann Arbor: University of Michigan Press, 1970. Pp. 88–101. (a)

Pastalan, L. A. Privacy as a behavioral concept. *Social Forces,* 1970, *45*(2), 93–97. (b)

Patterson, A. H. Criticism of Oscar Newman's *Defensible space.* Unpublished manuscript, Pennsylvania State University, 1974.

Patterson, M. L. Compensation and nonverbal immediacy behaviors: A review. *Sociometry,* 1973, *36*(2), 237–253. (a)

Patterson, M. L. Stability of nonverbal immediacy behaviors. *Journal of Experimental Social Psychology,* 1973, *9,* 97–109. (b)

Patterson, M. L., & Holmes, D. S. Social interaction correlates of MMPI extroversion-introversion scale. *American Psychologist,* 1966, *21,* 724–725.

Patterson, M. L., Mullens, S., & Romano, J. Compensatory reactions to spatial intrusion. *Sociometry,* 1971, *34,* 114–121.

Patterson, M. L., & Sechrest, L. B. Interpersonal distance and impression formation. *Journal of Personality,* 1970, *38,* 161–166.

Pedersen, D. M., & Shears, L. M. A review of personal space research in the framework of general systems theory. *Psychological Bulletin,* 1973, *80*(5), 367–388.

Pennock, J. R. Introduction. In J. R. Pennock & J. W. Chapman, *Privacy.* New York: Atherton Press, 1971. Pp. xi–xvi.

Pennock, J. R., & Chapman, J. W. *Privacy.* New York: Atherton Press, 1971.

Plant, J. S. Some psychiatric aspects of crowded living conditions. *American Journal of Psychiatry,* 1930, *9*(5), 849–860.

Plant, J. S. Personality and an urban area. In P. K. Hatt and A. J. Reise, Jr. (Eds.), *Reader in urban society.* New York: The Free Press, 1951. Pp. 574–592.

Proshansky, H. M. Theoretical issues in environmental psychology. *Representative Research in Social Psychology,* 1973, *4*(1), 93–109.

Proshansky, H. M., Ittelson, W. H., & Rivlin, L. G. (Eds.). *Environmental psychology.* New York: Holt, Rinehart and Winston, 1970.

Queen, S. A. The ecological study of mental disorders. *American Sociological Review,* 1948, *5,* 201–209.

Rapoport, A. Yagua-Amazon dwelling. *Landscape,* 1967, *16,* 27–30.

Rapoport, A. Some perspectives on human use and organization of space. Paper presented at Australian Association of Social Anthropologists, Melbourne, Australia, May 1972.

Rapoport, A. An approach to the construction of man-environment theory. In W. F. E. Preiser (Ed.), *Environmental design research* (Vol. 2). Stroudsburg, Pennsylvania: Dowden, Hutchinson and Ross, Inc., 1973. Pp. 124–136.

Rawls, J. R., Trego, R. E., McGaffey, C. N., & Rawls, D. J. Personal space as a predictor of performance under close working conditions. *Journal of Social Psychology*, 1972, *86*(2), 261–267.

Roberts, J. M., & Gregor, T. Privacy: A cultural view. In J. R. Pennock and J. W. Chapman (Eds.), *Privacy*. New York: Atherton Press, 1971. Pp. 189–225.

Rogler, L. H. Slum neighborhoods in Latin America. *Journal of Inter-American Studies*, 1967, *9*(4), 507–528.

Rohe, W., & Patterson, A. H. The effects of varied levels of resources and density on behavior in a day care center. Paper presented at Environmental Design Research Association, Milwaukee, Wis., 1974.

Roos, P. D. Jurisdiction: An ecological concept. *Human Relations,* 1968, 75–84.

Rosenberg, G. High population densities in relation to social behavior. *Ekistics*, 1968, *25*(151), 425–428.

Rosenblatt, P. C., & Budd, L. G. Territoriality and privacy in married and unmarried couples. *Journal of Social Psychology.* In press.

Rosenfeld, H. M. Effect of an approval seeking induction on interpersonal proximity. *Psychological Reports*, 1965, *17*, 120–122.

Ross, M., Layton, B., Erickson, B., & Schopler, J. Affect, facial regard, and reactions to crowding. *Journal of Personality and Social Psychology*, 1973, *28*(1), 69–76.

Russo, N. F. Connotation of seating arrangements. *The Cornell Journal of Social Relations*, 1967, *2*, 37–44.

Sainsbury, P. *Suicide in London.* New York: Basic Books, 1956.

Scherer, S. E. Proxemic behavior of primary school children as a function of their socioeconomic class and subculture. *Journal of Personality and Social Psychology*, 1974, *29*(6), 800–805.

Schmid, C. Suicide in Minneapolis, Minnesota 1928–1932. *American Journal of Sociology*, 1933, *39*, 30–49.

Schmid, C. Completed and attempted suicides. *American Sociological Review*, 1955, *20*, 273.

Schmid, C. Urban crime areas: Part I. *American Sociological Review*, 1969, *25*, 527–542.

Schmid, C. Urban crime areas: Part II. *American Sociological Review*, 1970, *25*, 655–678.

Schmitt, R. C. Density, delinquency and crime in Honolulu. *Sociology and Social Research*, 1957, *41*, 274–276.

Schmitt, R. C. Implications of density in Hong Kong. *Journal of the American Institute of Planners*, 1963, *24*(3), 210–217.

Schmitt, R. C. Density, health and social disorganization. *Journal of the American Institute of Planners*, 1966, *32*, 38–40.

Schorr, A. L. Slums and social insecurity. United States Department of Health, Education and Welfare, Social Security Administration, Division of Research and Statistics, Research Report No. 1, Washington, D.C., 1963.

Schroeder, C. W. Mental disorders in cities. *American Journal of Sociology*, 1942, *48*, 40–51.

Schwartz, B. The social psychology of privacy. *American Journal of Sociology*, 1968, *73*, 741–752.

Schwartz, D. T., & Mintz, N. L. Ecology and psychoses among Italians in 27 Boston communities. *Social Problems,* 1963, *19*(4), 371–375.

Selye, H. *The stress of life.* New York: McGraw-Hill Paperback, 1956.

Shaw, C., & McKay, H. D. *Juvenile delinquency and urban areas.* Chicago: University of Chicago Press, 1942.

Sherrod, D. R. Crowding, perceived control, and behavioral aftereffects. *Journal of Applied Social Psychology,* 1974, *4*(2), 171–186.

Shils, E. Privacy: Its constitution and vicissitudes. *Law and Contemporary Problems,* 1966, *31,* 281–305.

Silber, J. R. Masks and fig leaves. In J. R. Pennock and J. W. Chapman (Eds.), *Privacy.* New York: Atherton Press, 1971. Pp. 226–235.

Simmel, A. Privacy is not an isolated freedom. In J. R. Pennock and J. W. Chapman (Eds.), *Privacy.* New York: Atherton Press, 1971. Pp. 71–88.

Simmel, G. The metropolis and mental life. In K. W. Wolff (Ed. and trans.), *The sociology of George Simmel.* New York: The Free Press, 1950. (a)

Simmel, G. Secrecy and group communication. In K. H. Wolff (Ed. and trans.), *The sociology of George Simmel.* New York: The Free Press, 1950. (b)

Simmel, G. *The sociology of George Simmel.* (Trans. by K. H. Wolff.) New York: The Free Press, 1950. (c)

Simmel, G. The metropolis and mental life. In P. K. Hatt and A. J. Reiss, Jr. (Eds.), *Reader in urban life.* New York: The Free Press, 1951.

Simmel, G. *Brücke and Tür.* Stuttgart, Germany: K. F. Koehler, 1957. Cited in Schwartz, B. The social psychology of privacy. *American Journal of Sociology,* 1968, *73*(6), 741–752.

Smith, G. H. Size-distance judgments of human faces (projected images). *Journal of General Psychology,* 1953, *49,* 45–64.

Smith, G. H. Personality scores and personal distance effect. *Journal of Social Psychology,* 1954, *39,* 57–62.

Smith, R. H., Downer, D. B., Lynch, M. T., & Winter, M. Privacy and interaction within the family as related to dwelling space. *Journal of Marriage and the Family,* 1969, *31*(3), 559–566.

Smith, S., & Haythorn, W. W. The effects of compatibility, crowding, group size, and leadership seniority on stress, anxiety, hostility, and annoyance in isolated groups. *Journal of Personality and Social Psychology,* 1972, *22*(1), 67–69.

Sommer, R. Studies in personal space. *Sociometry,* 1959, *22,* 247–260.

Sommer, R. Leadership and group geography. *Sociometry,* 1961, *24,* 99–110.

Sommer, R. The distance for comfortable conversation: A further study. *Sociometry,* 1962, *25,* 111–116.

Sommer, R. Further studies of small group ecology. *Sociometry,* 1965, *28,* 337–348.

Sommer, R. Man's proximate environment. *Journal of Social Issues,* 1966, *22,* 59–70.

Sommer, R. Intimacy ratings in five countries. *International Journal of Psychology,* 1968, *3,* 109–114.

Sommer, R. *Personal space.* Englewood Cliffs, N.J.: Prentice-Hall, 1969.

Sommer, R. *Design awareness.* New York: Holt, Rinehart and Winston, 1972.

Sommer, R., & Becker, F. D. Territorial defense and the good neighbor. *Journal of Personality and Social Psychology,* 1969, *11,* 85–92.

Sommer, R., & DeWar, R. The physical environment of the ward. In E. Friedson (Ed.), *The hospital in modern society.* New York: The Free Press, 1963. Pp. 319–342.

Sorokin, P. A., & Zimmerman, A. T. *Principles of rural-urban sociology.* New York: Henry Holt, 1929.

Stea, D. Territoriality, the interior aspect: Space, territory, and human movements. *Landscape,* 1965, Autumn, 13–17.

Steinzor, B. The spatial factor in face-to-face discussion groups. *Journal of Abnormal and Social Psychology,* 1950, *45,* 552–555.

Stewart, G. T., & Voors, A. W. Determinants of sickness in Marine recruits. *American Journal of Epidemiology,* 1968, *89*(3), 254–263.

Stilitz, I. B. The role of static pedestrian groups in crowded spaces. *Ergonomics,* 1969, *12*(6), 821–839.

Stilitz, I. B. Pedestrian congestion. In. D. V. Canter (Ed.), *Architectual psychology.* London: RIBA Publications, 1970. Pp. 62–72.

Stokols, D. On the distinction between density and crowding: Some implications for future research. *Psychological Review,* 1972, *79*(3), 275–278. (a)

Stokols, D. A social psychological model of human crowding phenomena. *American Institute of Planners Journal,* 1972, *38,* 72–83. (b)

Stokols, D. Toward an operational theory of alienation. *Psychological Review,* 1975. In press.

Stokols, D., Rall, M., Pinner, B., & Schopler, J. Physical, social, and personal determinants of the perception of crowding. *Environment and Behavior,* 1973, *5*(1), 87–117.

Stratton, L. O., Tekippe, D. J., & Flick, G. L. Personal space and self-concept. *Sociometry,* 1973, *36*(3), 424–429.

Strodtbeck, F. L., & Hook, L. H. Social dimensions of a twelve-man jury table. *Sociometry,* 1961, *24,* 297–415.

Studer, R. G. The dynamics of behavior-contingent physical systems. In H. M. Proshansky, W. H. Ittelson, and L. G. Rivlin (Eds.), *Environmental psychology.* New York: Holt, Rinehart and Winston, 1970. Pp. 56–70.

Studer, R. G. The organization of spatial stimuli. In J. F. Wohlwill and D. H. Carson (Eds.), *Environment and the social sciences: Perspectives and applications.* Washington, D.C.: American Psychological Association, 1972.

Studer, R. G. Man-environment relations: Discovery or design. In W. F. E. Preiser (Ed.), *Environmental design research* (Vol. 2). Stroudsburg, Pennsylvania: Dowden, Hutchinson and Ross, Inc., 1973. Pp. 124–136.

Sundstrom, E. A study of crowding: Effects of intrusion, goal blocking and density on self-reported stress, self-disclosure and nonverbal behavior. Unpublished doctoral dissertation, University of Utah, 1973.

Sundstrom, E., & Altman, I. Field study of dominance and territorial behavior. *Journal of Personality and Social Psychology,* 1974, *30*(1), 115–125.

Suttles, G. D. *The social order of the slum.* Chicago: The University of Chicago Press, 1968.

Tesch, F. E., Huston, L., & Indenbaum, E. A. Attitude similarity, attraction, and physical proximity in a dynamic state. *Journal of Applied Social Psychology,* 1973, *3*(1), 63–72.

Thibaut, J. W., & Kelley, H. H. *The social psychology of groups.* New York: Wiley & Sons, 1959.

Thompson, B. J., & Baxter, J. C. Interpersonal spacing in two-person cross-cultural interaction. *Man-Environment Systems,* 1973, *3*(2), 115–117.

Thrasher, F. M. *The gang.* Chicago: University of Chicago Press, 1927.

Tiger, L. *Men in groups.* New York: Random House, 1969.

Tolor, A. Psychological distance in disturbed and normal children. *Psychological Reports,* 1968, *23,* 695–701.

Tolor, A. Popularity and psychological distance. *Personality,* 1971, *1,* 65–83.

Tolor, A., & Salafia, W. R. The social schemata technique as a projective device. *Psychological Reports,* 1971, *28,* 423–429.

Turnbull, C. M. *The mountain people.* New York: Simon & Schuster, 1972.

Valins, S., & Baum, A. Residential group size, social interaction and crowding. *Environment and Behavior,* 1973, *5*(4), 421–440.

Ward, C. Seating arrangement and leadership emergence in small discussion groups. *Journal of Social Psychology,* 1968, *74,* 83–90.

Watson, O. M., & Graves, T. D. Quantitative research in proxemic behavior. *American Anthropologist,* 1966, *68,* 971–985.

Watts, R. E. Influence of population density on crime. *Journal of American Statistical Association,* 1931, *26,* 11–21.

Weiner, M., & Mehrabian, A. *Language within language: Immediacy, a channel in verbal communication.* New York: Appleton-Century-Crofts, 1968.

Weinstein, L. Social schemata of emotionally disturbed boys. *Journal of Abnormal Psychology,* 1965, *70,* 457–461.

Weinstein, L. The mother-child schema, anxiety, and academic achievement in elementary school boys. *Child Development,* 1968, *39,* 257–264.

Westin, A. *Privacy and freedom.* New York: Atheneum, 1970.

White, R. C. The relation of felonies to environmental factors in Indianapolis. *Social Forces,* 1931, *10*(4), 498–509.

Whyte, W. F. *Street corner society.* Chicago: University of Chicago Press, 1943.

Wicker, A. W. Undermanning, performances, and students' subjective experiences in behavior settings of large and small high schools. *Journal of Personality and Social Psychology,* 1968, *10,* 255–261.

Wicker, A. W. Cognitive complexity, school size, and participation in school behavior settings: A test of the frequency of interaction hypothesis. *Journal of Educational Psychology,* 1969, *60,* 200–203. (a)

Wicker, A. W. Size of church membership and members' support of church behavior settings. *Journal of Personality and Social Psychology,* 1969, *13,* 278–285. (b)

Wicker, A. W., McGrath, J. E., & Armstrong, G. E. Organization size and behavior setting capacity as determinants of member participation. *Behavioral Science,* 1973, *17,* 499–513.

Wicker, A. W., & Mehler, A. Assimilation of new members in a large or small church group. *Journal of Applied Psychology,* 1971, *55*(2), 151–156.

Widgery, R., & Stackpole, C. Desk position, interviewee anxiety, and interviewer credibility: An example of cognitive balance in a dyad. *Journal of Counseling Psychology,* 1972, *19*(3), 173–177.

Willems, E. P. Behavioral ecology as a perspective for man-environment research. In W. F. E. Preiser (Ed.), *Environmental design research* (Vol. 2). Stroudsburg, Penn.: Dowden, Hutchinson and Ross, Inc., 1973. Pp. 152–166.

Willems, E. P. Behavioral technology and behavioral ecology. *Journal of Applied Behavior Analysis,* 1974, *7,* 151–165.

Williams, J. L. Personal space and its relation to extroversion-introversion. *Canadian Journal of Behavioral Science,* 1971, *3*(2), 156–160.

Willis, F. N. Initial speaking distance as a function of the speaker's relationship. *Psychonomic Science,* 1966, *5,* 221–222.

Winick, C., & Holt, H. Seating position as nonverbal communication in group analysis. *Psychiatry,* 1961, *24,* 171–182.

Winsborough, H. H. The social consequences of high population density. *Law and Contemporary Problems,* 1965, *30,* 120–126.

Winsborough, H. H., & Davis, J. E. Partial associations between intra-urban population densities and vital rates. *Population Index,* 1963, *29,* 227–228.

Wirth, L. Urbanism as a way of life. *American Journal of Sociology,* 1938, *44,* 1–24.

Wohlwill, J. F. Human adaptation to levels of environmental stimulation. *Human Ecology,* 1974, *2*(2), 127–147.

Wolfe, M., & Laufer, R. The concept of privacy in childhood and adolescence. Paper presented at the Environmental Design Research Association, Milwaukee, Wis., 1974.

Wolfgang, J., & Wolfgang, A. Personal space—an unobtrusive measure of attitudes toward the physically handicapped. *Proceedings of the 76th Annual Convention of the American Psychological Association,* 1968, 653–654.

Wolfgang, J., & Wolfgang, A. Explanation of attitudes via physical interpersonal distance toward the obese, drug users, homosexuals, police, and other marginal figures. *Journal of Clinical Psychology,* 1971, *27,* 510–512.

Wynne-Edwards, V. C. *Animal dispersion in relation to social behavior.* New York: Hafner, 1972.

Yablonsky, L. *The violent gang.* New York: Macmillan, 1962.

Zeisel, J. Symbolic meaning of space and the physical dimension of social relations: A case study of sociological research as the basis of architectural planning. In J. Walton and D. Carns (Eds.), *Cities in change: Studies on the urban condition.* Boston: Allyn and Bacon, 1973. Pp. 252–263.

Zeisel, J. *Sociology and architectual design.* New York: Russell Sage Foundation, 1974.

Ziller, R. C., & Grossman, S. A. A developmental study of the self-social constructs of normals and the neurotic personality. *Journal of Clinical Psychology,* 1967, *23,* 15–21.

Ziller, R. C., Long, B. H., Ramana, K. V., & Reddy, V. E. Self-other orientations of Indian and American adolescents. *Journal of Personality,* 1968, *36,* 315–330.

Ziller, R. C., Megas, J., & DiCencio, D. Self-social constructs of normals and acute neuropsychiatric patients. *Journal of Consulting Psychology,* 1964, *28,* 59–63.

Zlutnick, S., & Altman, I. Crowding and human behavior. In J. F. Wohlwill and D. H. Carson (Eds.), *Environment and the social sciences: Perspectives and applications.* Washington, D.C.: American Psychological Association, 1972. Pp. 44–60.

Zorbaugh, H. W. *The Gold Coast and the slums.* Chicago: University of Chicago Press, 1929.

Author Index

Subject Index